A SINHALA VILLAGE IN A TIME OF TROUBLE

OXFORD UNIVERSITY SOUTH ASIAN STUDIES SERIES

Oxford University South Asian Studies Series

A SINHALA VILLAGE IN A TIME OF TROUBLE

Politics and Change in Rural Sri Lanka

JONATHAN SPENCER

OXFORD
UNIVERSITY PRESS

OXFORD
UNIVERSITY PRESS

YMCA Library Building, Jai Singh Road, New Delhi 110 001

Oxford University Press is a department of the University of Oxford. It furthers the
University's objective of excellence in research, scholarship, and education
by publishing worldwide in

Oxford   New York

Athens   Auckland   Bangkok   Bogota   Buenos Aires   Calcutta
Cape Town   Chennai   Dar es Salaam   Delhi   Florence   Hong Kong   Istanbul
Karachi   Kuala Lumpur   Madrid   Melbourne   Mexico City   Mumbai
Nairobi   Paris   Sao Paolo   Singapore   Taipei   Tokyo   Toronto   Warsaw

with associated companies in Berlin   Ibadan

Published in India
By Oxford University Press, New Delhi

ISBN 019 565 0808

Typeset in Baskerville
by Taj Services Ltd, Noida
and printed by Rekha Printers Pvt. Ltd, New Delhi 110 020
Published by Manzar Khan, Oxford University Press
YMCA Library Building, Jai Singh Road, New Delhi 110 001

To the Memory of

Martin Earle
(1952–1984)

and

James Littlejohn
(1921–1988)

Acknowledgements

I have incurred many debts in preparing this book. In Oxford, Michael Carrithers and Nick Allen at different times provided encouragement and good counsel. I have many people to thank in Sri Lanka. In Kandy, Professor K. M. De Silva, Michael Roberts, and Mr B. L. Fernando. In and around Tenna, S. A. Karunatissa, Father Pia Ciampa SJ and Father Paul Fernando, Mr and Mrs Sunil Fernando, Mr J. S. B. Peliyagoda, Mr M. L. M. Aboosally, the Reverend Wikiliya Narada Thero and the Reverend Damahana Visuddha Thero. I have to thank all the people of Tenna for their generosity and help; those listed here are merely those whose special kindness brings them to mind as I write: W. Kiriappuhami and his sons, in particular W. Mohottihami and W. Podimahatmaya; K. A. Tilakaratnahami and D. G. Jayawardena; A. M. Abhayasinghe; T. D. Kiriyansa and his family; W. L. Mudalihami and his family; M. G. Cyril, M. G. Mudalihami, and M. G. Wijeratna; Lionel Fonseka and Ariyaratna Kongolla; E. A. Rankita; M. Baba Gura; R. M. Jayawardena and R. M. Sirimalhami; R. M. K. Wimalaratna; and S. K. Karunaratna and his fellow teachers.

My stay in Sri Lanka from 1981 to 1983 was supported by a studentship from the Social Science Research Council (now the Economic and Social Research Council). In 1984 I was able to return for a second short trip thanks to an invitation to attend a conference in Anuradhapura, jointly supported by the US Social Science Research Council and the South Asia Committee of the American Council of Learned Societies.

This book is a substantially revised version of a D.Phil. thesis originally presented at Oxford University in 1986; the examiners of the original thesis—Michael Gilsenan and Éric Meyer—helped me clarify some of its shortcomings. Earlier

viii / *Acknowledgements*

versions of Chapters Five and Seven were originally presented to audiences in Anuradhapura, London, and Sussex. Colin Kirk and Mick Moore in particular provided valuable criticisms of the first version of Chapter Seven. In addition Philip Thomas, Alison Tierney, and Elizabeth Nissan all read drafts of the final manuscript and helped to rescue it from needless obscurity and confusion. John Swannell not once, but twice, devoted his remarkable talents to turning the dross of social scientific prose into something more recognizable as the English language. Richard Gombrich did much to see this book into print.

As well as those already mentioned, the following all provided support and ideas at times when I most needed them; Colin Kirk, Elizabeth Nissan, Jock Stirrat, James Brow, Mark Whitaker, Rosemary Evans, Stuart Bradshaw. My parents, George and Maisie Spencer, have been a source of unfailing help and encouragement for far more years than seems reasonable. Julia Swannell, in some mysteriously unspecifiable way, really did make this book possible.

Contents

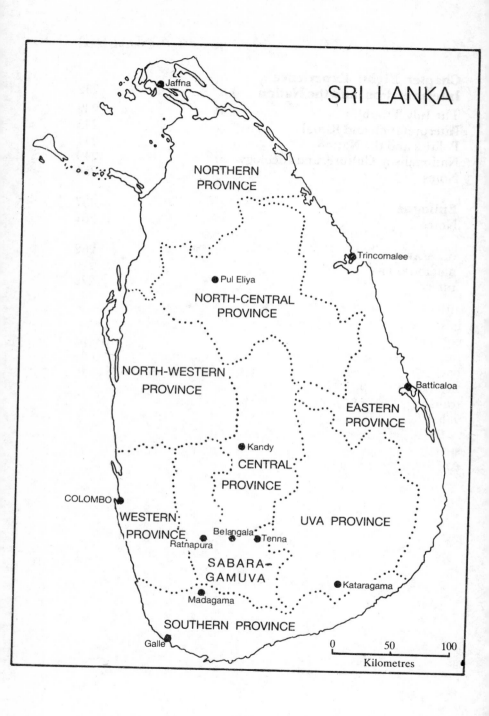

Transliteration

I have used a slightly simplified version of the standard transliteration of Sinhala. *t* and *d* are both dental consonants; *ṭ* and *ḍ* are retroflex. The macron *ā, ī* etc. is used to distinguish long from short vowels. *ä* corresponds to the vowel in English 'felt' or 'wet'. *c* is pronounced /ch/ as in English 'church'. *th, dh, kh*, etc., are, strictly speaking, aspirated consonants; I have retained the orthographic distinction here although there is no phonetic distinction in ordinary speech. I have not differentiated between the various classes of nasal consonant, nor have I retained the orthographic distinction (again unrecognized in normal speech) between front and back *l* and *n*. Double consonants are pronounced twice, rather as in the middle of English 'bookcase'. The phoneme transliterated here *v* is somewhere between English v and w in value.

Proper names and place names have not been transliterated strictly but have been written in the most conventional Anglicized form.

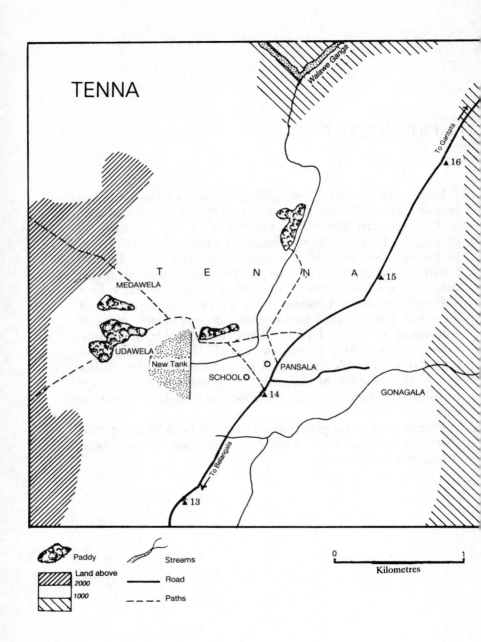

TENNA

T E N N A

MEDAWELA

UDAWELA

New Tank

SCHOOL ○   ○ PANSALA

▲ 14

GONAGALA

▲ 15

▲ 16

To Gantala

To Belangala

▲ 13

Walawe Ganga

Paddy

Land above
2000
1000

Streams

Road

Paths

0   1
Kilometres

Names and Abbreviations

In what follows all place names in and around Tenna have been changed, as have all the names of its inhabitants. I have, however, retained one or two real names in the historical parts of this work; they will be obvious enough to those historians interested in the area. Sri Lanka is a small country and allows only a limited amount of ethnographic disguise; I can only ask readers to respect the privacy of the people whose lives are central to this work.

Sinhalese and Sinhala are synonyms, referring both to a language and the speakers of that language; in what follows I use Sinhala to refer to both language and people. Sri Lankan and Ceylonese refer to all the inhabitants of the island of Sri Lanka (known until 1972 as Ceylon), including Sinhala and Tamil-speakers, Buddhists, Christians, Hindus, and Muslims.

I have used the following abbreviations in the notes and references:

SLNA: Department of National Archives, Colombo
AR: Administration Report

Preface to the Paperback Edition

A new edition is a dangerous temptation. It affords the author a golden opportunity to sound off at his or her critics, explaining what was really said and meant in the original and denouncing their various misreadings and, of course, uninformed criticisms. Somehow, though, this strikes me as a little undignified, not to mention counter-productive in many cases. The book you are holding is as clear as I could make it at the time and, while there are sections I would present rather differently now, the challenge ahead is to write new arguments, rather than to defend old assertions. Nevertheless, as the book is very much a product of a very specific time and a very specific place, it is probably worth spending a little time elaborating on the context in which it was written.

In the broadest terms, the existence of this book probably owes most to Mrs Thatcher, and especially to her government's assault on British universities in general, and the social sciences in particular, through the 1980s. This book was written in two intense bursts in the second half of that decade. In the summer of 1986 I wrote the bulk of the PhD thesis from which it was drawn. Two years later, after a taxing but stimulating year as a temporary lecturer at the University of Sussex, a period of under-employment allowed me time to rewrite the whole thing, bringing in a number of new chapters and restructuring the argument. It was especially important—then and now—that the book be read as a product of fieldwork carried out at a very particular historical juncture: specifically, in the years leading up to the 1983 anti-Tamil violence in Sri Lanka. I was not to know, when I alluded to 'a time of trouble' in my title, that the time in question would extend from months to years to decades. The low-level skirmishes between Tamil militants and the Sri Lankan security forces which punctuated my period of fieldwork in the early 1980s became, after 1983, something much more like a full-blown civil war. That war continues—despite occasional truces and peace initiatives—to the time of writing this Preface, at great cost to the country and its people. The full story is too long to detail here, but anyone seeking an accessible and judicious account of the causes and consequences of the war should start with Elizabeth Nissan's excellent recent introduction (1996), while an introduction to the academic responses to the conflict can be found in a recent co-authored article (Rogers, Spencer, and Uyangoda 1998).

This is a book about a village I have called Tenna, in the Sinhala-dominated rural south of Sri Lanka. It covers a crucial period in the island's politics, when the right-of-centre United National Party (UNP) consolidated its control of the country through a Presidential election and a Referendum to extend the life of the sitting parliament, both held in the second half of 1982. The Referendum was particularly notable for the widespread use of fraud and intimidation to deliver the government's desired vote. Within a year the same gangs of party supporters who had bullied the voters in 1982, were on the streets again, touring towns and cities like Colombo with electoral lists in order to identify Tamil homes and businesses for destruction. The elections of 1982 had such a profound effect on my understanding of the village in which I was living, that politics became a dominant theme of my research. The July 1983 anti-Tamil violence, and local reactions to it, forced me to think about the links between what I had seen at village level and the powerful forces of Sinhala Buddhist nationalism. This, then, is a book about politics, the state, and nationalism, as seen by an anthropological fieldworker living in a relatively poor and remote corner of the country.

Already, when I wrote the book, I realised that the social and political landscape had changed irrevocably in the village on which this book is based, as in other southern villages. The most important change was the spread of political violence across the whole island in the second half of the 1980s. The 1983 anti-Tamil violence, which occurred in the last months of my original fieldwork, provided a flood of new recruits for the militant separatists, in which the group known as the Liberation Tigers of Tamil Ealam (LTTE or simply the Tigers) asserted a brutal domination over their Tamil rivals. From being a tiny group of young men on bicycles, they were now strong enough to capture and control whole areas of the island, like the northern city of Jaffna. The Indian intervention in the conflict in 1987 (when Rajiv Gandhi's government foisted a peace agreement on the government and the LTTE), provoked fierce hostility in the south from young radical Sinhala nationalists. This hostility found expression in anti-state violence from a group called the Janata Vimukti Peramuna, or JVP, and in the next few years, thousands were murdered or 'disappeared' in the struggle between the JVP and the state. The manuscript of this book was completed in 1989, when that struggle was at its peak. At that point I had not been back to Tenna since 1984, and reliable news was extremely hard to obtain about events and conditions anywhere in the island. I knew from reports from passing visitors—anthropologists working elsewhere, development consultants who had passed through the immediate area—that Tenna was in a zone of bitter confrontation between the forces of the state and the young radicals of the JVP. I did not, though, know anything about specific events in the village or the fate of my friends there. These were the circumstances under which I wrote the Epilogue to this volume. There I sketched in the background to the violence of the late 1980s, but carefully steered away from specific comment or speculation on its effects in the village.

In late 1989 the main figures in the JVP leadership were tracked down, arrested and, in many cases, killed by the security forces. I returned to the island in 1991, and again in 1992, and was delighted to discover that Tenna itself had miraculously escaped the worst impact of the violence of the late 1980s. Terrible events had indeed happened in the neighbouring villages, but no one in Tenna itself had been killed, nor had anyone disappeared or been subject to torture. It is, of course, hard to discover why this should have been so, but it does suggest two qualifications to the analysis that follows. On the one hand, the general sense of a social order under intense pressure, a sense acquired during my fieldwork and reproduced and analysed throughout the book, seems with hindsight a perfectly reasonable reading of the situation in which I had worked, a reading which would be, if anything, even more applicable to other parts of rural Sri Lanka at that time. On the other hand, any sense that this particular village was, for whatever reason, more than usually divided or fractious, would seem to be disproved by its collective survival during the trauma of the JVP years.

No sooner had I finished this book, than I began to realise what it was I had really wanted to say. Immediately after I sent the manuscript off to the publishers, I wrote two papers reflecting on broader issues of nationalism and political violence in Sri Lanka. It has been their peculiar fate that one of them, on nationalism and the anthropological notion of 'culture' (Spencer 1990a), has become reasonably well known to anthropologists, while the other, on the links between collective violence and everyday practice (Spencer 1990b), is probably better known to regional specialists. Between them, though, they extend and refine the argument of this book. In particular, they go further than I do in these pages in trying to link what I had learnt from my fieldwork to the understanding of events like the 1983 anti-Tamil violence. Some of this was, of course, negative: that the 1983 violence had very specific political causes, and any analysis which failed to give proper weight to such causes was bound to fail. In other words, while ethnographic research can provide fresh perspectives, and yield unexpected insights, it is foolish and dangerous to pretend that it can be used as a substitute for broader, and more structured accounts of political economy and political process. More recently still, I have written a much more overtly reflexive account of my reaction to the events of the early 1980s, bringing the reader up to date on what had happened in Tenna between 1984 and my return in 1991 (Spencer n.d.).

My most recent return to Tenna was in 1997. Many of the old people who had told me most about the village's past were now dead. Electricity had come to the village in the late 1980s and more and more houses had televisions. Malaria, though, had returned to the area, and there were far more stories of young couples losing their children in infancy than I remembered from my first fieldwork. Suicides had also increased, in the village as in the island as a whole, especially among young people. The village school had continued to expand, and some of the young people I had spent most time with in the early 1980s were now employed as teachers, but it was still hard for all but the richest villagers to send their children to the secondary school in the nearest town. It was, of course, delightful to see old friends again, and my welcome was as warm as ever. But materially, life seemed to have improved very little in recent years, and I came away troubled by the obvious, but too easily forgotten, facts of rural poverty and its tenacious persistence. I now think of this as a book, in the end, about the tension between the promise of democratic inclusion, which has swept the post-colonial world in the second half of this century, and the dull realities of exclusion—economic, political, and cultural—which affect people so profoundly in places like Tenna. Put so bluntly, this seems a very general proposition, but the working out of this tension, in different places at different points in the last twenty years, has taken on a huge variety of apparently unpredictable forms. To understand this variety, we need sensitive, historically and culturally grounded, studies of the way in which people deploy local resources and local understandings in coming to terms with the promise of democracy and the inescapable pressures of social and political inequality. I hope that this book still provides one small example of what that kind of study can offer.

Edinburgh
July 1999

REFERENCES

Nissan, E. 1996. *Sri Lanka: A Bitter Harvest* London: Minority Rights Group.
Rogers, J., J. Spencer and J. Uyangoda 1998. 'Sri Lanka: Political Violence and Ethnic Conflict' *American Psychologist* 53 (7): 771-7.
Spencer, J. 1990a. 'Writing Within: Anthropology, Nationalism and Culture in Sri Lanka' *Current Anthropology* 31: 283-300.
——— 1990b. 'Collective Violence and Everyday Practice in Sri Lanka' *Modern Asian Studies* 24: 606-23.
——— n.d. 'On Not Becoming a Terrorist: Problems of Memory, Agency and Community in the Sri Lankan Conflict' in V. Das, et al. *Violence, Political Agency and the Self* Berkeley: University of California Press.

Chapter One

Introduction

In September 1982 I was walking along a road in rural Sri Lanka with a procession of chanting adults and schoolchildren carrying white flags and flowers. We were making our way toward the Buddhist temple in the village. The atmosphere was pleasant enough but hardly highly charged; it reminded me, as much as anything, of an English Sunday school's harvest festival.

But as we were gathering at the temple compound, the mood was suddenly broken by the sound of raised voices. Apparently one of the men leading the procession had been chased and punched by a young man from the crowd of spectators, and when various worthies tried to remonstrate with him he had responded with jeers and insults. In particular, he had singled out two individuals: the *grāmasēvaka* (the minor government official who filled the role of the old village headman) and a school teacher who was much involved in temple affairs: 'Just wait until the 20th of next month,' he shouted. 'We'll see you transferred to Batticaloa and Jaffna!'

It was an unexpected and puzzling incident. It should be explained that it took place in the sprawling settlement I have called Tenna, on the edge of the mountains in eastern Ratnapura District. Our procession was one of a series that had been held on the quarter-moon day of each month since the start of the rainy-season retreat of the *sangha*, the order of Buddhist monks, some six weeks earlier. But the motivation of the belligerent young man was not religious but political: 'the twentieth of next month'—20 October 1982—was the recently announced date of Sri Lanka's first ever presidential election. The young man, also a schoolteacher, turned out to be a leading supporter of the ruling United National Party (UNP), whereas many of the prominent figures in temple affairs were identified with the opposition Sri Lanka Freedom Party (SLFP). It should also be explained that the transfer of public servants as a form of punishment, on political grounds, was a well-established fact of Sri Lankan political life, and Batticaloa and Jaffna are both predominantly Tamil cities, where no Sinhala person, it was firmly believed in the village, could hope to survive.

Not that I realised all this at the time. (I return to this incident and its implications in Chapter 3 where, amongst other things, I make it clear just how little of it I actually saw, let alone understoood as it happened.) I was excited though, because at last something was happening in the village; for five months I had lived there pleasantly enough without ever feeling I had penetrated beyond the thick veil of everyday *politesse* and deference which seemed to accompany me wherever I went. But as I unravelled this incident and its implications in the following weeks, I felt my understanding of the village increase dramatically. What I came to understand above all, was the centrality of party politics to village life. It was only much later that I was able to relate this understanding to the other context of the incident: the centrality of Buddhism to village life. But although central party politics and the particular style of Buddhism embodied in the schoolchidren's procession are equally recent innovations in this setting; both can be said to have started in the closing years of colonial rule, just before the Second World War.

Ten months and two elections after this incident I experienced another crisis, even more intensely felt. For a week in late July 1983 the entire country was convulsed by violence and rumour. First came an attack by Tamil militants in the north in which thirteen Sinhala soldiers were killed; this was followed by a week of destruction and rioting in the south in which an unknown number of Tamil civilians (probably several thousand) were killed. A curfew was declared; the government amended the constitution to outlaw separatist parties (thus disenfranchizing all those Tamils represented by the main opposition party, the Tamil United Liberation Front); many Tamils fled as refugees from Sinhala areas; and others who had been sceptical before about separatism were swiftly radicalized.

The explanation for these events, and those which have since followed, should be sought in the history of national politics, again especially the politics of those last years of colonial rule. Where necessary, in what follows I have supplied some background on the national political context; but an anthropological contribution to the understanding of these events is inevitably partial and local. As an anthropologist, I can record one important fact—the tenacious hold of Sinhala Buddhist nationalism amongst the people with whom I lived at the time—and attempt an explanation of the social and historical circumstances which have made these particular nationalist ideas such a compelling force in local affairs. To understand this we need to understand both the processions of the chanting schoolchildren and the subsequent scuffle outside the temple gate. Most of all we need to understand the kinds of change—material and cultural—that have affected villages like Tenna in recent generations.

As a descriptive study this work is concerned with rural change and rural politics in Sri Lanka. It is based on fieldwork carried out between 1982 and 1984 in one village in eastern Ratnapura District. The field data have been supplemented with archival material from the Department of National Archives in Colombo and with comparative material from the growing literature on Sri Lankan rural society. I have not attempted to emulate the immensely detailed concern with land tenure and kinship structure which preoccupied those predecessors whose work has most influenced my research (Leach 1961a; Obeyesekere 1967; Brow 1978). Instead I have chosen to range over a superficially broader set of topics—including, for example, land tenure *and* religious change, the growing role of the post-colonial state in daily life *and* other changes in the texture of everyday affairs.

In this particular case, then, there are good analytic reasons for trying to hold firm to a broad perspective on the processes of change. I mentioned earlier my concern with material and cultural change, but in fact I do not believe that these are different 'things' requiring different methods of study. This is perhaps best illustrated by an example. The old men and

women in the community I am writing about grew up at a
time when the main basis of livelihood was a kind of swidden
agriculture called *hēn* in Sinhala, but usually anglicized as
'chena'. This was always unpopular with British colonial
administrators, who saw it as both a profligate use of natural
resources and a sap on the moral fibre of the cultivators.
Despite colonial hostility, chena remained the main economic
activity of most villagers until the last decade or so, in which
population pressure and more effective regulation have seen it
virtually die out in the immediate area. Obviously the demise
of chena marks an important change in the material circumstances of life in the village. But it is more than that. Chena was
not simply a matter of agricultural technique, nor even of
work and property relations; it also embodied values and
feelings and ways of interacting. The chena fields were
necessarily dispersed, although a group of neighbouring plots
would be co-operatively cultivated. For a young man, going off
to watch his own chena plot for the first time was a sign of
maturity and adulthood; to ask a young woman to accompany
him was public sign of sexual liaison, often the 'only marker
there was of impending 'marriage' and domesticity. The men
on the chenas would spend nights in their huts, calling out
songs and rhyming riddles to the occupants of neighbouring
huts—these were often on religious themes, sometimes inter-
twining the doings of the gods with features of the local
topography. At the harvest of the staple *kurakkan* (finger-
millet) the holders of neighbouring plots would join together
and cut their way across the whole cultivated area; again there
were special songs of celebration to accompany the process
and whole families would join in together.

Nowadays marriages are marked by new kinds of ceremonies learnt from the ways of the rich—visits, interdining,
and various new rituals, not least the visit to the office of the
registrar. The young men who, a generation ago, would have
been setting out to their own chena for the first time may now
be found in the secondary school in the nearest town, trying to
scrape the grades for admission to one of Sri Lanka's universities. Virtually none of them know the songs and stories their
fathers knew; but then few of their fathers absorbed their
religious values through studying for an 'O-level' examination

in Buddhism. And, in place of subsistence activities like chena, the young devote their time to intensive cash-cropping, digging for precious gems, and that area of petty trading and wheeler-dealing summed up in the English loan-word *bisnis*. Needless to say, the forms and patterns of co-operation in these new activities are often very different from those of the chena fields.

We can talk of changes in material life having cultural consequences; this is obvious enough if we think of recent changes in the technology of communications, for example the change from an overwhelmingly oral and largely local culture to a radio- and print-based national (and occasionally international) culture. Two recent commentators on national-ism, Ernest Gellner (1983) and Benedict Anderson (1983), have both sought to locate the material basis of modern nationalism in the forms of cultural reproduction. I shall look at their arguments in more detail in the conclusion to this book, but for the moment it is important merely to note, in any discussion of change, that while the chena field can obviously be contrasted with the gem pit, it can also be contrasted, somewhat less obviously, with the schoolroom. Similarly, paddy cultivation is not merely a matter of technology and labour organization; it too embodies (or embodied) values of hierarchy and equality, inclusion and exclusion. When the activity changes or fades away, those values may become open to different kinds of question and challenge.

It should be clear then that I do not see 'culture' as something which can be abstracted from the practical activities in which it is manifested. A style of working and a style of argument are both cultural phenomena: in both cases the possibilities for action are circumscribed by the inherited understandings of the past. So too with politics—which is both a kind of work and a kind of argument, as I shall show later—and religion. But understanding is itself a practical activity and a necessary part of being human. Changes in any area of life pose problems for our inherited understandings of the world; they may be met with either new understandings based on new materials or with changes in other, older ways of making sense of things. In either case the process is an active one, in which particular people in particular circumstances make sense of their world and act in it with particular resources. In my usage, the word 'culture' loosely embraces all the aspects of this active process.

The way I have chosen to talk about culture has been heavily influenced by the particular circumstances of my own field experience. Something which is usually glossed into English as 'culture' (Sinhala *sanskṛtiya*) is a much argued about and self-conscious part of the way in which many people in Tenna try to make sense of their world. Their use of the term is closer in some respects to the idea of a 'high' Culture, and thus different from the more total and less evaluative 'culture' of much recent anthropology. But both anthropological 'culture' and Tenna 'culture' share one important feature: a belief in a world of separate and bounded cultures and a lingering romantic faith in culture as the embodiment of the distinctive genius of a people, a nation, or a race. This belief is of immense heuristic value to anthropology; it gives us, after all, a subject-matter: 'other cultures' rather than other culture. But the study of nationalism, which is historically its Siamese twin, renders it analytically problematic; in this context the very term 'culture' itself becomes something that requires explanation rather than something that explains.

In seeking a way out of this impasse I have drawn on the intellectual tradition of both Marx and Weber. My apprehension of Marx has been mediated by arguments in Britain about culture and politics and history; the problems of change in Tenna are not always so very different from the problems of change in Britain in the 1980s. In my understanding of both I have learnt a great deal from the tradition of committed scholarship represented by the historians E. P. Thompson and Eric Hobsbawm, but above all by Raymond Williams whose sadly premature death was announced as I was completing this book. Writing in the early 1960s, Williams had this to say about images of society:

Our abstract ideas about society, or about any particular society, are both persistent and subject to change. We have to see them as interpretations: as ways of describing the organization and of conceiving relationships, necessary to establish the reality of social life but also under continual pressure from experience. In certain periods, the interpretations satisfy experience in such a way that there is hardly any dispute at this level: the descriptions and concepts are deeply built in and accepted. In other periods, there are degrees of discrepancy: a given description is felt to be inadequate, and is disputed; or a description is accurate yet is challenged by an alternative conception of relationships, so that the whole status and future of the society are put into question, usually with deep division and controversy. (Williams 1965: 120)

This book tries to describe how, in one particular place at a time of trouble and unrest, people's ideas about their own community and their place in it were, as Williams puts it, 'put into question,' and it is also about the different ways in which they tried to answer that question. But Williams's influence extends further. Throughout his career he wrestled with the problem of relating his own experience to the ever more sophisticated and potentially distancing language of socio-logical and political analysis. At the heart of this passage there is for me a double obligation: that as an ethnographer I should not let my description betray my own experience; and that I should acknowledge the indeterminacy of a world in which experience and interpretation are at constant odds.

In trying to write dispassionately from within a situation of mounting crisis, it is perhaps inevitable that I should draw most heavily on those whose work was born of similar circumstances. The long decay of German political culture in the decades before Hitler's rise to power was chronicled, analysed, and resisted by a small number of remarkable men and women. Of these the tragic figures of Max Weber and Walter Benjamin are exemplary, and their very different inspirations colour much of what follows. In his passionate defence of his pedagogic role, the essay 'Science as a Vocation,' Weber described the teacher's duty as follows:

The primary task of a useful teacher is to teach his students to recognize 'inconvenient' facts—I mean facts that are inconvenient for their party opinions. And for every party opinion there are facts that are extremely inconvenient, for my own opinion no less than for others. (Weber 1948: 147)

Anthropology is, above all, a repository of inconvenient facts. Much of what I encountered in Tenna struck me as very inconvenient for the writing of the kind of anthropology I expected to write. The task of recognizing such inconveniences, Weber argued, was a moral one. While I would not claim to share either Weber's acute sense of duty (upon which he reflected so often in his sociological analysis), or his political position, I agree on the importance of recognizing this moral obligation to face up to the inconvenient.

Weber's influence has been mediated for me, as for many of my anthropological cohort, by the stimulating and exasperating figure of Clifford Geertz. But, working in Sri Lanka, I have also been especially influenced by Gananath Obeyesekere, and have drawn on his creative reworking of Weber. *Medusa's Hair* (Obeyesekere 1981) was published just before I set out for the field, and it became one of a small number of books which I read and re-read while living in Tenna. Apart from purely local insight, it seemed to offer a way of talking about culture and change which allowed for the recognition of disagreement and creative agency. These were two features of their life that my friends in Tenna emphasized in discussions; many of the individual connections and analyses in this book arose in conversations in which they demonstrated the urgency of their own need to understand their changing world. 'The first thing you need to know about this place,' as one Tenna friend once told me, 'is that everyone has different ideas (*mata*).'

Politics

In her 40 years of post-colonial history Sri Lanka has been characterized in many ways. For many years she was described as a model democracy, in which the electorate ousted the sitting government at each election between 1956 and 1977 and, more or less peacefully, voted in a new government. More recently the dominant tone of outside description has been darkly apocalyptic: disintegration and decay are the commonest figures of journalistic rhetoric. Throughout this period, however, there has been a growing body of evidence for what has usually been described as a high degree of politicization in both rural and urban society (e.g. Robinson 1975; Morrison *et al.* 1979; Moore 1985; Brow

1988). In the villages, in particular, party political identification has grown into something of an obsession; as one political scientist has put it: 'Mass sports or entertainments are unknown in the villages and politics remains a consuming passion' (Jupp 1978: 162).

In the mid 1970s, an anthropological monograph was published documenting politics in a Sinhalese village with the same meticulous detail with which, a decade earlier, Edmund Leach had documented land tenure in *Pul Eliya*. This book, *Political Structure in a Changing Sinhalese Village* by Marguerite Robinson (Robinson 1975), was based on field-work from two separate visits in the 1960s; the author had also made a return visit in 1972. In 1970 a government of the left had been elected, with a mandate for radical change. While this new government faltered in its first year of power, its erstwhile supporters among the youth of the southern countryside maintained the radical momentum of the election campaign, and were increasingly at odds with the government they had helped to power. This momentum reached its climax in April 1971 with an event remembered as the '1971 insurrection', apparently a bloody failure to win state power by force, based in the southern rural areas, and led by an ostensibly Marxist group, the JVP (*Janata Vimukti Peramuna*— People's Liberation Front).

Not surprisingly, the author's concluding remarks reflect these recent events:

Insurgents and UNP members reflect the extremes; the majority of [villagers] are SLFP supporters who sympathize with the insurgents but who are not themselves active revolutionaries. My main impressions from this brief visit... in 1972 were that the SLFP [villagers] are rapidly becoming integrated into the regional structure, and that the insurgents have only begun their fight. (Robinson 1975: 281)

We have here a picture of a village habituated to political division, its population divided between the right (the then opposition UNP), the left (the SLFP, in power in Colombo at the time), and a revolutionary left represented by the insurgents. For a time, the extraordinary events of the early 1970s attracted much scholarly and non-scholarly attention and analysis outside the island; they seemed to represent almost a parody of Western leftist preoccupations of the day—the spirit of 1968 reborn in a Third World youth uprising of vaguely Maoist inspiration[1].

Ten years after Robinson's last visit, when I was starting my own fieldwork, a visitor would have had difficulty finding the village she described. The roads around it were dominated by the trucks and moving equipment of a firm of Swedish contractors who were putting the final touches to a huge hydroelectric scheme, while many of the inhabitants of the area were being resettled on newly irrigated land in the northern dry zone. But even more bewildering than these changes in the physical environment were the changes that had taken place in the political landscape—changes of which this project was but one manifestation.

The left-wing government of 1970 had survived seven years of growing unpopularity and internal division, largely through a regimen of constitutional amendment and emergency rule. In the election of 1977 it was swept aside by the UNP, led by the veteran right-of-centre politician J. R. Jayewardene. Since then all efforts had been directed towards the attraction of foreign (that is to Western) aid and investment. 'Development' and the 'open economy' replaced the 'socialism' and 'self-sufficiency' of the previous government's rhetoric. The wooing of Western financial institutions proved remarkably successful, as was shown by a host of high-capital development projects, like the dam scheme which threatened to cover the area of Robinson's fieldwork, or the skeletons of new international hotels under construction along the Colombo seafront. It was hard to see any signs of radicalism among the revolutionaries of the previous decade (many of whom were now committed supporters of the ruling party). Instead, such radical opposition as could be discerned emanated from the Tamil areas of the north (which had not been involved in the disturbances of 1971), where a small group of young men, the so-called Tigers, had taken up arms and were proving an increasing embarrassment to the government. It should now be obvious that someone like myself, arriving in a Sinhala village in 1982, would have had rather different experiences—leading, quite naturally, to rather different conclusions—from someone working in 1971, or 1965, or in the conditions of extended crisis that prevail as I write. This is an ethnograply based on work at one very specific moment.

Even so, there are some obvious areas of continuity in recent political history. In the period of the 1970–7 government, the political party became established as the key medium of patronage and power at the local level, with the MP acting as a conduit for the distribution of virtually all state resources within a particular constituency. After 1977 the UNP took over this role from the SLFP, and the influx of foreign assistance meant that the party had more resources than ever before to distribute to its following. Unlike its predecessor, it managed to retain much of its support during its first term of office. Meanwhile, though, the party also entrenched itself as a medium of power of a more brutal sort; sections of the UNP became associated with the use of violence and intimidation against their political opponents (just as sections of the SLFP had been in the 1970s). In 1982, six months into my fieldwork, Jayewardene won a second term as President. A few months later a referendum was held, which extended the life of the existing UNP-dominated parliament for a further term, a referendum marred by widespread intimidation and fraud. From December 1982 the UNP were confirmed in power, with their old majority intact but with their popular legitimacy badly weakened as a result of the suspicious tactics employed in retaining power. The moment of my work was one in which the ground rules of electoral politics were rewritten, not for the first time in Sri Lanka, to suit the party in power, while the growth of organized violence in the shadow of the state posed a further threat to the continuation of normal politics on the island.

Robinson's account of local politics is framed in a familiar way. Politics comes to her village from the outside, disrupting an older and relatively 'harmonious' order of things; the old headman is replaced by a new official—an outsider who is granted no respect and is swiftly reduced to impotence; disputes escalate and the village divides into bitter factions on party lines. I intend to discuss politics in a rather different way. I believe that there is a strong continuity between contemporary party politics in Sri Lankan villages and earlier uses of the state as a medium for the working out or resolution of local disputes. Villagers did not simply have politics thrust upon them; rather they appropriated politics and used them for their own purposes. Politics did not necessarily create divisions, they often provided a means of expressing divisions which already existed.

I am interested in what the people involved actually thought politics was *about*, and the dialectical relationship between the local idea of the political and the processes of local politics. What is first rendered problematic in such an enquiry is our own assumptions about the meaning of the word 'politics'. Political anthropology in Britain started from a position of certainty about its subject matter and has only slowly come round to the realization that the very idea of 'politics' might be ideologically charged and culturally contingent. Radcliffe-Brown, for example:

The State... does not exist in the phenomenal world; it is a fiction of the philosophers. What does exist is an organization, i.e. a collection of individual human beings connected by a complex system of relations... There is no such thing as the power of the State; there are only, in reality, powers of individuals—kings, prime ministers, magistrates, policemen, party bosses, and voters. The political organization of a society is that aspect of the total organization which is concerned with the control and regulation of physical force. (Radcliffe-Brown 1940: xxiii)

This formulation (which bears an uncanny resemblance to some of the thoughts of Mrs Thatcher) is not, needless to say, quite how the people of Tenna see it. Their view of the State more often accords with the philosophers' fiction, while their understanding of what politics is—of what politics might be *for*—seems to me to have relatively little to do with physical force, but a lot to do with intangible ideas of standing, worth, value, the pursuit of social esteem and, perhaps paradoxically, the unseemly, the morally questionable, and the breakdown of the collective moral order. To understand politics in Tenna it is necessary for us to understand what the people of Tenna themselves understand politics to be; and for that, we need to question our own anthropological assumptions about the nature of the political.

There is, of course, an alternative tradition in political anthropology, traceable to one of the earliest ethnographers of Sri Lanka, A. M. Hocart. Hocart's contribution was to transpose the basic terms of what was yet to become political anthropology; as his contemporaries were about to embark on a whole generation's work demonstrating the political functions of ritual and myth, Hocart announced a demonstration of the ritual and mythic origins of politics:

Ritual organization is vastly older than government, for it exists where there is no government and where none is needed. When however society increases so much in complexity that a co-ordinating agency, a kind of nervous system, is required, that ritual organization will gradually take over this task. (Hocart [1936] 1970: 35)

Kings are different from councillors after all, not to mention magistrates and policemen. What we can learn from Hocart is the important link between power, ritual, and symbols on the one hand, and the contingency of any connection between these and the administration of people's mundane affairs on the other. Politics in our sense is an inappropriate term with which to describe Hocart's examples: kingship was about power, but power was about divinity and fertility rather than the doings of prime ministers and parliaments.

Everything about Hocart's work—his ideas, his career, his methods—conspired to exclude him from the canon of British anthropology. Recently, though, his work has received renewed attention with the publication of more or less explicitly Hocartian analyses of pre-colonial kingship in India (Stein 1980),Thailand (Tambiah 1976), Polynesia (Sahlins 1985), and Bali (Geertz 1980). Sahlins and Geertz in particular have criticized the parochial assumptions of Eurocentric political theory: Sahlins tilts at 'the quaint Western concept that domination is a spontaneous expression of the nature of society, and beyond that, of the nature of man' (Sahlins 1985: 75–6), while in Geertz's Bali 'what power was was what kings were':

The notion that politics is an unchanging play of natural passions, which particular institutions of domination are but so many devices for exploiting, is wrong everywhere; in Bali its absurdity is patent. The passions are as cultural as the devices; and the turn of mind—hierarchical, sensory, symbolistic, and theatrical—that informs one informs the other (Geertz 1980: 124)

In Bali the state was embodied in the king and the king was

the fulcrum on which turned a whole intellectual and ritual order.

But kings are not prime ministers, and it is significant that this renewed interest in the 'symbolics of power' should be largely confined to examples from the eighteenth and nineteenth centuries.[2] As we read Geertz and Sahlins there is a strong temptation to say—ah, but that was *then*; what of now? Interestingly, I think there is a converging interest in the symbolics of power and the meaning of the political in the study of Western political experience. For example, a number of the survivors of the Marxist tradition in history, sociology, and anthropology are now concerned with issues of meaning and representation. Both Althusser's writings on ideology and Gramsci's concept of hegemony have redirected attention on the political left to the question of what is included in or excluded from commonsense notions of the political. We can glimpse some idea of this sort behind all the familiar political clichés of 'setting the agenda', 'hidden agendas,' and so on. More subtly, though, it has been used to turn attention back to political language, as in a recent collection of essays by the Marxist historian Gareth Stedman Jones[3]:

> In general... historians have looked everywhere except at changes in political discourse itself to explain changes in political behaviour.... The implicit assumption is of civil society as a field of competing social groups or classes whose opposing interests will find rational expression in the political arena. Such interests, it is assumed, pre-exist their expression. Languages of politics are evanescent forms, mere coverings of an adequate, inadequate or anachronistic kind, through which essential interests may be decoded. (Jones 1983: 21)

Jones's comments preface a fresh analysis of the Chartist movement in nineteenth-century England, an apparently class-based phenomenon which nevertheless persisted in putting forward political demands, seeing access to Parliament as the best safeguard against economic oppression: Marxist orthodoxy might dictate that class-interests are material interests, and class-demands should therefore concern the conditions of access to material resources, but the Chartists themselves saw their problems as political problems, which could be solved by access to the institutions of government. The reasons for this political diagnosis, according to Jones, lie in the 'language of politics' employed by the Chartists, the assumptions about the possibilities and limitations of political action embodied in political discourse. What people say about politics is one obvious clue to what they think politics *is*, and what they think politics is constrains the particular ways in which they act politically.

The most obvious area in which attention has been turned to the language of politics and the symbolics of power is the problem of nationalism. One recent Marxist commentator has commented that 'the theory of nationalism represents Marxism's great historical failure' (Nairn 1981: 329), while another has acknowledged that 'nation-ness is the most universally legitimate value in the political life of our time' (Anderson 1983: 12). One of the most striking features of nationalist argument is the glorification of the collectivity, the unthinking worship of society over the individual: *dulce et decorum est pro patria mori*. Yet, uncomfortably enough for both political left and right alike, the collectivity invoked rarely corresponds to the collectivity which might be predicted from a simple theory of political interests.

This is the source of Gellner's extended jibe about the 'wrong address' in history:

Just as extreme Shi'ite Muslims hold that Archangel Gabriel made a mistake, delivering the message to Mohamed when it was intended for Ali, so Marxists basically like to think that the spirit of history or human consciousness made a terrible boob. The awakening message was intended for *classes*, but by some terrible postal error was delivered to *nations*. It is now necessary for revolutionary activists to persuade the wrongful recipient to hand over the message, and the zeal it engenders, to the rightful and intended recipient. (Gellner 1983: 129)

The same point is rather more elegantly made in Barrington Moore's ironic comment on August 1914: 'Like their class comrades in France and England.... German workers marched off to the carnival of slaughter in perfect order' (Moore 1978: 173). Since when we might add Indian and Pakistani, Hindu and Muslim and Sikh, Israeli and Arab, Jew and Muslim, Iranian and Iraqi, Sunni and Shi'ite, Tamil and Sinhala.

If Western commentators in the last forty years have tended to describe our world as riven by familiar ideological differences—right and left, capitalist and communist—real fighting and real wars (whatever the meddling of the super-powers) as often as not appear to have their origins in impenetrably local ideas of belonging and community.

Confronted with the dismal history of our century, and the evidence of deep fissures in so many post-colonial societies, there are two common responses. The first is a cry of 'atavism' and the invocation of 'the primordial'; 'blood,' we are told, 'will out'. This is probably the most popular explanation of the rise of so many nationalisms and sub-nationalisms, whether linguistic, regional, or religious at base, if only because it usually corresponds precisely to the stated aims and motives of nationalists themselves. It is, though, palpably inadequate since all the historical evidence argues for the novelty of mass nationalist political mobilization: the language of power and legitimacy in pre-modern states tended to emphasize natural differences—not necessary similarities—between rulers and ruled (Nissan and Stirrat 1987; cf. Sahlins 1985: 73–103). A slightly more sophisticated variant of this response is the cry of 'false consciousness' and 'divide and rule': nationalist ideas are knowingly propagated by the rulers in order to distract the ruled and camouflage the 'real' class nature of their oppression. At its crudest this idea is as silly as it is popular, but since it is perfectly possible to imagine other criteria for political mobilization in modern society (of which class is one), it becomes possible to accept a watered-down version of this argument. Nationalist ideas come from *somewhere*, and, as we shall see, are characteristically propagated by sociologically distinct elements within the community. At the birth of nationalism these elements are unlikely to be the ruling elite, although it may become expedient or necessary at times for all would-be rulers to employ some of the rhetoric of nationalism. Nationalism is one possible medium for political mobilization, but there are usually alternatives on offer, and it is also often the case that nationalism, far from suiting anyone's self-interest, can lead both rulers and ruled into suicidal paths of action. This is one obvious but tragic lesson we can learn from the recent history of Sri Lanka.

If we accept the minimal premiss that we are talking of intelligent and rational human beings (rather than aliens possessed by dark atavistic urges)—the sort of premiss common enough in other areas of anthropology but glaringly absent in journalistic discussions of these matters—the problem can be refined even further. There must be some correspondence between the life-circumstances of the people to whom nationalism appeals and the kinds of things that nationalism says. At the very least we are looking for a Weberian 'elective affinity' between particular groups of people and a particular style of political discourse. And this brings us again to the problem of politics and symbols. It is telling that two of the most acute commentators from the left devote much of their argument about nationalism to the discussion of symbols and rituals: Eric Hobsbawm (1972) in discussing nationalism as 'civic ritual' and analysing its use of the metaphors of kinship; and Benedict Anderson (1983) in his emphasis on nationalism as a genre, rather than a theory, and his discussion of the 'imagined community' and its construction in rituals akin to the pilgrimages analysed by the anthropologist Victor Turner.

Although Anderson and Hobsbawm direct our attention to language and ritual, neither of them retreats into the kind of ahistorical idealism associated with some anthropological work on these topics. Both, in their different ways, hold on to the particular historical circumstances in which nationalist ideas first appear and are then propagated. Those circumstances are both cultural and material in the sense I spoke of earlier: in following their example my aim is to describe that active process I spoke of, 'in which particular people in particular circumstances make sense of their world and act in it with particular resources.' That involves describing both material change in everyday life, and change in the intellectual resources available to those living through that change. It also involves describing politics as action, argument and form of life, as well as the rituals of the imagined community to be found both at the temple *and* in the political rally. If, throughout this work, I invoke the idea of a fragmented world, this should not obscure the fact that there is a necessary unity in my choice of evidence.

Buddhism and Nationalism

One point of departure for the understanding of Sri Lankan politics is the peculiar circumstances of their birth. Unlike its counterpart in India, the nationalist movement in Sri Lanka was first granted a degree of power and *then* established a mass base. Spoils were available for distribution from the first, while there was never any pressing political need to assert a pan-Lankan solidarity against the colonial rulers. In 1931, despite some opposition from elite nationalists, the colonial government of Ceylon instituted a system of universal adult suffrage. Seventeen years later independence was granted, again without any sustained prior agitation on the part of elite politicians. The result was that the language used to appeal to the voters became very swiftly, and with only a few exceptions, a language of narrow communally-defined interest (see Russell 1982; Meyer 1982). Whereas Gandhi and Nehru, in their different ways, both tried to create a genuinely Indian identity and nationalism, the products of Sri Lankan resistance to colonialism were limited sectional nationalisms.

Modern Sinhala Buddhist nationalism is in large part a product of Sri Lanka's colonial experience. There are, though, important discontinuities in the history of Sri Lankan responses to colonial rule: 'primary' resistance in the early nineteenth century took the form of a series of rebellions, or would-be rebellions, focused on the figure of a pretender to the old Kandyan throne who promised his followers a return to the old days of kingship. This resistance, which was most bloody and prolonged in the 1817–18 rebellion following British annexation of the Kandyan provinces, was predicated on a popular ideology of Buddhist legitimacy, and much of the rebels' action involved the manipulation of powerful Buddhist symbols such as the tooth relic of the Buddha (Pieris 1950). Embarrassingly enough for latter-day nationalists, equally firm amongst the participants was the conviction that there could be no legitimate Sinhala claimant to the throne. The pretender, like his successors in later similar movements in the first half of the nineteenth century (analysed by Malalgoda 1970), claimed to be a member of the deposed South Indian (Tamil-speaking) Nayakkar dynasty. It is perhaps for this reason that popular versions of this episode in the Sri Lankan press now concentrate far more on the aristocratic participants like Keppitipola, and play down the role of the pretender himself. The last of such movements to cause the colonial government any serious concern was in 1848 (De Silva 1965); after that, while dreams of a liberating prince lingered on, there was no direct violent challenge to the authority of the colonial government.

What unrest there was, after the brief pathos of the 1848 rebellion, took the form of scuffles and disturbances between the congregations of different faiths in urban areas. Buddhist or Hindu mobs attacked Catholic religious processions or were attacked by Catholics or Muslims. The worst of these disturbances occurred in 1915, and involved Buddhists and Muslims. The heavy-handed response of the colonial authorities to the 1915 riots in turn inspired a new level of political resistance from the hitherto pacific local elite groups. But for all the colonial attempts to find anti-colonial sentiment at work in these events, the fact remains that violence was confined to one section of the colonized attacking another (or in some cases being pacified by a dubious militia hastily assembled from the European settlers). Although the incidence of such violence is related to the proto-nationalist revival of Buddhism in the second half of the nineteenth century, it is important to note that the antagonistic groups involved were defined by religious affiliation—Catholic, Hindu, Muslim, Buddhist—not by language and 'race' as in post-Independence violence (Nissan and Stirrat 1987; Rogers 1987b; Kearney 1970; Kannangara 1984).

The pretender movements were based in the peasantry of the Kandyan countryside. A second response to colonial cultural pressure was the revival of Buddhism in the nineteenth century, particularly in the low-country coastal towns south of Colombo. In fact, this revival can be traced back to the mid-eighteenth century, to the revival of the ordination tradition of the *sangha* from Thailand and the foundation of the Siyam Nikāya (the monastic order restricted to members of the highest *goyigama* caste[4]), encouraged by one of the Kandyan kings, Kirti Sri Rajasinha. From the early years of the nineteenth century, however, new ordination traditions were started in the low country, open to castes excluded from the Siyam Nikāya, and new styles of Buddhism developed, partly influenced by and partly reacting against Christian missionary activity. These in turn attracted the attention of Western figures like Colonel Olcott and Madame Blavatsky of the Theosophical Society, who came to Ceylon to contribute their ideas and organizational skills to the gathering anti-Christian movement in the last years of the last century. An English-educated member of a rich low country family, much influenced by the Theosophists, took the name of Anagarika Dharmapala, and in his speeches and writings made the most explicit connection so far between cultural resistance through Buddhism and nationalist political aspirations (see Obeyesekere 1979: 295–309; Malalgoda 1976).

There were different sources and styles of response, then, to colonial rule. Physical resistance was a peasant reaction which dwindled and died in the course of the nineteenth century. Cultural resistance, in contrast, emanated from sections of the population which had the greatest contact with colonial culture—low country, urban, aspirant groups. This never manifested itself in a direct political challenge to colonialism; but it did, however, provide a double legacy for future generations: a new style of Buddhism and a new vocabulary of belonging and identity.

The new style of Buddhism has been described by Obeyesekere as 'Protestant Buddhism'—a deeply resonant analogy which links changes in organizational style, often borrowed from Christian missionary example, and changes in ethical rationalization, which were justified by an appeal to a restored, original, and 'pure' form of Buddhism (Obeyesekere 1970; Malalgoda 1972, 1976; Southwold 1983). It is also a more public style of Buddhism, with greater emphasis on collective ritual and collective symbols. As such, it has provided a rich symbolic vocabulary for those politicians confronted from 1931 onwards with the necessity of finding common ground with a population from which they were hopelessly separated by class and education. In the course of the nineteenth century, and no doubt influenced by the colonial context, earlier ideas that legitimate sovereignty depended on the ruler's support for the *dharma* (teaching) and *sangha* of the Buddha—ideas explicitly stated in the Maha-vamsa, the chronicle compiled by *bhikkhus* (monks) from the sixth century after Christ (Mahavamsa 1960)—were infused with an increased emphasis on the ethnic base of religious affiliation. 'Buddhist' now came to mean 'Sinhala Buddhist', and the chronicle itself was interpreted as an account of the national destiny of the Sinhala 'race.' Early nineteenth-century assertions that there was no legitimate Sinhala ruler for the Kandyan kingdom were no longer acceptable; it was now argued, with this reading of the re-popularized Maha-vamsa in support, that the Buddha had himself entrusted sovereignty of the island to the Sinhala people so that they could protect and uphold his *dharma*.[5]

The Sinhala nationalist view runs something like this. Sri Lanka was colonized in the distant past from North India by a prince, Vijaya, and his followers, who founded the Sinhala nation. Vijaya arrived in Sri Lanka on the day of the Buddha's death. The Buddha, who had himself paid miracu-lous visits to Sri Lanka, enjoined the gods to protect Vijaya, as he had ordained that Sri Lanka was where his teaching would be preserved, and the Sinhala people, to whom he entrusted the island, would be the preservers of that teaching. Later the great Indian emperor Asoka sent a mission to Sri Lanka to spread the Buddha's teaching; from thenceforward the land was ruled by Sinhala kings, who protected the *sangha* and observed the *dharma* and built great works in honour of the Buddha and his teaching, works which can be seen today by visitors to the ancient capital of Anuradhapura. In later years Sinhala rule over the island was threatened by Tamil invaders, but warrior kings blessed by the *sangha*, of whom Dutthagamini is the most famous, defeated the Tamils and protected the island as the land of the Buddha. Eventually, in the twelfth and thirteenth centuries, Tamil invaders from India defeated the Sinhala kings, driving them into the mountainous centre of the island and destroying the northern dry zone civilization over which they had presided for more than a thousand years. Succeeding centuries saw the gradual decline of Sinhala power, finishing with the British take-over of the last Sinhala kingdom, that of Kandy, in 1815. But the Buddha's mission was not forgotten, and with Independence it was time for the Sinhala once again to claim their rightful position as rulers of the island of the *dharma*. In particular, other people (Tamils, Muslims, Christians) who had received preferential treatment from the British must learn to accept that the Sinhala too were to have their rightful share.

All sources agree in treating the rise of S. W. R. D. Bandaranaike's SLFP in 1956 as the second turning-point (after the introduction of the 1931 constitution) in the country's politics (Wriggins 1960; Peiris 1958). Bandaranaike had from the 1930s used the imagery of the Buddhist cultural revival to his political advantage, and his coalition's victory in 1956 has been generally viewed as a victory for Sinhala communal populism over the old Western-oriented political elite. In fact, viewed from Tenna, it looks rather more like a victory for that section of the elite with the firmer grasp of the idiom of communal politics; Bandaranaike was married to a daughter of the *radala* ('feudal' aristocrat[6]) family which owned much of the village land and whose members had served as key local intermediaries with the colonial regime. By the time of the election, both UNP and SLFP had committed themselves to a Sinhala-only language policy in government, which has so alienated the Tamil population that thirty years later the country is now poised on the brink of partition. When, two years after his election, Bandaranaike attempted to negotiate a settlement with Tamil political leaders, it was the supposedly 'Western-oriented' UNP, with a younger J. R. Jayewardene playing a leading role, that organized the campaign of opposition which destroyed Bandaranaike's deal. Since then, government after government has attempted to negotiate a soultion to the 'Tamil problem,' while opposition after opposition has been able to scare them into abandoning any agreement by popular campaigning for what is described as the defence of Buddhism and the Buddha's chosen rulers of the island, the Sinhala people.

Groups which opposed Buddhist hegemony in the colonial period have had to adapt to the new style of mass politics. Christian-Buddhist confrontation in the post-Bandaranaike years centred on the alleged privileges of the elite Christian schools and the State's moves to nationalize them. In 1962 the Catholic bishops called off a campaign of resistance by their congregations, and a thwarted plan for a coup by a group of Christian officers in the armed forces shortly afterwards was the end of Christian opposition to Buddhist political domination (see Horowitz 1980). Since then, Christian identity has been submerged in the Tamil-Sinhala confrontation, to the extent that the churches are now threatened with schism on linguistic lines (Stirrat 1984). Muslims too have been careful not to challenge openly the ideology of Sinhala Buddhist nationalism, and have used their numbers skilfully in elections to gain representation in all recent cabinets. They have won, among other concessions, the right to set up their own State-funded schools. In casual conversations all over the island, during my stay, I uncovered a great deal more anti-Muslim than anti-Tamil feeling, but this feeling was largely contained by the absence of public challenge to Buddhist power from Muslim political leaders.[7]

It is in the Tamil-dominated north and east that post-Independence Sinhala Buddhist domination has been challenged head-on. Resistance to the language reforms of the late 1950s provoked major violence in 1956 and 1958, and throughout the 1960s and 1970s Tamil politics were dominated by regional parties pledged to fight for Tamil rights against the attacks of the majority community. An indirect effect of the success of regional Tamil parties was that, possible linguistic discrimination aside, the Tamil areas lost out as state funds and jobs were increasingly distributed through the organization of the two national political parties. By the mid 1970s, after two decades of frustration and futile negotiation, a section of northern Tamil youth (in social origin reminiscent of the Sinhala insurgents of 1971) took to violence against the state, calling themselves the Tigers. (Since then the militant resistance in the north has fragmented at different times into a number of groups of which the Tigers are only one: see Hellmann-Rajanayagam 1986.) In 1977 the main Tamil party, the Tamil United Liberation Front, at least nominally committed to a separate Tamil state in the north and east of the island, became the official opposition to the UNP government.

UNP promises to hold talks to solve Tamil grievances once and for all were undermined both by the actions of Sinhala chauvinists within the UNP itself and by the increasing violence of the Tigers; violence which was met with heavy repression, including random attacks on civilian targets, from the Sinhala-dominated security forces. In May 1983, the Tigers publicly challenged the authority of the old constitutionalists in the TULF, forcing them to withdraw from local elections in Jaffna. In July, a Tiger attack on an army convoy in which thirteen soldiers were killed was followed by widespread anti-Tamil violence in the south, and eventual proscription of the TULF by constitutional amendment.

My first period of fieldwork closed, then, at a moment of national crisis. I returned in 1984, by which time Tamil secessionist attacks on the security forces had spread to the east coast. Since then, violence—including the systematic massacre of civilians on both sides of the communal divide—has become a constant feature of the dispute. In 1987 the Indian government intervened; the result was a peace agreement which sought to answer Tamil grievances in the north and east, guaranteed by the presence of Indian troops on Sri Lankan soil. Within months the Indians themselves were embroiled in serious fighting with the same Tamil groups who had plagued the Sri Lankan security forces for so long. At the same time, southern opposition to the agreement—seen as an Indian-imposed sell-out to the 'terrorists' who had been vilified for so long in the Sinhala press—started to coalesce around the revived (but again proscribed) JVP, which represented the same blend of Marxism and ethnic chauvinism as the Tamil groups in the north and east. In recent months the JVP has been widely blamed for the assassination of Sinhala politicians known to be sympathetic to the agreement. The other talk now (March 1988) is of elections and of the succession to the Presidency when the aging Jayewardene steps down. The future looks to be as troubled as the recent past but, even now, it is not unreasonable to hope for a return to peace one day.

These are the broad political and cultural influences that combined in that moment of argument outside the temple gate. Party politics had become a central area of village life, a medium for expressing tensions generated in other areas of life, as well as a source of frequent opportunities for reassertion of the symbols of Sinhala nationalism. The temple (*pansala*) is one of the most central of those symbols, and the ceremony which was interrupted' was one in which the village was celebrating its reimagined self as a village of Sinhala Buddhists, equal partners in the imagined community. But these things happened at a particular time and place, and gained their importance from the rootedness of these ideas in the lives of the participants. The place is the village I have called Tenna.

The order of the evidence is as follows. The next chapter introduces the setting and some of the main actors. The third chapter is the narrative of my anthropological progress— through temple rituals, fights, and elections—in the first nine months of my stay in Tenna. After that I attempt, in successive chapters, to disentangle some of the themes that emerged in those months: the loss of shared experience in radically shifting material circumstances; the tropes and figures of community and change; changes in the moral texture of everyday life; and finally the complex meanings of politics and the nation in the experience of the people of Tenna.

NOTES

[1] Goonetileke (1975) has recorded much of the literature that resulted from the events of 1971; Halliday (1971) is a good example of wishful thinking posing as analysis; a pamphlet by a fringe leftist group (Solidarity 1972) provides valuable evidence of the idiosyncratic style of the insurrectionaries; the most stimulating recent analysis is that of Paul Alexander (1981).

[2] Interestingly, this is far less true of the politics of post-colonial Theravada Buddhism: e.g. on Burma (Sarkisyanz 1965); on Thailand (Tambiah 1976); on Sri Lanka (Smith 1978, Roberts 1984, and Tennekoon 1988). It would, though, be true to say that all of these studies concentrate more on national symbols than on the processes of local politics. The area of political anthropology I am discussing was first mapped out by Geertz in a series of essays on politics in the 'New Nations' in the 1960s (anthologized in Geertz 1973: 193–341), although his subsequent work (e.g. Geertz 1980) seems to have become ever more firmly rooted in the past.

[3] The most useful—albeit general—discussion of hegemony is that of Williams (1977: 108–114; 1983: 144–6); Jones traces his ideas on the language of politics to the influence of Althusser (Jones 1983: 12). It is not my intention to endorse either of these approaches, but simply to point out an area of intellectual convergence.

[4] The *goyigama* (cultivators) are generally held to be the most numerous as well as the highest Sinhala caste.

[5] This is not the place to make a case for radical discontinuities in the recent history of political identity in Sri Lanka. Most sources still seem to accept the nationalists' own claim for a 2000-year history of Sinhala Buddhist nationalism. Bechert (1973) and Obeyesekere (1979) make rather different arguments to this effect; Gunawardana (1984) and Nissan and Stirrat (1987) provide powerful counter-evidence for the novelty of mass nationalism in Sri Lanka.

[6] The *radala* are a small subcaste of the *goyigama* who held a virtual monopoly of local administrative positions in this area during the colonial period.

[7] In Galle in 1982 anti-Muslim resentment surfaced in a brief riot in which a number of people were killed. Both Sinhala and Muslim politicians were at pains to play down the incident, and the trouble did not spread any further.

Chapter Two

The Setting

Arrival

That I came to work in Tenna was largely the work of chance. On the basis of a series of trips to the eastern side of Sabaragamuva Province, by early 1982 I had narrowed my search down to the area around the small town of Belangala. Even so, the choice seemed overwhelming: within a fifteen-mile radius of the town I could be in a village high on the mountainside, hemmed in by tea estates; I could work with casual labourers on the rubber estates in the wet valley bottom to the west; or I could be with settlers in their neat and disciplined lines of cottages on the government colonies beyond Gantota by the river in the east.

The minor road out of the town to these colonies in the east winds out through foothills, past villages which are now little more than suburbs of the town; yet, this being Sri Lanka, even within the town there are paddy-fields and tea bushes a few yards from the main street. About three miles from the centre of the town, by this road, is a huge modern wall-tile factory which employs 800, mostly young, local people. The other main feature of the first miles of this road is a number of ostentatiously new and grandiose houses, each marked by a clutter of parked cars and at least one television aerial. There is no great mystery about these disproportionately expensive dwellings, for signboards invariably announce which of the town's many gem-dealers is to be found within.

From the first to the fifth milepost on the road, the country is given over to paddy, tea, or house-gardens; from the sixth milepost, the tea ends and the paddy-fields are interrupted by increasingly frequent stretches of dry scrub, with occasional poor houses and vegetable gardens dotted about. From the thirteenth to the sixteenth milepost the road crosses a plateau ringed by low hills; this plateau is the place called Tenna where I lived and worked. Then, dramatically, it crests a ridge and descends steeply, dropping a thousand feet in the mile to the Walawe river at Gantota. From the start of this descent there is an enormous view, first of acres of river-fed paddy, then miles of scrub-covered plain, punctuated in the dry season by plumes of smoke from bush-fires and chena. In the far distance is an isolated line of small, neat hills, emerging, like rocky islands, from the shimmering jungle. At the foot of these hills, some forty-five miles away by dirt road, is the great holy place of Kataragama. It should be possible, turning to the south, to make out the sea, but the heat rising from the dry plain always seems to dissolve it in haze.

I first passed along this road in the company of a Sinhala Catholic priest, who was travelling out to say a monthly mass at the home of a Christian family in the new colonies. We stopped in Tenna on the way back to buy vegetables from a roadside stall and tea-shop, at the junction where a spur of road runs off toward an important and much visited Muslim shrine a mile and a half away at Gonagala; we were sold our vegetables by a young man called Appuhami, who was subsequently to become one of my closest friends and informants. The main road at this point was lined on both sides by houses and a handful of shops. A *pansala* was set back from the road a few hundred yards away; adjoining it was the house which accommodated the village's new sub-post office. A new school, I later discovered, had recently been built near the road. Spreading out from this centre were houses of mud and brick, some tiled, some roofed with corrugated metal, some thatched. In the centre of the village there were usually a few lazy cows, chewing by the side of the road, chickens, and a scrawny dog or two. Away from the road the houses were fewer and further apart, but they still spread across the whole plateau to the cliffs on one side and the low ring of hills on the other.

A few days later I returned by myself, and was directed from the same roadside stall to the home of the *grāmasēvaka* a mile and a half further down the road, who answered my questions about the area enthusiastically. I returned a day or two after this as part of a jeepload of minor officials led by the Assistant Government Agent (AGA), who had come to supervise the distribution of government drought relief. In order to make myself useful, I joined the line of officials and helped to check off names as cash and food-stamps were handed over to the small crowd squeezed into the open-sided preaching hall of the *pansala*. Some of those who saw me that day assumed, quite reasonably under the circumstances, that I was the source (or at least a representative of the source) of the relief funds, an assumption that both aided and hindered the early days of my village census. After the distribution was over, the *grāmasēvaka* led us off for lunch at a new house some distance from the road, where the parents and brothers of Appuhami, the vegetable seller I met on my first visit, lived. The house and the tea-shop and vegetable stall at the junction with the Gonagala road were the products of a series of forays into the gem business. While this new prosperity had not endeared the family to some of their neighbours, they remained on good terms with the *grāmasēvaka*, a single man who felt unable to cater on his own for quite such a grand company of visitors.

I had by now decided that I would move out from the town to try this village as a first base for my fieldwork. The day after the relief distribution I again returned by myself, and stopped at the same tea-shop, which seemed to constitute a natural centre to the settlement. I was quickly joined by a middle-aged gentleman called Mr Ariyaratna, whose English, while ill-exercised, was still a great deal more businesslike than my still rudimentary Sinhala. He was quick to approve my plan to stay in the village, and said that the villagers could provide a room for me to stay at the village *pansala*, just along the road from where we were talking. This was not quite what I had had in mind—I was hoping to arrange lodgings with a family—but it did offer me the advantages of centrality and a possibility of limited quiet and privacy. I failed to notice it at the time, but this was the 'point of entry' of fieldwork textbooks, and what at the time seemed to me no more than chance occurrences were to determine the shape of much of my subsequent work.

I stayed in my room at the *pansala*—it was in fact the *sīmāgē* (boundary house for meetings of the *sangha*), and a separate structure in the temple compound—from April 1982 to September 1983. I returned for three months from June 1984, this time staying with a friend who lived opposite the *pansala*. In all this time I worked by myself, except for three months in late 1982 and early 1983 when I employed a young man as an assistant to transcribe tapes and glean gossip. This experiment was not a success, and after that I never used a resident assistant but did all my work in the village myself; I did, however, give some of my taped interview material to a retired clerk who lived nearby to transcribe and prepare preliminary translations.

The Setting

Tenna is a new settlement raised on old foundations. Most of its population are immigrants, but some are the children of families which have lived and worked in this area for centuries. Its position defies easy categorization—it lies a few miles from the boundary of Sabaragamuva Province and Uva Province, a plateau on the very edge of the central mountains, in the area intermediate between the island's two great ecological zones—the wet zone and the dry zone. In what follows I shall try to place these facts in perspective.

Sri Lanka, known until 1972 as Ceylon, is a small island lying off the south-east coast of the Indian subcontinent. At its closest it is only twenty-five miles from the Indian mainland, close enough to be heavily influenced, both culturally and politically, but separate for all that. The island is tear-shaped, about 25,000 square miles in area, and about 150 miles from east to west at its broadest and a little less than 300 from north to south. At the time of my fieldwork the population was about 15 million, 11 million of whom were speakers of Sinhala, a language of north Indian origin; the remainder were mostly speakers of Tamil, a member of the great south Indian group of Dravidian languages. There were just over 10 million Buddhists, almost all Sinhala-speakers, somewhat more than 2 million Hindus, overwhelmingly Tamil-speakers, with over 1 million Muslims (predominantly Tamil-speakers) and a million Catholics (both Tamil- and Sinhala-speaking).

The island lies in that southern extremity of the region which receives not just the south-west monsoon on its passage to the north of the sub-continent but also the returning north-east monsoon. Much of the island, though, particularly the north and the east, receives little if any of the south-west rains, although the north-east rains fall throughout the island. The result is a great variation in regional rainfall. Those parts of the south-west which receive both monsoons are classified as the wet zone, the remainder, dependent only on the north-east rains, constitute the dry zone. In the distant past, before the coming of malaria and of the Europeans, the dry zone was the centre of population and culture, as is attested by the ruins of religious edifices and irrigation works with which it is littered. But for many hundreds of years now the bulk of the population has been squeezed into the wet zone of the south-west, where the rainfall is more dependable.

Communications focus on the capital Colombo. One of the main roads from Colombo travels east, parallel to the great river the Kelani Ganga, before turning south-east to the city of Ratnapura ('city of gems'), an administrative centre of the province of Sabaragamuva and blessed with the dubious benefit of the highest rainfall on the island. Much of this is due to the proximity of the mountains which rise dramatically behind the city, dominated by the sacred outline of Sri Pada (Adam's Peak). From Ratnapura the road continues in the shadow of the mountains, through a populous countryside of paddy-fields, rubber estates, and gem pits, before it starts to climb. Thirty miles from Ratnapura and ninety from Colombo is the town of Belangala, where I first based myself. It is 1600 feet above sea level, at the point where a broad river, the Walawe Ganga, crosses the road, which carries on to the southern edges of the mountains before forking, one branch leading on to the east coast, the other climbing up to serve the tea-growing towns of Haputale, Bandarawela, and Badulla.

Belangala is a small town with a cinema, a post office, a weekly market, a number of schools, a police station, a hospital, several mosques and temples, a Catholic church, a large number of shops strung along the main road, and what often seems like an infinite number of young men hustling gems in the main street. It is also the centre of a parliamentary constituency which stretches out to cover Tenna, and is the base for the Assistant Government Agent who is supposedly the main link between the people of villages like Tenna and the machinery of the State. His area of jurisdiction covers an older administrative unit formerly known as Meda Korale.

When the British arrived in this area in the early nineteenth century almost all the paddy grown was 'rain-fed', that is, dependent on the diversion of streams carrying water off the terraced hillsides. There were traces of older irrigation works, of small village tanks in the lower foothills, of canals along the great Walawe river that flows through the area. These were ruined and unused, although local tradition spoke (and still speaks) of great seas of paddy on the dry plains by the great river, and the land off to the east of the hills is littered with the remains of tanks and other constructions, a reminder that the south was also the site of a great (if less frequently recalled) civilization in the distant past. In the 1880s the colonial authorities invested in major irrigation repairs along the river two miles from Tenna at Gantota, and these have been added to by post-Independence governments so that now the river is lined on both sides by acres of lush paddy; these official 'colonies' are populated almost entirely by immigrants from elsewhere in the district. In Tenna itself there are about thirty acres of irrigated paddy land, most of it only cultivable for one of the two main paddy seasons in the year. Tenna men still work as sharecroppers on the lands of the original Gantota scheme, and a handful have been allocated land on the more recent colonization schemes further downriver.

The ninety miles from Belangala to Colombo take four hours by bus. The fourteen miles from Belangala to my home in Tenna took the best part of an hour, whatever the mode of transport; within living memory the only options were walking or bullock caravan (*tavalam*), and the journey, along narrow paths and over steep hills, was the best part of a day's work. For decades the irrigation investment at Gantota was wasted because of the heavy cost of bullock transport to the town of Belangala. Construction of the metalled road to Gantota, which passes through the middle of Tenna and constitutes much of its *raison d'être*, was started at the turn of the century but only completed in the 1940s. Now the road is comparatively busy with buses, the occasional official jeep, ramshackle trucks carrying rice, vegetables, and other produce to market, and the flashy new cars of the prowling gem buyers. The older ways, the caravan tracks across the hills and through the scrub and jungle, are shared, it is said, between wild animals and humans who are just as anxious to conceal their business; the area across the river to the east is famous for its swidden-cultivated *ganja* (cannabis).

Tenna

Tenna is a sprawling settlement which covers the plateau on the very edge of the last slope down to the Walawe river at Gantota. The settlement is largely a product of recent migration into the area, although its core is made up of the descendants of people from two older villages on the edge of the current village, which I have called Udawela and Medawela. These villages can be traced back to the seventeenth and eighteenth centuries respectively. In the nineteenth century Udawela was recorded as a *nindagama* (lords' village) of the local *radala* aristocrats based at Mahagasgoda, ten miles away. Medawela was a freehold village. These two old villages have now been absorbed into the new settlement which has grown up around them. Tenna itself is strung out in a 'ribbon' development along the road from Belangala to Gantota and, when I first encountered it, it was manifestly neither isolated nor 'traditional.'

Tenna is on the edge of the mountains, 1000 foot above the plain which starts at Gantota, and is on the very edge of the dry zone, with a rainfall of about seventy inches a year. The driest time of the year is the period of the south-west monsoon—June, July, and August—when the average rainfall at neighbouring Gantota is less than an inch a month; at Belangala, which is in the wet zone, the rainfall never falls below three inches a month (*Resources of the Walawe Ganga Basin* 1960: Tables 24, 47, 61). The people of Tenna refer to this as *iḍōra kālaya*, the time of drought, and the vegetation withers as a persistent, strong, hot wind blows off the mountains to the north, and the sky is lit up with the glow of bush fires almost every night. Without some method of storing and releasing water, the cultivation of paddy is (or was until the recent introduction of new fast-maturing strains) impossible for six months of the year.

Tenna is both physically and culturally on the edge of things. One kind of example springs easily to mind. I can remember on one occasion asking about dowry and being told, 'Oh no, we don't have that. That's an up-country [i.e. Kandyan] custom (*uḍa raṭa siritak*).' Yet on another occasion, when I was asking another informant about the secrecy that locally surrounds girls' puberty rites, described elsewhere as occasions for much public celebration, I was told that the public ceremonies were the low country way of doing things. In other words, the broad cultural distinction between up-country and low country, between Kandyan and non-Kandyan, was recognized and used in a wholly negative way, to emphasize what people knew they were *not* in terms of cultural identity, but never to affirm what they *were*.

Of course, the cultural distinction between low country and up-country is a colonial innovation in at least two senses: as a pair of cultural labels it was coined and employed by the British authorities in the nineteenth century; but the reality behind the label refers to the earlier division between colonized ('low country') and non-colonized ('up-country'). That my informants tended to avoid both labels for themselves can most easily be explained by the history of the area in the early colonial period. It would seem that 'control' of the area passed back and forth between the European powers and the Kandyan kings, although it was normally on the very fringes of the territory claimed by either, suggesting that the very idea of 'control' might well have been negotiable at a local level, depending largely on whose presence was most recently felt in the neighbourhood.

This is one point of change. The colonial government first started to take an active interest in improving this area in the second half of the nineteenth century, and this interest has been maintained by its post-Independence successors. The story of Tenna since the fall of the Kandyan power in 1815 is a story of steadily growing State involvement in local life. The eradication of malaria, new irrigated land, the opening of new roads (and with them new commercial opportunities): all of the factors which have brought migrants into this hitherto poor and lawless area have been the work of government. Tenna may be an 'informal' colony, but its history has been closely tied in with the actions of the colonial and post-colonial State.

Population

The population of Tenna, including the two old villages it has now swallowed up, has increased at least tenfold in the course of this century. Tenna's spectacular demographic growth has to be seen in the light of two major national trends: the general growth in population all over the island since the Second World War; and the growth of internal intra-rural migration, mostly from the wet zone to the dry zone, in the same period.

Since the late nineteenth century the population of Sri Lanka has increased steadily; victory over malaria in the 1940s accelerated this process, so that in the years between 1946 and 1981 the total more than doubled, from 6.7 to 14.9 million (see Table 2.1). All districts have shown a steady increase over the years, although the most spectacular post-Independence growth has been in formerly unpopulous dry zone areas, some of which have shown regular annual increases of more than five per cent. Although Ratnapura

TABLE 2.1

Ratnapura District, Sri Lanka Population 1871–1971

	1871	1881	1891	1901	1911	1921	1931	1946	1953	1963	1971
(10,000s) Ratnapura District	9	11	11	13	17	20	26	34	42	55	66
Sri Lanka	240	276	301	357	411	450	531	666	810	1058	1269

Source: Peebles 1982: Table II. 4
Estimates for 1981 are 79.6 and 1485 respectively (Department of Census and Statistics 1982: Table 12)

District's rate of increase since 1946 has been lower than this (2.7 per cent per annum), it has the third highest percentage annual growth of any District in the island over the whole period from 1881 to 1971 (Peebles 1982: Table IV.7 74).

As well as the rapid rise in the overall population, another aspect of the broad demographic trend needs to be noted. This is the very slight decline in the rural-urban balance in the period of rapid population increase; the rural sector has declined from 85 per cent of the population in 1946 to 78 per cent in 1971 (although estimates for 1981 suggest a slight *increase* in the rural proportion; Department of Census and Statistics 1982: Table 14). Even allowing for the inevitable problems of definition in assessing figures of this sort, it seems clear that Sri Lanka, in contrast to many other post-colonial societies, has not experienced any really large-scale urbanization in recent decades. The population has drifted, but the drift has been largely within the rural sector, often from the crowded wet zone area to the less populous dry zone. The existence of large-scale government colonization projects in the dry zone has, I suspect, served to disguise the extent of what could be called the 'informal colonization' of parts of the dry zone: the growth of unplanned settlements on encroached or licensed State-owned (Crown) land.

This unusual pattern of intra-rural migration is in large part a product of 'populist' policies on access to Crown land pursued by successive administrations since the 1930s; equally important in this respect is the lenient attitude to encroachment and squatting, and the state's liberality in the formal distribution of land. A second factor complements Crown land policy as a cause of rural migration: the virtual eradication of malaria in the 1940s, which caused the population explosion and pressure on resources in the more densely-settled areas, and at the same time removed the threat of disease which had been one of the major barriers to dry zone settlement in earlier years. The importance of these factors in the political economy of Sri Lankan rural change (as well as for the generality of the conclusions of the present study) is very considerable indeed.[1]

The demographic history of Tenna is as follows. From some time before the arrival of the British, people had lived and worked in the two adjacent villages of Udawela and Medawela, most of their houses clustered together amongst the paddy terraces on the hillsides which rise on the north-west of the plateau. The plateau itself was uninhabited, except for the occasional temporary chena cultivator's hut and the Muslim visitors to the shrine at Gonagala on the opposite side. In the 1920s a handful of men built permanent homes there: a couple of brothers of *beravā* caste who owned land at Medawela, but had been living in a village on the other side of the Udawela ridge; a *vahumpura* man and his brother who had done occasional work for the *raṭē mahatmayā* at Gantota and combined their own chena with cart transport between town and Gantota. They were joined by further kin in the 1930s, as were the *beravā* settlers. At least one of the *goyigama* old villagers also moved down to the plateau before 1930. In the early 1940s the combination of a war-time expansion in commercial chena, a new *pansala*, a fledgling school, and, crucially, the completion of a metalled road across the plateau, made the settlement a more attractive prospect, and little by little the residents of the old villages moved down to house sites (on Crown land) near the new road, until by the time of my arrival there were only a handful of houses left in the old villages, nearly all their former occupants having left to establish the centre of the new settlement by the road. The descendants of the old villagers of Udawela and Medawela are the people I have called the Old Tenna families.

Through the 1950s and early 1960s the new settlement continued to grow quietly, although the extension of the irrigation schemes by the Walawe Ganga meant that a number of old villagers left to work colony-land granted them by the government. In the late 1960s a second wave of settlement started (partly attracted by the prospect of gemming), and increased rapidly. At first the new settlers were mostly people from the overcrowded wet zone villages around Belangala, but soon they were joined by others from further afield—from Ratnapura or even the small towns scattered around Colombo—for many of whom this was merely the latest in a series of moves around the dry zone, working chena for cash or exploiting whatever other economic opportunities appeared. Some of these have moved on, but many have stayed, making what living they can from whatever was at hand—chena, gemming, wage-labour.

These newest settler households are largely to be found in the remoter edges of the settlement, living in recently assembled huts. The majority of the Old Tenna families have graduated to more substantial houses with tin, or even tiled, roofs, and compounds with fruit trees and spices, close to the school, stores, and *pansala* in the middle of the settlement. But despite their wanderings, the newest settlers are rarely alone; migration is often channelled through kinship, a brother coming to join another brother, then sending for their sister, who marries a neighbour's son, thus establishing a valuable network of new kin. Of all the new households on the plateau, less than ten did not have at least one fairly close kinsman or kinswoman living nearby, while some, by marrying into the fringes of the Old Tenna families, had established *de facto* kinship with many of their neighbours.

There are half a dozen Christian households among the new settlers, mostly the descendants of itinerant craftsmen from the low country who moved to the Belangala area during the colonial period. There are also two households of ex-estate Tamil settlers (one of these is also Christian). Around the shrine at Gonagala, and along the road that leads to it, are thirty Muslim households. Until twenty years ago, the only Muslims resident at the shrine were *bava*s (itinerant religious specialists); in the early 1960s a couple of families of Muslim traders established themselves as permanent settlers. Many of the newer Muslim settlers run small tea-stalls near the shrine, and most of their income from this source is crammed into the festival season at the shrine. Most do some gemming; a very few scrape a living from a combination of dry-land farming and wage-labour like their Sinhala neighbours. One trader, who owns a large estate near the centre of the village, acts as patron and protector of both the Sinhala and Muslim population; he and a kinsman both own patches of paddy land in the old villages which are worked by Sinhala tenants. Although both of these men are frequent visitors, neither of them is normally resident in the village; the Sinhala villagers, when they make general complaints about the Muslims, often specifically except one or both of these men as being 'unlike the rest.' Another long-established Muslim family runs a small *bidi*-manufacturing business[2], again using predominantly Sinhala labour. Relations between the two communities, although superficially friendly, have in the recent past been quite bitter at times; on one occasion in the early 1970s a group of young Sinhala men rampaged through the Muslim settlement committing whatever damage they could.[3]

To sum up the population structure of Tenna (see Appendix One). At its heart—physically and socially—are thirty *goyigama* families, who dominate the village politically and economically; I have called these the Old Tenna families. They include all the major resident landowners, the bulk of the political leadership, most of the dominant figures at the *pansala*, and most of the traders running stores in the village. They are either descendants, or the spouses of descendants, of the handful of families who lived and worked in the old villages of Udawela and Medawela which have now been swallowed in the new sprawling settlement across the plateau. The majority of the population, 167 households, are settlers who have established their homes on plots of Crown land on the plateau over the past sixty years. There are two well-established clusters of older settlers—the *vahumpura* families who came in the wake of a family of traders who settled in the 1920s, and the *berava* families who were the first people to make their homes permanently among the chena and jungle on the plateau in the early 1920s. Most of the rest have arrived since the early 1970s; the more recent arrivals are the poorest and most marginal, living furthest from the centre of the village, and least likely to be involved in 'central' economic activities like paddy cultivation. Their caste identity is often unclear to their neighbours. Overall it is a young population, 44 per cent are under eighteen, with a slight preponderance of males over females (cf. Kearney and Miller 1983).

My classification suggests a degree of precision which is never apparent in daily life in Tenna. Many of the settlers have married into local families. Given the ease of inclusion by horizontal reckoning in Sinhala kinship—my cousin's cousin is my 'brother' and so on *ad infinitum*—these marriages greatly extend the range of kinship between Old Tenna and settler households, pretty well obliterating any hard boundary between them in the process. Most of the settlers are reckoned to be *goyigama* (although most people remain largely untroubled about the specifics of caste as long as the person concerned is not intending to elope with their daughter), but no one is entirely sure of who everyone is on the fringes of the plateau, or where they have come from.

The central figures in the dramas that followed my arrival were, on the one hand, Mr Ariyaratna the schoolteacher and his friends and allies, and on the other, the leaders of the village UNP—Cyril, Lionel, and Uberatna. I have provided a fuller description of them and of the other named actors who appear later in the book in Appendix Two.

I arrived in Tenna on 12 April 1982, barely in time for the Sinhala New Year holiday—an extraordinary feast of family reunion, drink, gambling, and trouble, of which I remained almost entirely oblivious (see below pp. 202–4). In my first month I settled into a rhythm dominated by my attempts to improve the stilted Sinhala I had acquired earlier in Kandy. I arranged for a family to provide me with two meals a day; my morning meal was provided by whoever brought the priest's *dānē* (meal donated by the laity) to the *pansala*; in his absence I bought bread and dal at one of the two tea-shops close by. I spent the mornings working in my room, often watched by crowds of large-eyed small children, at intervals wandering down to one of these shops (called 'bars'—*barekka*—by the villagers) for tea and halting conversation with whoever happened to be around. In the months to come my vantage point at the *pansala* gave me a privileged view of public politicking, even as it cut me off from quieter domestic dramas. The dominant personalities in the Tenna I discovered were the powerful men of the old families at the centre of the village, not the more peripheral settlers, and not the women whose gossip at the well formed another, rather different medium for public drama.

Appendix One

Population

The population of Tenna has increased dramatically in the last twenty years. That much is clear. Unfortunately, the absence of village statistics from post-war census reports means that this increase must be demonstrated through a rather uneven hodge-podge of information. The general trend is summarized in Table 2.2[4]. There is a very slight increase during the years of expansion at neighbouring Gantota, and then a decrease until the 1930s. After the war Tenna emerges as a unit in its own right (but at the expense of the figures for Udawela and Medawela). The last official figure is the 1961

TABLE 2.2
Population 1848–1982

Year	1848	1871	1881	1891	1901	1911	1921	1931	1946	1961	1982
Village											
Tenna	–	–	–	–	–	–	–	–	30	100	926
Medawela	34	160	48	65	75	7	19	21	–	–	926
Udawela	32		45	41	30	–	46	48	–	–	
[Gantota]											
TOTAL	66	160	93	106	105	7	65	69	30+	100+	926

Note: Census figures are only available at village level until 1931; the 1946 and 1961 figures are from the Land Settlement report on Tenna (the figures for Udawela and Medawela in these years are not known); my own census in 1982 gives an aggregate figure for the whole settlement, including Udawela and Medawela within the Tenna figure. The apparently catastrophic drop in population in 1911 would seem to be an error; contemporary sources give no indication of an abandonment of the area on the scale suggested.
Source: SLNA 45/120 Extent of the Division of Sabaragamuva and Return of Headmen with Extent of Jurisdiction 1848; Census Reports 1871–1931; Land Settlement Final Report 1961; author's survey 1982.

total of 100 for Tenna; even if we allow a generous estimate of 100 for the separate Udawela and Medawela figures in that year (there were only eight households within their official boundaries in 1980), the population has increased more than fourfold in twenty years, from somewhere between 100 and 200 to something approaching 1000. The real increase in this period is probably closer to sixfold than four. If we compare the last complete official figure for the area—the 69 people in Udawela and Medawela in 1931—with my own total of 926 in 1982, we get the most reliable indication of the magnitude of demographic change: a thirteenfold increase in the population of Tenna in half a century, compared to just under a threefold increase in the population of the island as a whole.

Table 2.3 provides a breakdown of my 1982 census by salient social categories. The figure to note here is that for 'Old Tenna.' These are all the households in which either the husband or wife is a descendant of the inhabitants of either Udawela or Medawela; these thirty households with their population of 176 represent the 'natural' internal demographic growth of the settlement. They are all of *goyigama* caste. The other three categories are all, to some extent, newcomers.

TABLE 2.3
Tenna Population 1982

	Households	Male	Female	0–18	18+	Total
Old Tenna						
Goyigama	30	90	86	78	98	176
Settlers						
Berava	12	33	23	22	34	56
Vahumpura	14	33	28	24	37	61
Other Settlers	141	326	307	291	342	633
All Settlers	167	392	358	337	413	750
TOTAL	197	482	444	415	511	926
[Gonagala Muslims]	[30]	[47]	[36]	??	[83]	[83]

Source: author's survey.[4]

'Vahumpura' are members of an immigrant caste who moved here from the 1920s on; the fourteen households (61 people) are all kinspeople of the family of a man called Kiriyansa from Mahagasgoda who settled in Tenna in 1924, and who founded the Tenna *pansala* in the 1930s. 'Beravā' are interrelated members of the drummer caste, whose current settlement was founded in 1922, although those who are ancestral owners of land at Udawela obviously have older ties with the immediate area. 'Other Settlers' are a heterogeneous collection of different castes, all of whom have arrived since the 1940s. A number have established affinal links with members of the Old Tenna group; the criterion of descent for classification in the latter group has been imposed to cut a way through the otherwise endless horizontal ramifications of Sinhala kinship. From this table it can be seen that 85 per cent (167) of all households, or 81 per cent (750) of the population, are classified as settlers. Almost half of the households (80−48 per cent) had been here ten years or less; only five (3 per cent) were established before 1947.

Dramatis Personae

Mr Ariyaratna

The middle-aged English-speaking gentleman who suggested that I should stay at the temple was Mr Ariyaratna ('Ariyaratna Mahatmayā' to his fellow-villagers), a school-teacher at one of the secondary schools ten miles away in the newly settled colonies. He had come from his home village, where his family were middling-prosperous farmers and small landowners, as the new village schoolteacher twenty years earlier. His marriage into one of the Old Tenna families had given the village its first-ever government employee, and an early gemming success with his brother-in-law had provoked the first Tenna gem rush in the 1960s. He was the chairman of the society that oversaw temple affairs, as well as the dominant personality in many other village activities. When not working on his paddy-fields or garden land, he was always to be seen in the loose white banian and sarong of national dress, popularized by the assassinated nationalist politician S. W. R. D. Bandaranaike; for his journeys to school he added black western-style shoes, worn without socks. This ensemble, as everyday garb, is characteristic of two figures in Sri Lanka: the rural schoolmaster of the old generation and the politician of past and present. The first afternoon was the only occasion I was ever to see Mr Ariyaratna whiling away the time in the tea-shop; our meeting, I gradually realized, was not quite the accident I had taken it to be.

The grāmasēvaka

The *grāmasēvaka* who had been my first contact was also an outsider by birth, having been posted to the village in 1972.

His home village was ten miles away toward Belangala, and before he took this job he had been a clerk and a teacher. His father was a craftsman and small-scale contractor who had moved to the area from Kandy. As *grāmasēvaka* (literally 'village servant'), he was the local representative of the State, in theory a combination of policeman and parish clerk, recording complaints of law-breaking, maintaining census and electoral lists, and keeping a check on a myriad of minor official matters. The position was created as a part of the populist politics of the 1950s: 'village servants,' neutral bureaucrats without ties and interests in the area, were to replace the allegedly 'feudal'and oppressive headmen (*āracci*) inherited from the colonial administration. What authority had been passed on from the old headmen, however, was swiftly eclipsed by the power of a new breed of political bosses.[5] The Tenna *grāmasēvaka* continued to receive the deference due to any holder of a government post, however lowly, and indeed was still addressed by some villagers with his predecessors' honorific (*rālahāmi*), but no one entertained any illusions about the extent of his real power. Moreover his area of responsibility—his *vasama*—stretched beyond Tenna itself to include a number of smaller and more remote villages a few miles away, and much of his time was spent on business away from the centre of the village. A small unmarried man in his early forties, he lived some distance down the road from the temple and the school, where village activities tended to be centred. He would attend religious rites at the *pansala* in the spotless white banian and sarong of Buddhist piety; on official business, though, he wore an appropriately bureaucratic European-style shirt and trousers.

Appuhami mudalāli and his brothers

The tea-shop owner was a young man in his early thirties called Appuhami *mudalāli* merchant[6]), who lived with his recently-married bride in a tiny room partitioned off from the end of the shop. The shop-site had been bought in partnership with his elder brother a few years earlier for the extraordinary (for Tenna) price of 18,000 rupees (about £500); this brother, a self-styled gem-merchant and rather lackadaisical farmer, had advanced the money for a younger brother to set up a bakery, and they all combined to subsidize yet another brother, an arts student at University in Colombo. Another brother had a job with the archaeology department, and another worked an allotment of land on the new colonies along the Walawe river. The oldest brother had been left behind by his siblings' trading adventures and remained a poor sharecropper, getting most of his income from his tenancy of a couple of acres of paddy at Udawela. Their elderly parents, a former sharecropper from Udawela and his illiterate wife, lived in the family's new concrete-and-tile house, another product of gemming and *bisnis*. This family had risen from poverty as a result of the sons' involvement in gemming and trade, a fact which caused some jealousy (*irisiyāva*) among their neighbours.

The priest

Before settling, I made a point of seeking out another person whose approval struck me as important for my plans: the incumbent of the *pansala*. He was a forty year-old priest of the branch of the Amarapura Nikāya whose move into the area I document below (pp. 155–8). To find him I had to travel back to the next major village in the direction of the town, where he was a teacher at the government middle-school. An unusually shy man, he proved to be a rare case—a university-educated member of the *sangha* who, despite having a government job, showed no desire to disrobe.[7] His Sinhala-medium BA from the University of Colombo made him the best-educated and most widely-read inhabitant of the village. After graduating, he had taught at schools many miles away in the eastern dry zone, before moving to his present job and incumbency five years, earlier. When in the village he lived alone at the *pansala*; often though, he spent his nights at the bigger temple eight miles up the road, where he had been first ordained. He was a sharp and informed critic of the government, and in the evenings, when he was in the village, a number of men would regularly call by at the *pansala* to discuss local and national

politics. These men were predominantly, but not all, supporters of the SLFP.

Cyril, Uberatna, Lionel

In my first week in Tenna, on one of the days of the New Year
holiday I had sheepishly taken myself to the new tank to
bathe, and was none too pleased to be joined by an unfamiliar
group of men with bottles of arrack as well as bars of soap.
They were not themselves residents of the village, but had
come out from town to pay a New Year visit to their brother.
This brother, whom I was immediately taken to visit, was
Cyril De Silva, the Cultivation Officer, whose agrarian duties
covered the same area as the *grāmasēvaka*'s administrative
functions. He lived in a house between two of the village
shops, half of which he leased to the Belangala Co-operative
Society for their store. His father had been a trader in
Belangala, and he came out to Tenna in the early 1970s to run
a small shop; in a few years he had married into one of the Old
Tenna families. He owned his giddy rise to his present
position less to his agricultural expertise than to his standing
as *de facto* boss of the village UNP. In this he was hardly
disadvantaged by the fact that his elder brother, who lived in
Belangala, was the agent and right-hand man of the area's
MP.
  Cyril cut a rather different figure from his enemy Mr
Ariyaratna. Like Mr Ariyaratna, he was a skilled public
speaker, but his oratory was altogether more fiery, and his
appearance, on big public occasions, trousered rather than
'traditional.' He was also better known for his partying than
his piety, his opponents often grumbling that he wheedled
support out of people by means of a liberal supply of free
alcohol. Cyril's two closest associates during my stay were two
unmarried young men called Uberatna and Lionel. Uberatna
was the younger brother of Cyril's wife, and lived in the next
house. He had been given a job as a teacher—at the same
school, ironically, as Mr Ariyaratna—after the UNP election
triumph in 1977. His mother had been killed in a shooting
accident (see note 3) when he was young, and some villagers

blamed his short temper on the absence of a mother who might have taught him proper restraint. Uberatna started the fight outside the *pansala* that night in September. Lionel was a cousin of Uberatna, one of a group of brothers who between them owned a relatively large holding of the Udawela and Medawela paddy lands. He had made money in gemming and built a large new house for himself, his mother, and his two unmarried sisters. He continued to make money from gem dealing and, it was whispered, from organizing illicit felling of timber in what remained of the jungle on the hillsides behind Tenna.

Farmers

Before the administrative reorganization which brought the new figure of the *grāmasēvaka* to Tenna in the 1960s, the only resident link with the government was the irrigation headman (*vel vidānē*), whose job it was to co-ordinate the cultivation of the old village fields and supply information on the harvest to the government. There were two old men in the village who had at different times held the post, and who were still respectfully addressed as '*vidānē mahatmayā*'. One was Kirisanta, a *vahumpura* immigrant to Tenna in the 1920s, whose father had founded the *pansala*. He was a highly respected man who still worked an acre of sharecropped land at Medawela every year. He was an active figure in the organization of temple affairs, and also a public supporter of the UNP. After the 1977 election a sub-post office was established in the village, and his daughter was given the job of postmistress.

The second farmer *vel vidānē* was an old man almost bent double with age. This was D. G. Mohottihami, whose eldest son Mudalihami was the biggest paddy farmer in the village. His daughter was married to the other genuinely prosperous paddy farmer in the village. Some of the land worked by Mohottihami and Mudalihami was inherited by Mohottihami's wife; some was acquired by Mohottihami during his tenure as *vel vidānē*; and much of it was owned by outsiders but worked (often at terms very favourable to the tenant) by Mudalihami. Mudalihami also owned all the buffaloes used for ploughing and threshing; as a result he received at least some share from every plot of paddy harvested in Udawela and Medawela. Another son, Podimahatmaya, was, beyond all question, the village success story. His cleverness had won him successive scholarships to schools in Ratnapura and Colombo and to university at Peradeniya, then to the United States for a postgraduate degree. This had earned him a well-paid job in Colombo, but he was dissatisfied with what he saw as political obstacles to further promotion and was already making plans in 1982 to return to his American university to complete his doctorate. He left soon after; unfortunately for my research, he did not return to the country during the rest of my stay.

Kapu mahatmayā

In a corner of the *pansala* was a small shrine (*dēvālē*) to the local deity, Mangara. People who called to make vows to the god would seek out an old man called Kirikattidiya, who was the *kapu mahatmayā*, the man who acted as intermediary for the deity. As well as his occasional duties at the *dēvālē* Kirikattidiya also performed at major rituals to Mangara, known as *kirimaḍuvas*. He was the last of the original *beravā* caste settlers to arrive in Tenna in 1922. His house was behind the *pansala* and was surrounded by the houses of the children and kin who had settled around him. This cluster of *beravā* dwellings was the only caste-specific residential unit in Tenna, and the *beravā* themselves, usually respectfully addressed as *gurunännsē*, were the only caste identifiable as such in everyday interaction.

Member mahatmayā

Before the 1977 election, Tenna's representative on various local bodies set up by the SLFP government was a young man who, at the time of my fieldwork, was still the secretary of the Tenna SLFP, and was still generally known as 'Member Mahatmayā' in honour of his former position. His father had originally settled in Tenna in the late 1940s from a village a few miles down the road toward Belangala. Now Member Mahatmayā and his married brothers and sisters lived in a cluster of houses around his father's house half a mile from the centre of the village. He, like his brothers and brothers-in-law, worked as a sharecropper and occasional cash-cropper. The family were related in various ways to the Old Tenna families and were active at the *pansala*.

NOTES

[1] This pattern is confirmed both at the level of local studies and in national census figures. Martin Southwold reports of a bazaar settlement in Kurunegala District in the 1970s that 77 per cent of household heads were born outside the village (Southwold 1983: 21 n.10). Obeyesekere calculated from genealogical data that, from the 1880s onward, about half the males born into one of the constitutive hamlets of Madagama (in the remote northern hills of Galle District) had migrated out of the village (Obeyesekere 1967: 265). In Ratnapura District 14 per cent of the population in 1971 had been born outside the District; another 13 per cent of those born in the District had taken up residence in other Districts. Most of Ratnapura District is in the populous wet zone; really spectacular gains in population are reported from the remoter dry zone Districts: in Monaragala District (just across the provincial boundary from Tenna) 27 per cent of the 1971 population were immigrants; in Trincomalee the figure is 29 per cent, in Vavuniya 36 per cent, in Polonnaruva 48 per cent (Kearney and Miller 1985: 98; cf. Kearney and Miller 1983). These figures, in registering movement between the relatively large administrative Districts, leave unreported the large shifts of population between villages within the same District.

[2] A *bidi* is a kind of cheap local cigarette.

[3] The cause of this attack was the accidental killing of a village woman, by a Muslim who mistook her for a deer while out hunting; when his relatives effected a hasty payoff to remove him from police custody, the local young men decided to exact their own revenge on Muslims in general. The background to this, and to much else beside, is the continuing dispute over ownership of the Gonagala shrine itself, which since the 1930s has been claimed as a Buddhist shrine by certain communal zealots; in the early 1970s one such man, a Buddhist monk, took up residence at the shrine under police and army protection. In 1977 a prominent local Muslim and chief lay custodian of the shrine was elected as UNP Member of Parliament for the area; since then the Muslims have enjoyed an uneasy peace at the shrine itself.

⁴ The figures I present are based on a census conducted between June and October 1982. My intention at first was to cover the entire plateau on either side of the Belangala–Gantota road between the thirteenth mile post and the beginning of the descent to Gantota at Bogala three miles further on. It is characteristic of a settlement like this that no one, least of all government officials, knows exactly who is there at any one time, especially on the fringes. Towards Belangala there is no obvious physical or social boundary, and my eventual cut-off point was of necessity somewhat arbitrary. I carried out nearly all of this work unassisted, and the questions were restricted by my then limited linguistic abilities: the names, ages, relationships, and places of birth of household members; whether or not they had any relatives nearby, and, if so, who they were (the answers were then cross-checked); and when they first settled here. The data are imperfect, though probably not significantly more so than those from official sources (the more recent of which were not in any case available to me).

The figure in square brackets for Gonagala Muslims derives from the electoral register for 1981, and includes all residents over eighteen, but no children. I found it impossible to survey the thirty Muslim households around the shrine at Gonagala by the same means; a few of the Muslims understand neither Sinhala nor English, and casual calls on Muslim women alone at home, I quickly sensed, were a less acceptable mode of enquiry than they had been with Sinhala households. On a number of grounds—culture, language, kinship, religion—Gonagala is a quite separate community with considerable ethnic boundaries from the Sinhala settlement, and this, I hope, justifies its partial exclusion from this book. The most common contact between the Sinhala and Muslim populations is economic, and this is dealt with, where appropriate, below.

⁵ Cf. Robinson (1975: 192–99).

⁶ The term *mudalāli* (from *mudal* meaning 'money') is variously applied to anyone involved in buying and selling things, from people operating little run-down stalls by the road to the big gem merchants of the town with their Mercedes Benzes and their palatial dwellings; there is an excellent discussion of the term and its uses in Brow (1978: 129–30 n.15).

⁷ Unlike Thailand, Sri Lanka has no history of institutionalized temporary ordination into the *sangha*. In practice a very high proportion of those ordained, especially the university-educated, disrobe and re-enter lay life. There were at least five ex-priests among the settler population in Tenna.

Chapter Three

Rituals of Unity, Carnival of Division

In this chapter I aim to introduce the reader to Tenna by telling the story of my own introduction, of the nine months from my arrival in April 1982 until the UNP's referendum victory in December of that year. The chapter hinges on that moment in September when a fight was allowed to disrupt the schoolchildren's procession to the temple, and this ethnographer lost the first layer of his political innocence. The main events which disturbed the carefully constructed routine of my first months in Tenna occurred at the *pansala*; they in turn were eclipsed by village and national politics. Thus the first half of the chapter describes rituals of unity, the second what I have called the carnival of division. The first half is focused on the temple, and starts with a description of the temple as a physical space and the relationship of *sangha* and laity as a social fact. The second part concerns politics and describes the two election campaigns of 1982 in Tenna. For me, the formalized amity I watched enacted in the temple rituals was mirrored by the equally formalized animosity embodied in electoral politics. Both, in different ways, were moments when people in Tenna publicly acted out their own opposed images of the village—presenting it to themselves (and to this outsider) as a community of fellow Buddhists and Buddhist fellowship, then watching as, under the hypnotic effect of national politics, the Hobbesian 'reality' of private hostility and disorder took over.

The Pansala

The Buddhist year in Sri Lanka has a concentration of public ceremonies—generically known as *pinkama*[1]—in the six months between the secular festival of the Sinhala New Year (*avurudda*) in April and the beginnings of the north-east monsoon in October and November. These follow the lunar calendar, in which full-moon, new-moon and quarter days (*poya* days) are regularly singled out for worship at the *pansala*. A month after the New Year, the full moon of Vesak is said to commemorate the triple anniversary of the Buddha's birth, enlightenment, and death. The next month, Poson, is the anniversary of the coming of Asoka's emissary Mahinda to Sri Lanka, which is to say the bringing of Buddhism itself to the island. This is followed by the month of Äsäla and the great pageant in the old royal centre of Kandy (*Äsäla perahara*) as well as the festival of the god at Kataragama. The next three months are those of *vas*, the rainy season retreat for the clergy, the end of which is marked by the *kathina pinkama*, a collective ritual at each temple. The only occasion for large-scale collective devotion between then and the following New Year in April is the pilgrimage season to Adam's Peak (Sri Pada—the mountain-top shrine of the Buddha's footprint) from late December to the following Vesak. My first six months in the village were thus regularly interrupted by ritual and ceremonial.

The focus of this chapter is the *pansala*, so it is appropriate for me to start by describing this more fully. What I have so far called the 'temple' is in fact a collection of whitewashed and tiled buildings set in about half an acre of land adjoining the main road. The temple compound is fenced with wire to keep out stray animals, with a gate opening onto the road. On either side of the gate is a decorated concrete post; that on the left is inscribed with the full name of the *pansala*, that on the right houses a box used for offerings (usually of coins, occasionally small gems and silver figures of the god's buffaloes) to the deity Mangara. A huge bo tree (*ficus religiosa*) worshipped in honour of the Budda's enlightenment under its branches is the first thing to be seen on the left inside the gates. It is a large tree with odd tatters of coloured flags, past offerings, hanging from some of its lower branches. The tree is ringed by an ornamental wall (replaced at great expense during my stay); a small concrete shrine with a statue of the Buddha built into it faces the road. Here people would sometimes offer flowers, incense, and shallow coconut-oil lamps (*pahana*) to the tree itself. The tree, as is often the case (Gombrich 1971: 77), is far older than the rest of the *pansala*, and was the object of veneration before the rest of the temple was assembled around it.[2] One night in the mid-1930s, Kirisanta's father had a dream while sleeping at the foot of this tree, in which he was told to organize the building of a *pansala* here. At first this consisted of only the rudest of shelters, in which a young monk from the larger temple at Galpitiya (eight miles away toward town) could spend the rainy-season retreat. But with the passing years, the incumbent has become almost a permanent resident, and the buildings themselves have been added to and improved.

Beyond the bo tree, looking from the road, is what I have called the image-house (*pilimagē*—'statue-house'—sometimes referred to as the *vihāra*). This is a square, tiled structure, with an outer cloister and an inner room with doors closing it from the outside. On one side of the outer cloister is the *dēvālē* (shrine) to Mangara, little more than a cupboard, enclosed behind a locked door and covered with a curtain. Inside is a statue of the god in the form of a handsome prince with a buffalo behind him and with a noose in one hand and a staff in the other; behind the statue is a mural depicting the tale of his death and rejuvenation. The central, inner chamber of the *pilimagē* houses a large painted statue of the Buddha in meditating posture, with a table in front to receive the flowers and other offerings of worshippers.

The largest building, beyond the *pilimagē* and furthest from the road, is the *pansala* proper, the dwelling-place of the incumbent (Southwold 1983: 217; Gombrich 1971: 75). A large house, it has an open front verandah, two inner rooms with beds for the incumbent and any visiting monks, another room used for small meetings, a back room in which meals are taken, and a dark, rude kitchen in a lean-to beyond the building proper. Closer to the road, and opposite the image-house across the beaten-earth compound, is a smaller building, surrounded by a ring of sixteen stone stumps set in the earth. This is the *sīmāgē* ('boundary-house'), and the sixteen stones constitute the boundary (*sīmā*) essential for the performance of certain formal acts of the *sangha*, such as higher ordination (*upasampadā*). In fact most such acts take place at the larger *pansala*s in the area, and the building is normally used for storage and, for eighteen months in Tenna, housing the visiting anthropologist.

Finally, closest to the road and opposite the bo tree, is the *bana sālāva*, the preaching-hall. This is a large, open-sided room with a table, chair, and lines of benches. It is used for acts of formal preaching (*bana*), meetings of various societies and committees (it was here that the drought relief was dispensed by the AGA on my first visit), at one stage for private English classes run by a boy from Belangala, later for *daham pāsala*, Buddhist 'Sunday school' for the small children of the village.

The whole compound is dotted with coconut, lime, orange, and mango trees, some carefully tended medicinal plants and shrubs planted so as to be available for all who might need them, and a certain amount of unkempt grass. The whole complex is usually referred to as the *pansala*, less commonly as the *vihāra*, although those terms could be reserved for the monk's dwelling-house and the house of the Buddha image respectively. The complex of buildings is an embodiment of certain social and symbolic relations, between the village as a collectivity of lay Buddhists, on the one hand, and the tripartite division of organized Buddhism into Buddha, *dharma* (teaching), and *sangha*, on the other.

In this work I have used the two terms 'monk' and 'priest' (each misleading in its way) to describe members of the *sangha*. A strict translation of village discussions would refer to them as 'lords'. *Bhikkhu*, the term employed in virtually all ethnographies, is never used to refer to a member of the *sangha* except in learned and rather bookish contexts. The most common word in everyday usage—both as term of reference and term of address—is *hāmuduruvō*. *Bhikkhu* is a Pali word meaning 'mendicant'; the simplest gloss for *hāmuduruvō* might be 'lord'. The word is an honorific plural, like the equivalent *rājjavurō* ('kings' for 'king'). When, as is often the case, English-speaking Buddhists in Sri Lanka refer to 'lord Buddha,' they are translating the ubiquitous Sinhala expression *buduhāmuduruvō*. Moreover, a term like this is accompanied by a whole lexical subset of honorific replacements for day-to-day terms: a monk does not 'come' (*enavā*)—or go, or eat, or die—in the same words as a lay person, he 'arrives' (*vaḍinavā*—the semantic nuances are untranslatable), repasts, passes away, in a separate lexical universe. This honorific vocabulary is the one applied in the past to kings (Carrithers 1982: 48; cf. Carrithers 1983: 140). The term *hāmuduruvō* itself was also used in the past for *radala* figures—the old *raṭē mahatmayā* (the local official with responsibility for the Belangala area) was referred to as *disā hāmuduruvō* ('lord *disāva*') by older villagers in their reminiscences—and important members of the colonial administration. Interestingly, though, it is not in my experience used to refer to anyone of equivalent position at the present time—MPs, Ministers, landlords—but has become restricted to the *sangha*. Its removal from secular discourse, with all that implies, leaves the *sangha* alone at the apex of local society.

The veneration and separation of the *sangha* extends further than linguistic usage; it is also given regular physical expression. It is unthinkable in most contexts for a lay person to sit on an equal level with a monk: if the monk is seated, the lay person must either stand or squat on the ground (large monastic establishments keep diminutive stools—above the ground but lower than a normal chair—for important guests); if they are seated, and are joined by a monk, they must rise, or else settle themselves on the floor. A priest arriving at a villager's house would be greeted by an act of 'worshipping' (*vandinavā*) involving complete prostration at the priest's feet (a gesture used also by children to their parents on very formal occasions such as marriages), and offered a seat, covered, if at all possible, with a white cloth. Anyone arriving at the *pansala* greets the priest by worshipping him in this way before proceeding to their business.[3]

The asymmetry in these gestures of deference and respect is given material expression in the language of prestations. The principle here is simple: all transactions in a formal context require a material transfer from laity to clergy; this direction can never be reversed. Formal alms-givings (*dānē*) to the *sangha* are part of the rites of death and of the commemorative rites on anniversaries of a death, as well as part of *pinkama*s at temples or after *pirit* (protection) rituals. These always take the form of a lavish meal served with great deference to a specially invited group of monks; often small gifts are given to the individual monks afterwards. Food which has been formally received by a group of the *sangha* is called *sanghika* and no self-respecting lay person would accept it. Left-overs after a big *dānē* are given to poor Indian Tamils or members of the very lowest *roḍiyā* caste—both groups held to be outside the normal moral universe. In return for this constant flow of material support to the *sangha*, the laity receive merit (*pin*) and edification through preaching of the *dharma* and the presence in their midst of the exemplary spiritual life which, above all, is what the *sangha* represents.

The Tenna temple is relatively newly established and poor. The only productive land it owns is subject to a continuing use-right by the widow of the donor. Its sole incumbent spends most of his days away teaching at a school down the road, and almost half his nights at the bigger monastery at Galpitiya, eight miles away, where he was first ordained. For most of the year his meals and other necessaries (betel leaves, areca nut and chewing-tobacco, paraffin, soap) are organized according to a monthly rota (*dān vata*) of thirty households, each of which is allotted one day on which to provide the priest's meals. If, as is often the case, he is not there on the appointed day, they simply wait their turn until the next month. If a household in the village is holding a commemorative (*mataka*) *dānē* for a dead member of the family, the rota will usually be adjusted so that they can provide the priest's morning meal at the *pansala*, as well as the midday *dānē*.

Of the thirty regular households, the majority are wealthier Old Tenna families prosperous enough to bear the cost of regular donation, but they also include both Kirisanta and Kirikattidiya, the *beravā* and *vahumpura* patriarchs. The system is co-ordinated by the secretary of the temple committee (now known as the Buddhist Protection Society *sāsanāraksa samitiya*[4]), a young unmarried man who, with the aid of his father and a tiny wizened *beravā* man known universally as *upāsakā mahatmayā*[5] because of his simple piety, ministers to the monk's various minor needs each day, making tea and filling the oil-lamps.

Vesak

I arrived back in Tenna from a trip to Kandy on the eve of the Vesak full-moon *poya* to find that the *pansala* had been transformed. The usual waist-high grass around the back of the buildings had been cut back and trimmed, and the earth floor of the compound between *pansala*, image-house, and road had been swept meticulously clean. Flags and streamers had been festooned around the bo tree, and fringes of coloured paper stuck along the eaves of the various buildings, while a small stage had been built out from one side of the preaching hall. Over the main gateway was a large arch (*torana*) made of decoratively matted and woven leaves and fronds. On either side of the road outside the gate were knocked-together tea-stalls selling cigarettes and soft drinks to the passers-by. Hanging everywhere were the five-coloured Buddhist flags invented in the late nineteenth century by the American Theosophist Henry Steel Olcott.

The Vesak ceremonies started to take shape in the course of that afternoon itself. In late afternoon, a number of drummers assembled outside the image-house and started to play. Children gathered, dressed in their best white school clothes. At one point I found myself talking to Mr Perera the village postman, who was dressed resplendently in a white sarong; he explained to me that, although a Christian himself, he liked to support the Buddhists in the village. Meanwhile the drummers were competing vigorously with a pair of loudspeakers blaring raucous Buddhist pop songs from the *bana sālāva*. As the sun went down, just after six, the children were sorted into a column which set off along the main road toward Gantota.

In front were a number of boys, on bicycles dressed up with plumes of torn and coloured paper, wheeling along in circles and figures of eight. Next were two men bearing flaming bundles of kerosene-soaked rags (*gini bōlaya*—fire balls) on the end of long poles which they twirled around them as they proceeded. They were followed by lines of children waving Buddhist and national flags, crying '*Apē gamē budu perahara*'. ('Our village's Buddha procession'). Behind them were a man on a new government-donated invalid tricycle and two groups of drummers and dancers, the most magnificent of whom were wearing the tooled metal breast-pieces, ankle bells, and red cummerbunds of traditional Kandyan dance; all had red or red and white turbans. Then came another crowd of schoolchildren, clutching white paper flags, and shouting '*Sādhu, sādhu, sā*' (an untranslatable but ubiquitous piety perhaps closest to 'hosanna' or 'amen') followed by a 'Landmaster' single-wheeled tractor towing a trailer bearing a relic (*dhātu*) which had earlier been drummed out of the image-house with regal ceremony; those carrying it out of the building walked carefully, heel-to-toe, on cloths, while four men held a canopy of material over it.

Behind this was a group of schoolgirls in identical skirts and bodices, with rouged cheeks—a teacher's idea of traditional women's dress—performing a popular 'folk dance' with sticks. They were followed by one of the village's shopkeepers, with a tape recorder and a pair of loudspeakers on the back of his motorcycle; these provided jumpy, brassy music for four dancers bearing decorated arches (*kāvaḍi*) honouring the god of Kataragama. The dancers on this occasion were two young women dressed as men and two young men dressed as women; the spirit of their dance was one of boisterous good humour, a far city from the teeth-gritting penance of Tamil Hindu *kāvaḍi* dancers. Even so, at least two people made a point of telling me that this—*kāvaḍi* dancing—was not a Sinhala custom but a Tamil practice, and really had no part in the procession at all (cf. Obeyesekere 1977, 1978).

After the dancers came a group of small (and not so small) boys dressed up as primitive Veddas,[6] with bows and arrows and skirts of leaves and branches. One young man, with a painted face, a borrowed brassiere, and a skirt of twigs, was the Vedda queen, and he was accompanied by a Vedda king. Others, with crude masks, were demons (*yakō*), rushing at the crowds of spectators to produce howls of dismay from the smaller children watching. Behind the Veddas came a young couple dressed as Prince Vessantara and his young wife, figures from the most popular of the Jātaka stories of the Buddha's earlier lives. And behind all these came a shuffling crowd of older spectators. As the whole crocodile wound its chanting, dancing, drumming way along the road, someone blew repeatedly on a conch.

Two miles from the *pansala*, just before the sixteenth milepost, the *perahara* veered off the road and up a steep path to a bo tree, somewhat smaller and less grand than the one at the *pansala*, which stood alone in a recently-cleared patch of scrub. With some confusion and bumping together of bodies, the *perahara* wound its way around the tree and back down the path to the centre of the village. On the back it was joined by the knots of spectators, so that by the return to the *pansala* a considerable crowd had gathered. Once back, the *perahara* circumambulated the compound, behind the bo tree and image-house, while the dancers did a final turn in front of the preaching-hall.

Eventually the crowd formed itself into a line stretching from preaching-hall to bo tree to image-house for a *budupujāva* (offering to the Buddha). Offerings prepared by a group of women and young girls in the preaching-hall were brought out in succession and passed in front of this line of spectators so that all could reach out and touch each one on its way, thus sharing the merit (*pin*) of the donation equally amongst the participants. First the Vedda king brought a large bunch of joss-sticks, followed by five or six girls carrying shallow baskets of betel leaves, flowers, and cooked rice, all of which were taken into the image-house proper and offered to the statue of the Buddha inside. All this while, the drummers kept up a rhythm of homage from their position just inside the outer gallery of the image-house.

With the completion of these collective offerings, the incumbent of the *pansala* made his first, and last, public appearance of the day. He hurried across from the entrance of the *pansala* proper, from where he had been watching the proceedings, to the doorway of the image-house. After the offerings had gone into the building, the crowd had re-arranged itself around the doorway, facing the position of the priest, women and small children clustered together on the side nearest the bo-tree, men and small boys nearer the preaching-hall. All sat or squatted with their hands in front of their faces, palms together in the attitude of prayer. First they whispered to themselves familiar words of homage to the Buddha. Then, repeating each line after the priest, all said the thrice-repeated words of refuge ('I take refuge in the Buddha,

I take refuge in the *dharma*, I take refuge in the *sangha*') and the Five Precepts (*pansil*—promising abstention from destroying life, theft, sexual misconduct, lying, and intoxication). The enunciation of the Three Refuges and the Five Precepts, which starts the day on the state broadcasting system and punctuates virtually all public gatherings, is the essential mark of the lay follower of the Buddha's teaching. After these there was a period of collective prayer, led by the monk reciting familiar lines of Pali, some of which were repeated by the congregation, others the signal for equally familiar responses from the crowd. After some twenty minutes of this the monk returned to the *pansala*, and the crowd broke up into small groups, chatting and greeting each other.

After the *pujāva* (offerings) and prayers, attention shifted to the preaching-hall, where the two young men from Belangala who had brought the public address system had started an auction, in which the crowd was invited to 'bid' for flowers and other offerings to be given to the Buddha. This was followed by a long, long play called 'Mind Control,' written and performed by a group of young men from the village.

There must have been between 200 and 300 people in the temple compound by now. There was a slightly higher proportion of women than of men, a fact made even more obvious by the limited mingling of the two sexes in the crowd. A few young couples would arrive together and stay together, but the older adults tended to arrive in groups, men and women separately, and remain apart, even from their own spouses in many cases, until they left. Unmarried young men and women were dressed up for the occasion, the men in brightly printed new sarongs and the girls in European-style frocks, and there was much would-be meaningful eye-contact between them as the men rather self-consciously horsed around and the small gaggles of girls whispered and blushed.[7]

The elderly, by contrast, were less easily distracted from the proprieties of the occasion. On the day of the full-moon itself, a group of elderly, white-clad men and women, with white towels over their shoulders, stayed aloof from the proceedings, spending much of the day sitting quietly or reading from popular religious tracts on the verandah of the *pansala*. The clothes and demeanour marked them out as *upāsakā*s who had taken the Eight Precepts (*aṭasil*) for the day, adding most notably the abstention from food after midday to the usual layman's five. The ten or fifteen such *upāsakā*s on a major day like Vesak *poya* would dwindle to half a dozen on the quieter full-moon days of the year, when, free of the *pinkama* crowds, much time would be spent sweeping and resweeping leaves in the *pansala* compound. On the other quarter days it would be most unusual for anyone to go so far as to take *aṭasil*, but a few elderly people would come to the *pansala*, perhaps make an offering quietly at the image-house and sweep a few leaves up before going home.

The play ended around 3 a.m., and the following day—the full-moon *poya* itself—began before dawn with drummers at the image-house beating out a *sabda pujāva* (sound offering) that was to continue all day except for brief interruptions to allow the monk to address the worshippers. A number of people I met told me that they had not bothered to sleep after the end of the previous night's activities. At 10 a.m. there was another offering, this time of flowers (*mal pujāva*), with a line of (mostly) women and young children again linking the preaching-hall with the image-house, as baskets of flowers were carried along it by a group of girls. After this the drumming continued in competition with the loudspeakers while couples and families stopped by to make individual offerings at the *vihāra* and bo tree.

By mid afternoon, the few exhausted drummers who had been maintaining a desultory rhythm inside the image-house were joined by fresher colleagues, and moved outside to the compound to engage in competitive displays of gymnastic drumming and dancing, while children and the other *perahara* participants gathered around them. Again the relic was carefully carried out of the image-house, and set on the same trailer as the night before. The *perahara* was almost identical to that of the previous night, only this time it turned from the *pansala* gate in the opposite direction and headed for another large bo tree half a mile away. As it made its way in this direction the crowd would every so often have to force itself hard to one side of the narrow road, to allow the passage of buses taking Muslim pilgrims who were using the public holiday as an opportunity to visit their shrine at Gonagala.[8]

After its return to the *pansala* there was another *pujāva* and another 'auction' like that of the night before. After midnight, the monk came over to the preaching-hall, where to an audience of fifty or so, predominantly women, he preached a formal sermon (*bana*), unmoved by the fact that within a few minutes many of the audience were asleep. It is thought by some to be sufficiently meritorious simply to be in the presence of such preaching—to pay attention constitutes a considerable bonus. And so, with a priest preaching in stylized rhythmic prose to a room full of sleepy and sleeping adults and children, while the auctioneers dismantled their public address system, the festival came to an end.

The Sil Campaign

The next major event at the *pansala* was held on Äsäla full-moon *poya*. This was a *sīla viyapāraya* (*sil* campaign), organized by another village body centred on the school, the *Pāsal Sanvardhana Samitiya* (School Development Committee). The taking of the Eight Precepts (*aṭasil*) is usually held to be a sign of exceptional piety, of a sort most likely to attract the epithet *upāsakā*. In addition to the usual pledged avoidances of the Five Precepts, the taker also promises to avoid food after midday, the use of high beds and chairs, and attendance at public entertainments. These last three constitute a fundamental and particularly public part of the descipline of the ordained priest; those who observe them are halfway between the lay world and the world of the *sangha*. Until very recently, their observance was left to the very old and the very pious, like those who had spent the Vesak celebrations at the *pansala*; now, under the encouragement of schoolteachers and local politicians and enthusiasts, campaigns are organized for the mass observance of these Precepts, especially by the young, on particular *poya* days.

With some encouragement I agreed to take part in the campaign, and to join the others in observing the Eight Precepts on Äsäla *poya*. The first thing I learnt (from the horrified reaction that met my attempt to pass the day in my normal clothes) was that the point of the *sil* campaign was not simply to encourage the observance of the precepts; it was also to encourage their observance as a public spectacle. One had to be seen to be participating, and this meant dressing properly. Proper dress for a male was a white banian and sarong, with a white towel-like cloth (*piruvaṭaya*) thrown diagonally over the shoulder. So it was that I found myself being coached in the tying of sarongs while a search went on for a banian commodious enough to accommodate me.

Sil was taken—by reciting the Eight Precepts after the monk—at the *pansala* on the morning of the full-moon day. The first group to take *sil* consisted of the usual dozen elderly *upāsakā*s and *upāsikā*s who could be expected on any of the bigger full-moon days. Then, accompanied by the school principal and his two lady teachers, a gang of about 100 village children arrived, aged from six to fifteen and dressed in various approximations of the *upāsakā*'s garb. They took the Eight Precepts in unison together before returning to the school for a morning meal, provided by a group of younger men, including Cyril, Lionel, and Uberatna, the triumvirate of the village UNP, as noticeably present now as they had been noticeably absent at Vesak. The same men provided the midday meal, also at the school. Meanwhile, the older participants returned to the *pansala*, and the children were kept occupied by a series of talks and prayers.

After the midday meal, the children offered flowers at the image-house in a *mal pujāva* before listening to a preaching (*bana*) from the priest at the school. In the early evening, all but a hardy handful of the older children released themselves from their eight promises by reciting *pansil* at the *pansala*. The older children and the adults maintained their promises until the following morning. That the main material difference between the Eight Precepts and the five is the abstention from food after noon, and that most of the small observers were released from this in good time for their evening meal, further reinforces the importance of the public aspect. The purpose of the campaign is not so much the simple encouragement of a pious observance of the Buddha's rules, as the encouragement of visible displays of that piety.

Vas

The three-month rainy season retreat for the Buddhist clergy known as *vas* or *vas väsima* begins on the full-moon *poya* after the month of Äsäla—in 1982 this fell in early August. Ironically enough, this is the middle of what the Tenna villagers call *iḍōra kālaya*—the drought time between May and late September, when the scrub is bleached dry in the sun and the night-time hillsides are lit by wandering bush-fires. *Vas* is essentially an element in Buddhist monastic discipline; its timing betrays Buddhism's north Indian origins (where the rains really do fall at this time of year) as well, perhaps, as revealing a characteristically Theravada respect for the letter rather than the spirit of the law. Its origins are said, in fact, to lie in Jainism, in particular the Jain practice of avoiding movement in the wet monsoon days so as not to harm the myriad small creatures splashing around on the flooded paths and roads. That is certainly how the Tenna priest explained it in his *bana* at the start of *vas* during the two years I was present. In practical terms *vas* is understood by the villagers as a series of rules restricting the movements of the priest. For the three lunar months of the season, he must confine himself to his home *pansala*; he is allowed to spend a night away only in the event of serious illness (his own or his immediate family's). Whatever the emergency, he must spend no more than seven nights away from the *pansalas*; failure to observe this rule is tantamount to a breach of his vows (*sil*).[9]

But although the idea of a retreat suggests an increased withdrawal from the world, *vas* in fact represents an opportunity for intensifying the links between the village laity, the *pansala*, and the *hāmuduruvō*. When the *pansala* was first constructed in the 1930s, an incumbent was sought for the months of *vas*; it was only in later years that a full-time resident was expected to be present. Just as it is the priest who makes a *pansala* a *pansala*, so it is during *vas* that this aspect is most insistently stressed.

The *vas* arrangements were settled at a special meeting of the temple committee held after the successful *sīla viyapāraya* at Äsäla. The first problem was how to expand the monthly alms rota so that all 147 members of the temple society could offer at least one meal in the course of the three months of *vas*. (It was suggested, half-jokingly, that I should take up robes in order to provide an opportunity for twice as many donations.) At this stage, then, *vas* was an opportunity for the expansion of the ties of dependence between village and *pansala*; in particular, the decision to allot one meal per society member for donation brought in far more of the newer and poorer settlers who could not afford to undertake a regular monthly donation. But the links at this stage were relatively atomistic, only involving, at any one time, one specific household.

The second decision was the appointment of someone to the office of *kapa karu dāyakayā*, a combination of guardian and overseer appointed each *vas* to look after the incumbent's needs and comforts. In 1982 the position was given to a successful Old Tenna farmer, the son-in-law of the old *vidānē* Mohottihami. Usually the office rotated among the religiously-inclined old men of the centre of the village; at fifty, the 1982 *kapa karu dāyakayā* was unusually young and vital, although his active participation in temple affairs and close friendship with the incumbent qualified him in other respects. He was to have an unexpectedly busy time of it in the event.

The village marked the start of the retreat on the evening after the full-moon. As the sun was setting, drummers started a *sabda pujāva* at the image-house. A crowd gathered; there was a *budupujāva*; and the priest led the squatting crowd of about 100 adults and children through the usual sequence of precepts and verses, before retiring to the *pansala* while lights and seats were organized in the preaching-hall. Then, preceded by a pair of drummers and a boy carrying a Buddhist flag, and under a white cloth held over his head by Mr Ariyaratna and the Tenna school principal, the priest was led in procession across the compound from the *pansala* to the preaching-hall; again the ceremonial accompaniment was regal in its symbolism. Inside the hall was a crowd of about 100 (with, as ever, slightly more women than men), who stood to greet him. The priest sat at a large, cloth-covered chair behind a table while his audience settled themselves on the floor: women and the smaller children on one side, men on the other, with some of the younger men hovering just outside the hall itself, whispering jokes and fooling around. The proceedings were initiated by Mr Ariyaratna with a speech announcing the start of *vas* and inviting the agreed candidate to be *kapa karu dāyakayā*. The *dāyakayā* rose and vowed (*bāra ganavā*) to take on the job so as to bring *pihita* (blessings or succour) to all in both worlds (*delova*), this and the next. He then presented the priest with the *vas goṭuva*, a cone-shaped cup made from a large leaf, containing robes (*sivura*), betel, and other necessities. After another brief speech from Mr Ariyaratna, the priest, holding his preaching-fan in front of his face, began a long rhythmically spoken sermon (*bana*) retailing the history and background of *vas*. Some of the congregation dozed off; the man known as Upāsaka mahatmayā occasionally cried '*sādhu, sādhu, sā*', and Mr Ariyaratna crossly shushed a group of boys giggling at the antics of a stray dog that had wandered into the hall.

A week later it was the quarter day (*aṭavaka*) *poya*, a day which in a normal month would pass almost unnoticed at the *pansala*. But this time a *perahara* was organized, followed by offerings and preaching (*bana*) at the *pansala*. Each quarter-moon day was to follow this pattern until the end of the three-month retreat. Every week a *perahara* was to be organized from a different 'quarter' of the village. The following week it started from the bo tree near the sixteenth milepost, under the combined organization of the *grāmasēvaka* and the school principal. The next week there was a breakdown of communication, requiring the frantic assembling of a crowd at the thirteenth milepost bo-tree at the last minute. Mr Ariyaratna, ever-present on these occasions, quietly explained to me that, 'These people [i.e. the settlers near the thirteenth milepost] have not been here long and are still not united,' and he shouted at the children who had turned up, ordering them to spread out along the road to make their numbers look more impressive.

This was the worst organized and least impressive of the weekly *vas peraharas*. Two weeks later the *perahara* was organized by Appuhami *mudalāli*, Cyril (in what was to be his last involvement with *pansala* affairs for a year), and the other traders in the middle of the village. The route went along the side road in the direction of Gonagala. The Muslim families gathered in their doorways to watch as the procession passed (one Muslim man even being so moved that he carried his small son on his shoulders at the back of the *perahara*). On this occasion a certain Babanis, the fire-ball man from the Vesak celebrations, was prevailed upon to lead the way with his ever-impressive twirling bundless of flaming rag.

Interestingly, apart from the short detours around the two peripheral bo trees, all the routes went along the tarred road. No attempt was made, for example, to venture off along the paths in the direction of the old villages or the paddy-fields or the newest areas of settlement. And the 'quarters', as organized, involved a degree of geographical fiction, so that people resident along the road in the centre of the village were aligned with different outlying sections: Appuhami and Cyril with the Gonagala area, Mr Ariyaratna with the thirteenth milepost squatters, the school principal with the *grāmasēvaka*'s neighbours near the sixteenth milepost. Even though the organization expressed the links between the *pansala* and all sections of the settlement—even Muslim-dominated Gonagala—control and initiative still came from the centre.

Rituals of Unity

The *perahara*, particularly the famous *Äsäla perahara* at Kandy, has long been known as an exemplary means of representation in Sri Lankan society, or at least in sections of that society. At Kandy the pre-colonial *perahara*, held once a year, 'seemed to sum up the kingdom's social, political, economic and religious systems' (Seneviratne 1978: 112; cf. Nissan 1988). In this respect the events described so far in this chapter require little further interpretation. The *perahara*s I witnessed in 1982 were an attempt to represent Tenna to itself (and to outsiders like the Muslims and the anthropologist) as a unified community of Sinhala Buddhists.[10] But whereas the Kandy *perahara* represented Kandyan society in terms of caste and hierarchy, indeed emphasized these features, the *perahara*s in Tenna did not recognize caste, or any other divisions within the community, other than the spatial criteria employed in the division into 'quarters.' The arrangements for *vas* took this further; the *dānē* rota was reordered for the three months of the retreat such that the community supported the *sangha* both as households, then in the *kaṭhina pinkama* (described in the epilogue to this chapter), as a unity giving to the *sangha* assembled as a whole.

The symbolism of the Vesak *perahara*—the most elaborate of those described—was a ragbag of nominally 'traditional' elements, Jātaka stories, Veddas folk-dances. Only the 'Tamil' *kāvaḍi* dance was singled out for me as new and inappropriate in this context. But the 'tradition' to which the other elements belonged was not the oral culture of the old villages but the print culture of the schoolroom and news-paper (hence the prominent role of schoolmaster like Mr Ariyaratna), and the rituals themselves were novel assemb-lages of local initiative and borrowed ideas. The *peraharas*, like the acts of collective worship at the *pansala*, the *budupujāva* and the *sil* campaign, were very recent innovations in Tenna, having developed in the previous ten years (or so I was told much later; cf. Malalgoda 1972). Even the *pansala*, so impressively central in so many ways, was only a generation or two old, and had grown in symbolic import as the settlement around it grew ever more culturally diffuse.

What I was witnessing was the symbolic making of a community from the socially heterogeneous elements de-scribed in the previous chapter. The makers—the organizers of the temple society, the fund-raisers, the ritual innovators—were predominantly Old Tenna. Indeed they were largely drawn from a section of the Old Tenna population which has recently started to rise in wealth and ambition above its neighbours and kinsfolk. But the participants in these rituals were drawn from all sections of the village—men and women, young and old, settlers and established villagers, even Christians (but rarely Muslims). The success of the rituals, and with them the overwhelming impression of unity and amity I gained in these first few months, can be largely attributed to the symbolic idiom from which they were drawn. This idiom is the language of reformed Buddhism—what Obeyesekere (1970) calls 'Protestant Buddhism'—which is so prominent in contemporary Sri Lanka.

As well as introducing new emphases and organizational patterns within Buddhism, many of them influenced by

Christian teaching and practice in the colonial period, Protestant Buddhism is associated with a renewed emphasis on the social implications of Buddhism. In Sri Lanka the effort to make the country into a Buddhist society is inextricably bound up with the belief that Sri Lanka is, by the Buddha's express wish, the land of the *dharma*, itself the heart of contemporary Sinhala nationalist ideology. The idea that the country is, or should be made to be, a community of fellow Buddhists is endlessly repeated in political rhetoric, in classrooms, in popular songs and fiction, and in films. It was not a view I ever heard challenged by a Sinhala inhabitant of Tenna during my stay (although all manner of other beliefs—religious or political—were regarded as potentially open to sceptical question); it therefore represented a strong core of unanimity in a settlement which was soon to prove itself deeply divided.

In the next sections the story continues with many of the same protagonists, and the use of the same public and symbolic space; but, as in the country as a whole in the second half of 1982 (and seemingly ever more with each passing year since), the theme is one of fracture, dislocation, and break-down. In fact, as I shall argue later, we are looking at two sides of the same coin. When a community signifies itself to itself, as Tenna did in those months of 1982, in such a strikingly Durkheimian way, there is no reason to suppose that it is telling the truth.

The National Context

In September, with the elaborate *vas* arrangements only half completed, national political developments overtook Tenna and its dozing ethnographer.[11] The possibility of an election was a recurring topic of conversation throughout the first months of my stay in the village. What was announced in early September was unexpected: instead of the parliamentary election everyone was expecting, the Presidential election was to be brought forward and held in October. This was a shrewd move, designed to capitalize on the fact that President Jayewardene's personal popularity was much greater than the sum of its party and parliamentary parts, since grievances had grown up in many constituencies over the handling of State resources by MPs and their local agents. At the same time, the tortured internal politics of the SLFP were reaching a new climax; with Mrs Bandaranaike barred from office, her son Anura seemed the obvious party candidate, but he was un-popular with the party's left wing. Eventually, Hector Kobbe-kaduwa, an uncharismatic ex-minister, was made the party's surprise compromise-candidate. His support from Anura Bandaranaike's wing of the party was lukewarm, and no agreement was reached with other left-wing parties (except the Communist Party), so that there were other candidates of the left to split the vote against Jayewardene. The Tamil opposition, the TULF, decided to abstain, but a splinter Tamil party also put up a candidate in the north. The victor was to be chosen on a single transferable-vote system, electors marking their ballot papers in order of preference and votes being shuffled and recounted until one candidate emerged with more than fifty per cent of the total. In the event no such juggling was called for, as Jayewardene took just over fifty per cent of the first-choice votes.

Although Jayewardene proved an easy victor in the Presidential poll in October, there still remained the problem of a parliamentary election to be held within the next year. The government was presented with something of a problem. The constitutional removal of the first-past-the-post system for parliamentary elections, and its replacement with a system of proportional representation based on a district list, was no longer the attractive idea it had seemed in the first flush of the 1977 victory. It was decided to make unexpected use of one of the other provisions of the 1978 constitution, originally designed to prevent a repetition of earlier excesses. This was the clause requiring a referendum to endorse any constitution-al amendment extending the life of a parliament. What the government announced in the aftermath of the Presidential election was just such a referendum, to prolong the life of the existing parliament for a second term without a general election. If the government could win a simple majority of the votes cast (which had also to exceed a third of the total of registered electors) it would retain its existing huge parliamentary majority, at minimum risk. If it lost the referendum it simply meant that it would have to face a general election which, even without this expedient, would have been inescapable.

Even so there was no guarantee that it could win such a vote. Despite a partial boycott in Jaffna, the combined votes of the opposition candidates in the Presidential election came perilously close to the fifty per cent required to defeat the proposal. With a full Tamil vote (almost entirely against the proposal) and the replacement of Jayewardene's personal attraction with the far more dubious charms of some of the sitting MPs, the opposition seemed in with a very good chance of success. But the UNP launched an extraordinary campaign—still the subject of dispute and recrimination as I write—which, by one means or another, won the day for the government in December. In retrospect, this evasion of the electoral process marked a new phase in Sri Lankan political culture; within a year a whole section of the population—the Tamils of the north and east—had been effectively disenfranchized by constitutional amendment, and people were asking whether there would ever be another election in the south. In the long-range view it is possible to see this as the culmination of a process started after the 1970 election, in which politicians of both parties have tinkered so heavily and so frequently with the electoral principle that it may be now irreversibly damaged.

From my point of view in Tenna, the effect was rather more immediate. From early September until the end of December village affairs were dominated by public politicking. Even the UNP victory in the referendum was not the end of the matter, for the grievances of the defeated lingered on for months, while the optimistic expectations of the victorious—for new jobs, new government money, contracts—were equally slow dying in the new year.

First Moves

Until the middle of September the village had maintained a remarkable, almost seamless, appearance of collective solidarity and affability in my presence. It is true that I had seen one brief and trivial scuffle by the bus-stand involving Uberatna (the young schoolteacher and brother-in-law of Cyril, the Cultivation Officer). But odd incidents like this were quickly submerged in the still waters of day-to-day pleasantness.

I had occupied myself with the census which, after two months, was taking me further and further from the centre of the village as I discovered ever more clusters of settler houses out on the edges of the plateau. I had also spent time in the paddy-fields noting ownership and harvesting arrangements. Apart from one exhausting and baffling ritual for Mangara, the only regular events to disturb my days were the meetings at the *pansala* of the new temple society and 'good works society'. These were held fairly regularly at the *pansala*, and were dominated by Mr Ariyaratna—who made at least one substantial speech at each meeting—and a few of his younger friends. The meetings themselves were usually attended by between fifty and one hundred people, with more men than women at the co-operative society and more women than men at the temple society. Proceedings were studiedly formal, with the reading of minutes, proposal of motions, and a great deal of what sounded to me like stilted oratory. I attended more from a sense of duty than from any great ethnographic expectation; I had yet to realise that these meetings, and the newly reformed societies in general, were of obvious real importance for the people who devoted so much effort to them, however dull and prosaic they might look to an outsider with exaggerated expectations of the thrills of fieldwork.

Rural politics and the effects of electorally-dependent power on local hierarchies were areas I intended to explore when I first arrived in the field. This sort of interest was not encouraged by my new neighbours. The *grāmasēvaka* asked me what kinds of things I was interested in finding out: 'You don't want to know about politics, do you? Politics are not a good thing.' That politics were 'not a good thing' remained the general view throughout my stay, even or especially amongst those most involved in politics, and what I found out about politics was based either on events I witnessed directly or someone's attribution of all manner of chicanery to a political opponent. Nobody, though, boasted of political skill, or drew my attention to some particularly adroit political manoeuvre; indeed, I had to spend most of my time fending off more or less explicit protestations of political innocence.

In conversations about national politics at the *pansala* I had picked up the erroneous impression that most people in the village remained supporters of the opposition SLFP. In May the SLFP had held a rather poorly attended meeting in the village, which was addressed by their prospective parliamentary candidate. I noted who was there (the quickest and simplest assessment of political allegiance, as I was to discover)—quite a number of worthies prominent in temple affairs, and a handful of new settlers. I also noticed a number of people sidling past on the road, obviously interested in what was going on but not prepared to come into the compound where the meeting was being held. Amongst these were Lionel and Cyril and old Mr Kirisanta, the postmistress's father. It was some months before I realized, looking back at my notes, that these were leading figures in the Tenna UNP.

The election campaign began properly in Tenna four days after the last *vas perahara* I have described. Posters had appeared announcing a meeting to be addressed by the UNP MP at the Co-operative Store. On the morning of this meeting, a group of men, enthusiastically led by Cyril, set about decorating the main street for the meeting with polythene banners and flags in the party's colour green. The meeting itself was held at midday, and when I arrived I was immediately appropriated by the organizers and seated alongside the village party officials, the MP, and the MP's chief companion on the trip, Cyril's brother, the district UNP organizer (effectively the MP's election agent). Hovering on or about the verandah which was being used as a platform were Cyril, Lionel, and Uberatna, ensuring that the more important guests had seats and providing them with glasses of warm, brightly-coloured soft drinks. From behind the speakers I was able to survey the crowd of fifty or sixty that had gathered, noting names and faces and absorbing their implications for village political alignments. There were quite a few Muslims from Gonagala, as well as most of the village's Christians, including Mr Perera the postman, who made a hesitant opening speech in his capacity as an office-holder of the village UNP.

He was followed by the MP himself, who spoke for about ten minutes, explaining the election and why it had been called, referring to the benefits the current government had brought to the village, and making frequent references by name to Cyril and Lionel as the proper people to be thanked for these things. His speech was calm and unhesitant, although he said to me, on resuming his seat, that he had difficulties because Sinhala was not his first language. In contrast, the next speaker, Cyril's brother from town, was fiery and demotic, attacking and ridiculing both the national opposition candidates and their prominent local supporters.

After Cyril's brother's speech, the MP rose again and asked if there were any particular problems or questions the villagers would like him to deal with. This was met with burning silence. We were ushered into the living-room of Cyril's house (adjacent to our meeting-place at the Co-operative Stores) where, in contrast to their usual loud jocularity, he and his friends set about serving their guests with a meal in a spirit of careful deference. The MP asked for my opinion on the outcome of the election, before suggesting that my task in the village would be very difficult: 'These people,' he said in English to seal off our conversation from those around us, 'are very hard to get to know; if you ask them something they always give a reply but they never tell you what they are really thinking.' He was referring to a paradox of political life; the very deference that his position as MP inspired deprived him of the information on which local politics so crucially depend. As in a Greek tragedy, no one wanted to be the bearer of bad news to the great man. That (among other obvious reasons) was why he needed a rough-tongued companion like his agent, whom people would be far less hesitant in putting their grievances to. I could sympathize with his dilemma; no one wanted to spoil my vista with bad news either.

Trouble

Three days later it was the new-moon quarter day (*māsa poya*) and the occasion for another procession, *pujāva*, and *bana* at the *pansala*. This time the *perahara* was organized from the sixteenth milepost by the *grāmasēvaka* and a few of his neighbours. There was the same mixture as before of decorated bicycles and shouting children with flags, led, as the previous week, by Babanis with his fire balls. The procession made its way from the sixteenth to the fourteenth milepost, where it turned back along the main street to the *pansala*, watched by people gathered in front of the shops and houses.

As it did so, something happened. I was about ten yards behind the front of the procession, where the disturbance occurred, and by the time I had caught up, whatever had started seemed to have finished; very few people actually saw the incident that sparked off the later trouble, but all were involved in its later ramifications. Babanis, who was leading the procession, did something to anger Cyril's young brother-in-law, Uberatna, who had been watching the *perahara* from in front of his house. As I passed the house, an obviously incensed Uberatna was being forcibly restrained by his companions. Babanis, looking a little shaken, continued to lead the *perahara* in through the gateway to the temple compound and round the back of the image-house.

As the crowd gathered in the compound for the *pujāva* and prayer and the priest made his way over from the *pansala* itself, there came the sound of raised voices from the gateway. Mr Ariyaratna came rushing over to the *grāmasēvaka* and told him to come quickly, as there was trouble (*karadara*). The shouting continued, the priest seemed unsure whether or not to proceed with the prayers, while efforts were made to coax the bystanders away from the source of the noise and back to their position in front of the *vihāra*. A start was eventually made, trays and baskets of offerings were brought around, *sil* taken, prayers chanted in unison, all punctuated by angry noises from the direction of the road. About halfway through, a shaken *grāmasēvaka* returned and tried to pick up the threads of the half-completed ritual.

What had happened was this. As Babanis went out of the compound to the road to extinguish his bundles of flaming rags, he had been set upon by Uberatna (notorious, as I later learnt, for his temper), still angry at the incident in the village street. When Mr Ariyaratna and the *grāmasēvaka* tried to

intervene, Uberatna treated them with contempt. He turned
to the *grāmasēvaka* and said, 'If you are the big man here, why
don't you go and tell the police?' The answer was painfully
obvious to all present: the *grāmasēvaka*, for all his official
standing, had little or no political pull as long as the current
government stayed in power; and without political backing
there was no point in complaining to the police about someone
with Uberatna's political connections. Uberatna continued
his harangue: 'All you government servants,' and here he
turned to include Mr Ariyaratna and, by implication, the
priest waiting over by the *vihāra*, 'just wait until the twentieth
of next month [election day]—we'll see you transferred to
Batticaloa and Jaffna.' The places mentioned are towns in the
Tamil-speaking part of the island, where, local folklore had it,
any Sinhala person walked in constant fear of attack from
vicious and unmerciful terrorists.

When I asked afterwards what the trouble had been about,
one friend simply replied (using the English word) 'drinks.'
Mr Ariyaratna, whom I had never before heard utter a
critical word about his fellow villagers, was a great deal more
forthcoming:

Uberatna has done this sort of thing before. I never wanted to tell you about
this before but those people—Uberatna, Cyril, Lionel—the villagers will not
associate with them. They are Buddhists but they have no religion. They do
not join any of the societies or come to the temple. I told Uberatna that he
was a stupid fool.

Having thus explained to me what he thought was going on,
he set about organizing an emergency meeting at the *pansala*
after the evening's ceremonies were complete. The *grāmasēvaka*
called by on his way home from this meeting, but he too was
reluctant to be drawn any further than the word 'drinks' on
the subject of what he thought the trouble was all about. He
did reveal, though, that it had been decided to enlist the help,
not of the police, but of the chief priest (*māha nāyaka*) of the
Tenna priest's home temple; this was the same priest who,
forty years before, had come to Tenna as the first incumbent
of the new *pansala*. He was also a leading supporter of both the
UNP and of the current Muslim MP.

The decision to take the matter to the *māha nāyaka* and from him to the MP was confirmed at a lengthy meeting of the temple committee two days later. The intervening days had been very tense. Cyril, Lionel, and Uberatna had been very visible around the centre of the village; when one of their opponents from the temple committee happened to pass, both sides rather ostentatiously avoided each other's glance and eschewed any normal greeting. At the second meeting at the *pansala* Mr Ariyaratna opened the proceedings with his account of what had happened. One point he stressed rather heavily was that during the previous week at least one Muslim man had come to the *pansala* to watch the *perahara*. An outbreak of trouble like this would only frighten them away, and undo such healthy signs of village unity. Nobody wanted this trouble to spread and turn into a Sinhala-Muslim confrontation. These public utterances were at apparent variance with Mr Ariyaratna's frequently-expressed personal distaste for the Muslims; his reference to a possible Sinhala-Muslim clash (no Muslim was at all involved in this except the MP on whose position Uberatna and friends were so dependent) must have appeared to some as a thinly veiled threat.

There was no disagreement about the strategy of approaching the MP by way of the *māha nāyaka* and asking him to come to the village to settle the trouble, and the meeting devoted most of its time to deciding exactly who was to make up the delegation. In the end it was decided that six members of the committee should go, three UNP members and three SLFP members (in case anyone should think this was a political matter). As my friend Appuhami's brother, the bakery proprietor, explained, Uberatna had started fights on a number of occasions in the past; the problem was that he had no mother, no ties, no responsibilities. Besides, he and his friends were obviously jealous (*irisiyāva*) because more people had come to the *perahara* than had attended their party's rally earlier in the week. But, he insisted, this was not a problem for the SLFP in the village (of which he was a keen supporter) but for the village as a whole; the politics were, as ever, the concern of his enemies, he was simply worried for the common good.

Alignments

My own understanding of the situation and its sources was only arrived at later with the benefit of hindsight; the version which follows is my interpretation, and I have included in it a number of salient facts about my own position in the village which I know to have affected my perspective on political alignments. First of all, I was hindered by the fact that those on one side in the dispute—Uberatna, Cyril, and Lionel—while remaining perfectly affable, were reluctant to acknowledge to me that there was a dispute at all. Meanwhile their opponents were almost queuing up to unleash to me their feelings about the others. There was not a great deal I could do about this, for in the last analysis my physical location in the *pansala* would always identify me to some extent with the party that had staked out that side of the village as its territory.

There were in fact at least two prominent divisions within the centre of the village. The first was that of political party—ruling UNP against opposition SLFP. Party identification often, but not always, followed from family; one group of adult siblings might all be SLFP while another cluster of related families could be all UNP. A second division, less clear-cut, and partly overlapping with the first, combined age and style of life. In ideal typical terms I described the two sides at the time in my notes as the 'wide boys' (of whom Uberatna was quintessentially one) and the 'good Buddhists' (led by the relentlessly pious Mr Ariyaratna). In part this was a division between the older, richer villagers, whose lives had been built around farming and whose social activity centred on the *pansala*, and those younger men, wrapped up in gemming and business, whose predilection for drink and partying was in marked contrast to the public pieties of the temple-oriented.[12]

The divisions I describe make most sense at the extremes, which is to say the leaders. Mr Ariyaratna, as well as being the single most prominent figure in the SLFP camp, was also the accepted leader in matters relating to the *pansala*. The incumbent of the temple, while careful to remain aloof from public political activity during my stay, was well known for his privately expressed hostility to the government. Clearly aligned with these two were prosperous farmers like the *kapa karu dāyakayā* and his brothers-in-law. But just as prominent in temple affairs were older UNP supporters like the *vahumpura* ex-*vidānē* Kirisanta, whose political affiliation in no way affected his distaste for the antics of his younger fellow UNP members. Other young men though, like Appuhami's brothers, combined public sobriety and piety with SLFP support and good works. And the SLFP secretary in the village, Member Mahatmaya, managed to be young and concerned with temple affairs and not at all averse to a drink with the opposition. Political differences could and did cut across ties of kinship, friendship, and caste. People were not necessarily enemies just because they were in different parties; more often they had ended up in different parties because they were enemies, a point which I will explain in more detail later.

The dominant force in the Tenna UNP was the triumvirate of Cyril, Lionel, and Uberatna. The other office-bearer in the party was Mr Perera the postman: both a Christian and a famous drinker, he nevertheless escaped censure from Mr Ariyaratna and his friends because he never grew aggressive and threw his weight around, and was always willing to help with the various temple-centred committees and societies. Kirisanta was a pillar of sobriety and respectability who identified with the party. Also there were the Gonagala Muslims, who were solidly UNP, as was only to be expected in a constituency with a Muslim UNP MP.[13] But whatever the other consequences, their presence and their single powerful connection precluded the likes of Cyril from appealing too strongly to the ever-popular symbols of Sinhala Buddhist political and cultural hegemony. That area was necessarily left by default to the opposition.

From 1956 to 1977 the relationship between the village and the wider political arena had been relatively harmonious. That is to say, the constituency, like the village worthies, remained steadily committed to the SLFP regardless of national changes in the party of government. From 1960 to 1977 the MP was a member of the *radala* family which still owned many of the old village fields. In 1977 everything changed. The new MP was a Muslim and a UNP man; his allies in the village were the Gonagala Muslims, semi-outsiders like Cyril, and a few disaffected young Old Tenna men like Lionel. The Old Tenna families, at least that majority of them that remained identified with the SLFP, found themselves cut off from local power, while the unprecedented flow of jobs and resources that came with the new government was channelled through hitherto powerless and insignificant neighbours. People like Uberatna and a Muslim neighbour of his became schoolteachers, Mr Perera became the new postman, Kirisanta's daughter the postmistress. Cyril the trader became Cyril the Cultivation Officer, and his store was profitably rented to the Co-operative Society. Only Lionel did not take up a job, but his political protection served him well both in gem-dealing and in illegal timber-felling, his other major source of income.

If the nature of their local electoral alliances prevented the UNP leadership's overuse of the symbols of Sinhala Buddhist supremacy, the opposition suffered no such qualms. Indeed, with the arrival of the current priest in 1979, a source both of learning and of sharp-tongued criticism of the government, the *pansala* became an obvious centre for regrouping and opposition. As well as the new temple committee in early 1982, the same group set up a 'good works society' (*subhasādhika samitiya*) based at the *pansala*, which recruited from all sections of the village, Old Tenna, Muslims, settlers. Members paid a monthly due, and the society provided help with funerals as well as serious illnesses and other emergencies. This, like the parallel push for large-scale temple improvements and the whole ceremonial celebration of Vesak and *vas*, could be seen in part as attempts by those cut off from the external power and resources of a newly-beneficent state to cultivate their own alternative centres of power and resources within the village.[14] These centres were, moreover, perfect examples of the first rule of village political discourse: that the stated purpose of any politicking is always 'to bring the village together', to unite it. Which is not to say that these ventures, which had their fair share of UNP supporters (but not Cyril and his friends), were not genuine attempts to improve the lot of the community as a whole. They were. But they also provided opportunities for leadership and standing for many of those frustrated by what they felt sure was the temporary success of their political opponents.

When I arrived in Tenna in April 1982 I too was a new resource, a not inconsiderable source of prestige for my hosts. Before I had any idea what was happening I was installed in the *pansala* by Mr Ariyaratna and his allies. It was from this position, a difficult one to say the least, that I met Cyril and his associates. At times—as, for example, at that first rally attended by the MP—they were quite happy to include me on their side, but my physical location at the *pansala* (not to mention the unfortunate impression of sanctimoniousness which I must have given in refusing their offers of village-made hooch) was always going to distance me. I remained on friendly terms with all of them, but I do not think there was ever any question of my gaining their complete confidence.

In retrospect, it is clear that the circumstances of the opening months of 1982 must have frayed the nerves of the UNP leaders. At the *pansala* there was an unprecedented and apparently unending stream of meetings, ceremonies, rituals, festivities, all of them dominated by their political opponents. Then there was the arrival of the bizarre but glamorous (because rich, because European) outsider, who, before they even knew he was coming, had been also installed in the *pansala*. Whatever the exact circumstances that provoked Uberatna to take on Babanis—and a fair amount of drink coupled with an inherently lethal temper undoubtedly played their part—his action merely brought into the open a long-simmering crisis.

Unfortunately for Uberatna's party, it did so in a way that could only favour their opponents. An attack on a procession of Buddhist schoolchildren outside the gates to the *pansala* on a *poya* day (by a drunk to boot) was hardly a guaranteed vote-winner. More to the point, with a Muslim MP, himself the victim of constant sniping from Buddhist chauvinists in a constituency with a large Buddhist majority, it was the last thing the local party wanted. There was almost an air of glee in the SLFP leaders' savouring of the outrage in the days that followed. The SLFP tactics, too, could hardly have been better. The *māha nāyaka* was not only an old friend of the village, he was also a crucial supporter of the MP, providing a much-needed air of Buddhist legitimacy to a man who was otherwise perceived as representing a much-disliked minority. Nor were the complainants seeking retribution; they simply wanted to stop any trouble escalating to the eventual detriment of the village as a whole. This is probably how the UNP delegates from the temple committee really saw the situation. But the interests of the SLFP majority were intermittently visible, as for example in their immediate attribution of responsibility for the affair not to Uberatna but to Cyril, the party leader (who had not even been present at the first scuffle).

The meeting which chose the delegation to see the *nāyaka* represented the climax of the affair, at least as a public scandal. Contact was never openly established with the MP, but his secretary accompanied the *nāyaka* to the village, where he was seen by all to have an admonitory word with an unusually sheepish-looking Cyril. The *aṭavaka poya* a few days later was unmarked by processions of any sort, although a small crowd assembled to hear a *bana* preached at the *pansala*. Under the election law, I was told, all processions were forbidden until the end of October. A week later the *nāyaka* himself came to preside over the temple society meeting on the full-moon *poya*; he promised that there would be no more trouble and urged all present to continue their good work for the temple and the village. But the year's rituals of village unity had ended a fortnight before, and the village was by now deeply engaged in that odd ritual of local disunity, a Sri Lankan election campaign. And I had lost my ethnographic innocence; in a matter of days the everyday pleasantries I had grown used to had been swamped in accusations and rumours and threats.

Politics

The launching of the referendum campaign hard on the heels of the Presidential election, had the effect of prolonging the abnormalities of heightened politicking from October through into December. I shall now give some idea of what this means, by describing what politics—*dēsapālanaya* in modern Sinhala—means in a village like Tenna.

Politics can be described both as a string of events and as a particular orientation to the world. It is at once a matter of eminently public history—meetings, speeches, elections, and the distribution of material spoils—and a mode of being (what I have called politicking) which permeates, and at times dominates, the everyday world. What follows is an account of one particularly eventful day in the October campaign. In the morning of the day in question, a week and a half before polling day itself, there was a large UNP rally some six miles from Tenna at one of the largest new colony settlements on the flatlands to the east. In the afternoon the Tenna SLFP was to hold its sole rally of the campaign, in the compound of one of the poorer Old Tenna sharecroppers (Appuhami *mudalāli*'s eldest brother). The north-east monsoon had broken some weeks before, so the morning rally was held in intense humid heat, and the afternoon attendance was limited by the regular 2 p.m. deluge.

I travelled to the morning rally by motorcycle, accompanied by my next-door neighbour, a committed UNP supporter. Another dozen or so people from Tenna, who had come by bus, were amongst the crowd of around 500 who greeted us at our destination. The star speaker was to be a young and charismatic cabinet minister, who, it had been announced in advance, would be arriving in his own helicopter. (SLFP supporters grumbled that most of the crowd had come to see the helicopter rather than its occupant; meanwhile I spent the waiting time discussing the relative merits of airconditioned Range Rovers and their Japanese competitors with the minister's extremely well-heeled secretary.) Waiting at the rally were the local MP and his aides; the minister arrived with a very popular film star, who gave a brief speech in support of the President.

I watched all this, either from backstage, where as an almost-VIP I was made welcome in the local party boss's house, or from among the crowd in front. The house itself, which was immediately behind the stage, served as a discreet venue where local party officials could meet, talk, and, especially, drink. Occasionally they would be interrupted by the arrival of a supplicant eager to see a letter (a favour? a job? a pending criminal case?) passed on with a favourable word to

the MP or even the minister. A feature of these encounters was
the extreme humility with which the favour-asker approached
the politically-connected; I was later to see similar deferential
behaviour when villagers met one of the big Belangala
gem-dealers, or, on occasion, when a poor villager approached
one of the shopkeepers for credit or a loan. This backstage
deference was in contrast to the formality of the various
politicians' speeches to the crowd. In these, for example, the
audience would always be addressed by the politest form of
the second person pronoun, *tamunnänsēlā*, which is almost
extinct in daily conversation. The pregnant ambiguity between the surface *politesse* and the acknowledged realities of
power is best exemplified in the politician's characteristic
gesture of greeting to a rally crowd: on the surface this is the
usual palms-folded two handed gesture of worship and
welcome; but when turned into a flourished salute it is
triumphal rather than supplicatory, and is more like a boxer's
arm raised in belligerent victory.[15]

The afternoon meeting in Tenna was altogether on a
smaller scale. Even the prospective SLFP parliamentary
candidate billed to appear somehow failed to arrive. Instead,
as the heavens opened, the crowd of fifty or so spent much of
the time huddling under the same corrugated iron shelter as
the guests, leaving the speakers to address themselves
outward into the rain and mud, with most of their audience
behind them under cover. The meeting was opened by the
most politically-visible priest in the Belangala area, speaking
on why he ought to be free to speak in these contexts: 'You
hear that the *sangha* should not involve itself in politics, but
what about X and Y [naming two prominent clerical
supporters of the UNP], do they keep out of politics?'

Half an hour later, one of the SLFP's district organizers was
halfway through a denunciation of the government's neglect of
Tenna and of the area in general when he was interrupted by
slurred but angry cries from the direction of the road which
passed just below the house compound. The source of the cries
was Cyril, now returned from his own party's rally in the
morning; he was well fortified by his colleagues' drink, and
incensed at the slights he had just heard directed at his party's
performance. He was at this moment mounted unsteadily on

the handlebars of a bicycle, which was being rather shakily wobbled backwards and forwards by a young man who was just as drunk. The speaker tried to continue with his theme, but this was too much for Cyril, who, furious by now, jumped off the bicycle and marched into the compound. Glaring straight at the speaker, he began to accuse him of lying and worse: 'What about the new school? What about the water-pipe? Who gave you these? We did. We do all this work to improve the village, then you people come and tell lies about it.' The priest who had been speaking minutes earlier rose to his feet to rebuke Cyril, shouting and wagging his finger at him. Cyril started to shout back, then, clumsily checking himself as he realised he was, after all, addressing a man of the cloth, he stopped in mid-accusation and offered a brief lopsided gesture of worship before returning to his harangue. (It is, I believe, precisely to avoid such moments of cultural incongruity—the worship offered to the *sangha* in the midst of a stream of profane invective—that most people deplore the involvement of the clergy in public political activity.)

At this point Member Mahatmaya tried to assuage Cyril, putting his arm around him and addressing him as *macan* (a rather coarse word which comes between 'cross-cousin' and 'mate' in meaning), all the while trying to edge him away from his confrontation with the guests. Sensing that we were on the edge of violence, which could only bring down more misfortune on all concerned, I took Cyril's other arm and cajoled him back to the road and the bicycle. The meeting ended soon afterwards with Member Mahatmaya leading the damp crowd through a few choruses of 'Kobbekaduwaṭa *jayavēva!*' (victory to Kobbekaduwa, the SLFP candidate). Uberatna's earlier threats seemed to have worked: neither Mr Ariyaratna nor any other government employee from Tenna attended the meeting. Afterwards, commenting on Cyril's behaviour, a friend made a revealing comment: 'When he takes drinks, he doesn't know fear (*baya*) or shame (*lajja*).'

Cyril's interjections also reduced village political discourse to its barest essentials: look what we have done for you. What seem to be clear ideological differences between the major parties at national level dissolve in personal acrimony as we approach the village. Village politics are dominated by promises and reminders of the flow of good things from the state to the village, not by attempts to mobilize the population behind one or other competing vision of the good society. The image of the good society *par excellence* is provided by the rhetoric of Buddhist nationalism, with which neither party dares show disagreement, even should they want to (cf. Brow 1988). This image provides a kind of background of unanimity behind the sharper and more divisive elements of village political rhetoric.

Elections

The Presidential campaigning closed on 17 October with dancing in the streets at a huge UNP rally in Belangala. Public meetings, processions, and the sale of alcohol were all banned for the period of the election itself. The national press, much of it government-owned, was almost solidly behind Jayewardene and the UNP. On the eve of the election fly-posters appeared everywhere bearing the slogan: 'Do you eat gravy without chillis? Drink tea without sugar? Are we going to 1970?' (All references to shortages of essential foodstuffs under the SLFP regime.) SLFP posters, slogans, and propaganda were less visible, and if they appeared anywhere they tended to disappear rather rapidly. As a final indicator of the direction the wind was blowing, almost every house along the road—regardless of what if any political allegiance the occupants claimed—started to display posters with Jayewardene's photograph.

Cyril's house was the scene of a great deal of frantic activity over the following days. Uberatna's car, a venerable Peugeot which had never been seen to move after the day he bought it following a lucky break in the gem trade, was dusted off and tried out, scaring cyclists and chickens as it rattled up and down the road. At any time there might be anything up to a dozen UNP workers in and around the house, dashing off from time to time on new and urgent errands. There was no equivalent display of organization from the SLFP camp. Indeed there was not even a camp, the prominent SLFP supporters mostly keeping to their homes and the circle of their close friends.

The first event of note on election day was the dawn departure of the priest for the big temple up the road at Galpitiya. As if determined to demonstrate his awareness of Uberatna's threats of transfer for government employees after the election, he very conspicuously chose not to use his vote at all. Nor, whatever the rules for keeping the rainy-season retreat, would he return to Tenna after the election. It was another four days before the *kapa karu dāyakayā* could persuade him it was safe to come back. He later told me that he had been frightened that the UNP would cause trouble, possibly even going so far as to attack the *pansala* itself. His was but the most visible example of the village SLFP's fears; friends I spoke to were convinced their homes would be attacked, possibly by mobs from other villages sent in by the village UNP to escape detection. Nothing of the sort happened in Tenna, although similar incidents had certainly occurred after other Sri Lankan elections.

To join the small team of polling-officers who had come from Colombo with a police guard, the major parties sent scrutineers to watch the ballot. The turnout in Tenna was over 80 per cent, many wearing their newest and smartest clothes to attend the poll. Some, like Appuhami's brother the bakery-owner, waited for an astrologically auspicious time (*näkat*) before casting their votes; others, like his father, went to the *pansala* to pay obeisance to the Buddha before voting. On the way everyone had to pass Cyril's house, where lists of those voting were being checked off. But apart from a couple of carloads of favour-bedecked (and drunk) party supporters cruising up and down the road, the standard of electoral decorum was high. At this stage, the new frocks and sarongs, and the general atmosphere of slightly nervous restraint, were more reminiscent of a *pinkama* at the *pansala* than of the rowdiness of the big rallies.

The first results were announced early the next morning and continued, District by District, throughout the day, although by mid-afternoon it was not only clear that Jayewardene had won but that he had achieved the necessary 50 per cent on the first count. Nor can anyone have been ignorant of the fact; from dawn every radio in the village had been tuned in to the same frequency and each announcement of an addition to the UNP vote was greeted with cheers and the spatter of fire-crackers from Cyril's house.

I paid my first visit to the victorious party's headquarters at about 9 a.m. The more important supporters had been provided with chairs on the verandah, and a considerable crowd was lounging around waiting for new results. Those who were not already blind drunk were at least merry—or Muslims. Cyril greeted me with the announcement that I too had joined their party. Then, after much whispered conversation, I was invited into the house, where, in a room right at the back and well out of the public view, Cyril produced a bottle of local hooch (*kaṭukambi* 'barbed wire,' as it is appropriately known) from under a mattress where it had been concealed. It is peculiarly instructive that, for all the visibility of it effects as the day wore on, the heavy weight of shame (*lajja*) associated with village drinking meant that the bottles themselves remained hidden in the back room while their owner danced down the street (cf. Meyer 1984: 150).

By the early afternoon the scene at Cyril's house had changed. The cheers from each result had lingered and met, producing a continuous noise; occasionally this would resolve itself into a chant such as 'Kobbekaduwa *apiṭ epā*' (we don't want Kobbekaduwa), but more often it was just a general roar. Someone was banging out a dance rhythm on a hand drum, and even the worthies had given up their dignified seats of the morning to join in the dancing and singing. Cyril and Lionel were conducting the proceedings from the counter of the adjoining Co-operative Store. From there the crowd spilled out into the street, where Cyril, sarong hitched into his underwear, stalked up and down acting the part of 'Kobbeka-duwa *yakā*' (the Kobbekaduwa demon) while a friend mimed his exorcism.

During all this time the SLFP supporters stayed indoors, although one or two of the braver ones would occasionally saunter down to look at the celebrations from a safe distance. The dancing, singing crowd of drunken adults and sober children made its way down the street to the Gonagala junction, where Cyril buckled the Muslims' signboard in an effort to secure a perch from which to make yet another speech. Uberatna's car had now been brought out to the road, and

with a couple of drunken friends hanging from the bonnet, it
led the crowd, by now over one hundred strong, and including
a few women as well as men and children, in a victory
procession which followed the route and—transposed to the
register of disorder—the form of the *vas peraharas*. The
procession disappeared along the road in the direction of the
sixteenth milepost; as they passed the houses of well-known
opponents, taunts were chanted and shouted at them. After
about an hour the procession returned to the centre of the
village, with nothing worse to report than the start of
hangovers and much hurt pride on the part of the defeated
opposition. The party was quietened to listen to the President's victory broadcast on the radio, and as darkness fell the
village gradually returned to an uneasy peace.

The pattern of the referendum campaign in December was
broadly similar in the village. The UNP held a rally at which
the MP offered his explanation of why the government had
chosen this course rather than a general election. There were
bigger rallies in Belangala. The most significant difference in
the campaign was the demoralization of the opposition. The
SLFP organized no rallies in the district at all, and many of
their supporters in the village (rather surprisingly) saw the
result as a foregone conclusion. The UNP had won a majority
of the village's votes in October, and a growing number of
SLFP supporters publicly defected to the UNP.

I was not able to witness the December poll in the village.
When I returned, I was told that messages had been sent by
Cyril to all the remaining SLFP supporters warning them not
to attend the poll as scrutineers. One by one, the party
supporters found pressing business elsewhere that day; only
the *kapa karu dāyakayā* attended the poll as a SLFP scrutineer,
striding defiantly past the UNP leaders at Cyril's house. The
UNP won again—although the tactics employed remain the
source of much controversy in the country—and the Tenna
celebrations even outshone those in October. The opposition
symbol on the ballot-paper was a water-pot; Cyril and his
friends ceremonially smashed a large number of these and
then—and this was whispered to me as especially shocking—
Cyril dropped his sarong and danced down the main street in
his underwear.

Carnival of Division

These months of heightened political activity were obviously important to the village. The old leadership grouped around the *pansala* now had to face the fact that their opponents' ascendancy was more than temporary. Cyril, Lionel, Uberatna, and their power, would all have to be lived with. But there is another reason why I have chosen to describe them in the detail and style I have used here. I left the village a few days after the Presidential election feeling physically and emotionally drained by the intensity of the events of the preceding weeks. Nor was I alone in this reaction. Friends, especially the politically uncommitted, frequently apologized for the unseemliness of the village during those days. 'It's all right,' they would say, 'this trouble will finish with the election. After that the village will return to normal.' This can be compared with the *grāmasēvaka* assuring me, months earlier, that I really did not want to know about politics, as they only meant trouble.

What kind of trouble? And what is meant by normal? I suggest that village politics are seen by many villagers as a condition of collective moral disorder. Running parallel with the election was a second public drama in Tenna: the possession of an adolescent Muslim girl by a host of disturbing demons and ghosts. Dealing with this unprecedented eruption of the demonic proved a further test for the unity of the settlement. The case was eventually taken on by a Buddhist priest from a neighbouring village; at one point he insisted that the patient should hear *gihi pirit* (*pirit*—protective verses—chanted by laymen) every day. When I called on the patient on the evening of election day, no *pirit* was being said, and I asked one of her (Buddhist) neighbours why this was so; he explained that because of the elections people's minds (*hita*) were not good, and *pirit*, to be efficacious, must be recited with a good, pure mind. Such a condition was unattainable in the midst of all this politics.

The most striking contrast to me as an outsider was between the long, slow months of public *politesse* with which my fieldwork had started and the brief, flaring moments of violence and argument brought on by the elections. One way to describe the latter is to borrow my friend's description of

Cyril's drunkenness: the forgetting of fear and shame. Shame (*lajja*) might, for reasons I discuss below, be better translated as 'restraint' or 'holding in check.' Drink, like politics, or, most of all, a combination of drink and politics, allows for the suspension of the heavy imperatives of face-to-face constraint which dominate everyday life in a community like Tenna. Again and again, when violence or anger broke through, people would describe this eruption of abnormality in a political idiom, translating what struck me as simply personal disputes into differences of political alignment.

Moments of political agitation are moments when, in contrast to 'the normal,' it is not so much accepted as expected or assumed that you will say what you like about your enemies. It is therefore often expedient to choose the political side that allows the best prospect of getting at a particular group of close enemies, a strategy which goes some way to explaining the volatility of political allegiance in rural Sri Lanka. Village politics with their attendant electoral rituals, like those I have just described, are a kind of carnival of ill-fellowship, turning upside down the normal world of oppressively insistent good fellowship. Nowhere is this clearer than in the drunken victory procession, a parodic reversal of so many temple-based rituals of unity, with splenetic taunts at individual enemies taking the place of unison chants celebrating 'our' village, 'our' procession. Perhaps the form of the procession was a deliberate attempt to lampoon their enemies' earlier use of the *pansala* and its rituals as a political resource. Certainly the contrast was dramatic enough for me. After five months of too-placid introduction, I had felt life in Tenna was too calm and nice to be entirely credible. Two more months and the reverse seemed to be true; surely the stylized animosity of the victory parade was, in its way, just as improbable a representation of the village. I shall return to this theme in Chapter Six, which goes further into the strains, pressures, and contradictions of the 'normal' moral order.

Epilogue

After the Presidential election it was as if the village was picking itself up and dusting itself off; there was a sense of hangover and of a need to pick up the threads of whatever had been happening before this untoward interruption. What had been happening was *vas* and its Durkheimian rituals of village unity. There still remained a few weeks before the end of the retreat which is marked by the *kathina pinkama*, held in each *pansala* and carefully arranged on a different day in each village, so as to allow as many members of the *sangha* as possible to attend each *pansala*. A secondary effect of these arrangements is a degree of inter-village competition, as each tries to outdo its neighbours in the magnificence of its offerings.

For after the fragmentation of both *sangha* (each to his own *pansala*) and village (each household in turn providing), the *kathina pinkama* is the moment in the year when the village as a whole makes its offerings to the *sangha* as a whole. Tenna had divided itself into households and quarters in the previous months of *vas*, now was the time to join these together again. As well as the trappings of other *pansala* rituals, an all-night *pirit* ceremony was held in the preaching-hall, relays of monks taking it in turns to keep the recital of the protective verses going, while the lay audience clutched the thread (*nul*) through which the power of the verses is thought to be transmitted.

The following morning the *kapa karu dāyakayā* gave a new robe to the *sangha*, as the start of the biggest alms-giving of the year. A previous incumbent of the Tenna *pansala* (and well-known SLFP supporter) made a brief speech with a clear allusion to the UNP's reprehensible attack on Buddhism in previous months (by which he meant Uberatna's scrap outside the gate). As well as an enormous feast, each of the priests present was given an individual gift from the village. *Rodiya*s (the lowest beggar caste) from a village near Belangala had come to clear up the scraps of *sanghika* food among the leftovers. With these quintessential outsiders acting out their part in the proceedings, the cycle of rituals ended in Tenna. Apart from the allusion in the visiting priest's speech, and the conspicuous absence of a few political leaders, there was little indication of the fragility—so recently and so vividly revealed—behind this display of apparent unity.

NOTES

[1] *Pinkama* means literally 'merit-making' (from *pin* 'merit'), and is used to describe any act of medium-scale to large-scale Buddhist devotion.

[2] There were at least two other bo trees on the plateau which were the focus of devotion during my stay, one near the sixteenth mile-post, and the other near a collection of squatter dwellings called Pihimbiyagala. Both were the object of *pinkama*s, organized in the neighbourhood, and seemed likely in the long term to be built up into *pansala*s in their own right.

[3] Practical exceptions are made to this rule: urban eating-houses and buses (although all buses have a front seat reserved 'for clergy' and someone will always give up a seat if a monk boards) and the platforms of political rallies. On one occasion I was sitting in a village tea-shop when a monk arrived to wait for a bus; amidst the flurry of preparation (getting a chair and spreading a cloth on it) I rose with the other customers. I was told that I should sit down again, as 'only we (i.e. Sinhala Buddhists) have to do this, you don't.' It is odd that one recent writer (Southwold 1983), eager to demonstrate the extreme paucity of ritual in Buddhism, fails to mention this area of highly ritualized conduct.

[4] Until early 1982 there had in fact been two parallel men's and women's societies concerned with the management of the *pansala*, but they had been merged into one new body shortly before my arrival. Mr Ariyaratna and a number of the older Tenna farmers and traders were stalwarts of the society, as were the *beravā* and *vahumpura* patriarchs, Kirikattidiya and Kirisanta. New ideas and energy were provided by younger educated men like Appuhami and his younger brother, the bakery proprietor. Although Lionel and Cyril were both listed as founder-members of the society, they and their cronies never attended its meetings and played little or no part in the cycle of *pinkama*s that followed my arrival. Members had to pay a small monthly subscription, and held monthly meetings in the *bana sālāva* every full-moon *poya*. Of 147 members in September 1982, 58 were from Old Tenna households (including in-marrying settlers), 20 were from *beravā* households, 13 *vahumpura*, and 56 new settlers. (Another 16 were recently-dead villagers whose monthly subscriptions were paid by relatives to gain merit for them.)

[5] The term *upāsakā* (fem. *upāsikā*) is strictly speaking applicable to any lay Buddhist, but in practice reserved for the exceptionally devout (see Gombrich 1971: 65).

[6] Veddas are the supposedly primitive autochthonous inhabitants of Sri Lanka; for an excellent history of the term and its shifting meaning see Brow (1978: 3–39).

[7] This aspect of proceedings was by no means universally approved: the following year both the *grāmasēvaka* and the principal of the village school complained to me that the young no longer knew how to behave properly at the *pansala*.

[8] There is no doubt that the increased flow of Muslim pilgrims on Buddhist public holidays spurred the village Buddhists to greater and more public religious displays.

[9] These are the rules as explained to me by a couple of leading members of the temple committee; they do not correspond to the monk's actual movements during *vas*, as will become clear. (Cf. Gombrich 1971: 279–80).

[10] Compare the development rituals described by Tennekoon (1988).

[11] There are a number of good secondary sources on recent Sri Lankan politics. Wilson (1979), Jupp (1978), and the closing chapters of De Silva's history of Sri Lanka (1981) all tell the story up to the arrival of Jayewardene's government. More recent events are often most accessible in the foreign pages of the international press but Manor (1984), especially the contributions by Obeyesekere (1984b), Meyer (1984), and 'Priya Samarakone' (1984), covers some of the same ground as this chapter from a national perspective; see also Tambiah (1986).

[12] Nationally, the UNP's wooing of disaffected youth in the waning days of the Bandaranaike administration provided it with cadres of young workers in the 1977 election; many of these were rewarded with jobs (Uberatna became an unlikely schoolteacher) and privileged access to power. By 1982, there was concern about the growth of political thuggery among the UNP's supporters; in 1983 they were blamed for an escalating series of incidents, including much of the communal violence in July of that year (Obeyesekere 1984b). It is, though, hard to extrapolate Tenna political divisions to the national context; there had been (and somewhere probably still are) SLFP 'wide boys' in the 1970s, suggesting that here we are dealing with an aspect of power rather than an aspect of party.

[13] The Muslims, especially in recent years, are said to have exploited their block voting power in bargaining with both major parties, resulting in what is widely seen (by non-Muslims in Sri Lanka) as a disproportionate representation in both parliament and the government. Crucially, and unlike the northern Tamils, they have avoided all public challenge to Sinhala Buddhist cultural hegemony. As they are only too aware, this calls for a difficult and dangerous balancing act.

[14] I am grateful to Robert Jones for first making this point to me. In a parallel use of Buddhism as a surrogate political arena, Mrs Bandaranaike, barred from campaigning in the Presidential election, embarked instead on a series of well-publicized *pujāvas* at temples in the south. Whatever the crowds she drew, no government could afford to be seen barring a widow from her devotions.

[15] One day at the village school, I was invited to watch a group of nine-and ten-year-old children improvising little dramatic skits. One boy was told to act the part of a politician. His inspired performance reduced the political style to its functional necessities: a mimed speech of great violence

and much finger-jabbing, a quick transformation into a treacly-smiling 'worship' of the imagined crowd, before reverting to the belligerence of the speech as he waved his pressed palms above his head, while the other children, equally familiar with what was expected, rushed forward with pretended garlands and imaginary chits to press into his hand.

Chapter Four

Work and Difference

In the rest of this book I shall build up a series of overlapping contexts in which we can situate the experiences recorded in the last chapter, starting here with the material circumstances of life in Tenna. Early in the introduction to this work I used the example of chena cultivation to demonstrate the inseparability of 'material' and 'cultural' evidence. Ways of working can never be wholly separated from social relationships and valuations; economies are, like it or not, *moral* structures governed by shared assumptions of reciprocity, justice, fairness, and so on. At times of change different parties may appeal to different assumptions to justify their actions: the newly rich, for example, defend themselves in terms of necessity and the norms of the market, while the poor try to assert their rights in terms of older expectations of justice and entitlement (Scott 1976, 1985; Thompson 1971; Moore 1978). But even at moments of little apparent conflict, the world of work is a world structured by cultural assumptions, in which ideas of identity and personhood are embodied and made manifest.

In this chapter I describe certain features of economic change in Tenna over the last 150 years. The theme—as in the following chapters—is of the threat of dislocation and the effort made to put back together what time and circumstances have attacked. I contrast a picture of the past in which everyday work at once created, embodied, and reinforced a set of shared assumptions about inequalities and equalities, similarities and differences in local social life, with a present in which those particular assumptions have lost much of their force in the fragmentation of common experience in newer kinds of work. Paradoxically, the best evidence for these older assumptions can be found in accounts of dispute, while one modern response to the fragmentation I document is the creation of rituals of unity like those I described in the previous chapter. At the same time my dependence on older villagers' memories of the past lends an unavoidably romantic tinge to parts of this chapter. In the next chapter I return to the problems of memory; the discussion there should further erode the temptingly simple opposition of present and past in terms of division and harmony, individualism and community—an opposition which sometimes threatens to dominate this chapter.

Land and Person

In order to place my evidence in a wider perspective I shall start by drawing out certain implications from two of the best-known earlier ethnographies of rural Sri Lanka, Obeyesekere's *Land Tenure in Village Ceylon* (1967) and Leach's *Pul Eliya* (1961a). As Obeyesekere's work was in part designed as a response to Leach (Obeyesekere 1967: x), the two share sufficient common ground to be profitably read as two approaches to some very similar material. But in order to grasp those similarities it is necessary for us to isolate the source of the apparent differences between the two. Apart from obvious differences of time and place—Leach talks of a village in the northern dry zone in the early 1950s, Obeyesekere of an isolated village (Madagama) near the border of the Southern Province and Sabaragamuva in the early 1960s—the two studies are separated by biographical differences. Leach, it has to be remembered, was writing within (and, to a large extent, against) Cambridge anthropology of the time, while Obeyesekere was working within that Sri Lankan structure of feeling I shall describe in the next chapter, the concern with the impact of colonial rule on village communities and the imagery of disintegration and loss. Where Leach's project impels him to seek out evidence of stability and continuity, Obeyesekere's concerns direct him towards change and insecurity. But it is possible to tease out of both books a set of assumptions about work and belonging, community and persons, which seem to be common to both villages and which

I found still remembered in Tenna. This, I believe, represents an old idiom in local sociology in which important social differences are represented in terms of differences in access to certain key local resources.

Pul Eliya is clearly a book with an anthropological axe to grind. Ethnographically, as Leach repeatedly points out, it is about one village at one very specific point in time; theoretically it is about the nature of social structure and the source of observable regularities in social life. Oddly enough for a book published in the same year as the proto-structuralist *Rethinking Anthropology* (Leach 1961b), the tenor of *Pul Eliya* is overwhelmingly positivistic and empiricist. The structure of Pul Eliya society is *what is there*, and what is there is a group of people making a living from a determinate set of resources. The limitations of the resources determine the shape of local society. Norms and rules, in this context, have only statistical meaning; jural rules are *ex post facto* rationalizations of the harder realities of property and economics. Leach's adversaries are those he sees as the successors to Radcliffe-Brown, idealists of various sorts who attribute 'mystical' powers to society and 'social solidarity.'

The evidence Leach adduces in support of these assertions, and which gives the work its continuing value in Sri Lankan ethnography, concerns land tenure and inheritance, in particular the transmission of rights in wet rice-land. To be accepted as a full member of Pul Eliya society one should be a member of the same *variga* (subcaste) as other Pul Eliya people, and such membership depends on two criteria: ownership of some property right in the Pul Eliya fields, and acceptance of some kinship connection (usually through marriage) with other members of the *variga*. The fact that the ideal of *variga* endogamy can be manipulated in order to allow in acceptable outsiders is the key to Leach's argument that facts of kinship are here subordinate to facts of property.

Obeyesekere is less concerned with arguments within British anthropology and more with arguments within Sri Lankan society. His study is intended to provide local, empirical evidence for the more generally held view that village social structure had been unwittingly devastated by various colonial reforms: Crown-lands policy had deprived

villages of the opportunity to expand in response to demographic pressure; inheritance law reforms led to the alienation
of property rights out of the community with out-marrying
women; rural taxation (especially the compulsory commutation of the Grain Taxes in the 1880s) forced peasants to sell off
their holdings to outsiders. Where in the past it had been an
attainable ideal for each village to be a kin-based community
of equal co-parceners in a common piece of village land, there
was now inequality of access to village land, loss of economic
and kinship homogeneity, and considerable demographic
pressure on resources.

Leach manages to demonstrate an impressive continuity in
the pattern of control of village resources: although almost
half the plots of land in Pul Eliya had changed hands at least
once by sale between 1890 and 1954, the proportion of village
lands controlled by non-villagers had actually declined in that
period.[1] Obeyesekere, on the other hand, demonstrates a
steady seepage of land ownership out of the village; in the
preceding eighty years one group of related outsiders had
gained control of more than half of the land in one of the two
constituent hamlets of Madagama; in the other hamlet about
forty per cent of the land was held by outsiders at the time of
Obeyesekere's fieldwork (Obeyesekere 1967: 227).

But there are problems in the evidence offered by both
Leach and Obeyesekere. Few of Obeyesekere's factors of
change can be shown to have had the kind of impact he
claims. Crown-lands policy, although enacted from the 1840s
onward, was hardly enforced until the Land Settlement
Department drew up the Final Village Plan for Madagama in
1915 (Obeyesekere 1967: 101). (Madagama, like Tenna and
Pul Eliya, is far away from the area of European and
Ceylonese plantation expansion in the nineteenth century.)
No Madagama lands were sold for non-payment of the Grain
Tax in the 1880s (Obeyesekere 1967: 125). Leach's argument
runs up against the theoretical objection that 'property' is
itself a complex jural notion (although he is right to point out
the futility of trying to disentangle kinship from property as
distinct and separate 'things'). More to the point, both the Pul
Eliya fields and the value placed on their control and
cultivation are pre-eminently social facts. Paddy is not the

only source of subsistence in this part of Sri Lanka; most people living in the area of Pul Eliya have, for most of the time for which we have records, depended at least as heavily on shifting cultivation as their chief source of subsistence (Brow 1978: 92–100; see below pp. 104–7); yet it is paddy which is singled out as the area of life within which assertions about standing, belonging, and community are made. And if ownership of a portion of the Pul Eliya fields is, as Leach argues, a necessary condition for acceptance as a full member of the village, it is not by itself a sufficient condition; the traders who buy into the fields are still regarded as outsiders, unless they choose to claim some degree of kinship and unless the other villagers choose to acknowledge that claim.

What we are left with in both cases is a consistent set of village ideas linking paddy ownership and cultivation, kinship, residence, and village 'citizenship:'

[In Chapter 4] we saw how the people of Pul Eliya, the Pul Eliya *minissu*, stressed their membership of a common *variga*—a group of endogamous kin; but we also saw that membership of this common *variga* did not really depend upon common descent. Anyone who was acceptable as a Pul Eliya landowner and was also acceptable in the capacity of brother-in-law to an existing Pul Eliya landowner would, in practice, be treated as of 'our variga.' (Leach 1961a: 303)

Thus 'without the Old Field, the Pul Eliya community itself would be without a *raison d'être*; kinship alone could not hold the community together' (Leach 1961a: 304). If we agree with Leach that 'kinship structure is just a way of talking about property relations' (Leach 1961a: 305), we must also recognize that property relations in this context are themselves the means of 'talking about' many things beside the drudgery of everyday subsistence: things like standing or status, gender, caste, ultimately what manner of person you profess to be.

It is this area which Obeyesekere charts quite superbly in the latter sections of *Land Tenure*. Quite early in his analysis he points out that divisions of standing within the dominant *goyigama* caste are based in their 'relation to the soil': non-cultivating owners at the top, owner-cultivators next, and tenants at the bottom (Obeyesekere 1967: 15–17). It is not simply 'the soil' which is at stake, it is the control of paddy land as an idiom of social standing: 'power, prestige and authority is perceived by the Sinhalese as overlordship of an estate (*gama*) and its inhabitants, and its associated ceremonialism' (Obeyesekere: 220–21). The whole set of values derives from pre-colonial conditions:

There are limits (*sīmā*) to the power of each landlord. Each centre is a repository of power and authority: the ultimate repository of power is the king. The chiefs pay *däkum* [respects] to him and acknowledge him as their overlord. Since he is owner of all the soil of Lanka, he is the overlord of all: all citizens render service or *rājakāriya* [literally 'king's work'] generally devoted to public works and military services. These services are qualifications of citizenship. (Obeyesekere 1967: 220).

'Citizenship' within the polity, 'citizenship' within a village (Obeyesekere 1967: 267): both are ways of talking about personhood couched in the language of landholding (cf. Selvadurai 1976).

What I have described as the language of landholding can be traced back to the pre-colonial polity. Consider, for example, Knox's description of property and service in the late seventeenth-century Kandyan kingdom:

The Countrey being wholly His, the King Farms out his Land, not for Money, but Service. And the People enjoy Portions of Land from the King, and instead of Rent, they have their several appointments, some are to serve the King in his Wars, some in their Trades, some serve him for Labourers, and others are as Farmers to furnish his House with the Fruits of the Ground; and so all things are done without Cost and every man paid for his pains: that is, they have Lands for it; yet all have not watered Land enough for their needs, that is, such Land as good rice requires to grow in; so that such are fain to sow on dry Land, and Till other mens Fields for a subsistence. These Persons are free from payment of Taxes. . . But if any find the Duty to be too heavy, or too much for them, they may leaving their House and Land, be free from the King's Service, as there is a Multitude do. And in my judgement they live far more at ease, after they have relinquished the King's Land, than when they had it. (Knox 1681 [1911]: 68–9)

Knox is describing a division of labour oriented to the figure of the king and rooted in the holding of paddy land. He goes on to describe how the same pattern is reproduced in the division of labour around 'Noble' landholders; a pattern, we could add, which can still be found in the division of labour in modern temple villages, where the royal focus is provided by the deity who holds the land (Kendrick 1984). But we should also note Knox's observation that tenants of other men's fields and workers of 'dry land' (i.e. chena) are outside this order, and his apparent surprise that, as a result, they appear to be materially better off. This surprise is dispelled if we remember that the value of landholding in such an order is never simply economic. To be a holder of paddy land is to participate in a ritual order organized around the king, in which service is offered upward in return for the trickle down of the value embodied in the person of the king (cf. Hocart 1950, 1970). Anyone can cut free from this system by going off and cultivating chena; but this also involves cutting themselves free from the whole order of caste and social personality which was focussed on the person of the king and articulated through the control of paddy land.

Even now this control of paddy land is never simply an economic proposition based on criteria of profitability; it connotes potential control over people (or, at the minimum, personal autonomy from the control of others) which in turn is the clearest available index of position (cf. Neale 1969). Poor cultivators are not only motivated by subsistence requirements: 'They are partly motivated to cultivate the fields for the prestige and dignity associated with the role of peasant cultivator' (Obeyesekere 1967: 214). At the other extreme, the rural rich have been known to invest in property of little or no simple economic value; they continue to buy up tiny shares in village paddy lands, which are let out to sharecroppers, although 'hardly any of the produce is given to them' (Obeyesekere 1967: 209), while the pursuit of land disputes can cost far more than the land itself is worth (Selvadurai 1976: 83; cf. Leach 1961a: 41).

It is possible from this position to make sense of a number of mysteries in the reporting of rural change in Sri Lanka. If, as I believe, both Leach and Obeyesekere were attempting in their different styles to render sociologically intelligible what is a dominant rural social idiom, we can understand better the almost complete absence of the landless from their books;[2] denied 'citizenship' in this local idiom, they become sociologically invisible. This may also go some way to explaining the fact that their existence has been barely acknowledged in post-Independence tenurial reform (Moore 1985: 62). If the landless disappear in national statistics, there is a compensatory proliferation of 'farmers' to deal with. During my early village census I asked at each house for the head of the household's occupation; virtually everyone answered 'farmer' (*goviyā*)—the exceptions were holders of more prestigious government posts—seemingly regardless of their main source of real income, be it labouring, gemming, bidi-rolling or whatever.[3] A similar misapprehension at national level misidentifies the entire rural population as paddy producers (Moore 1985: 87; cf. Vitebsky 1984).

The relevance of all this to the situation I encountered in Tenna will become clear in subsequent sections. If the past was clearly describable in this idiom of landholding and local 'citizenship,' by the time of my stay it was applicable to some aspects only of present circumstances. Whole areas of life and whole sections of the population were of necessity excluded by it. The result was a potential lacuna in local sociology; new criteria were needed for both statements of social difference, and statements of social equivalence. In the past ideas of position and status were based in the shared experience of everyday work, and as earlier writers make abundantly clear, disputes (often violent) were generated and worked through in precisely this area of common concern—the area of land and property. Shared experience included the experience of inequality, exploitation, and discord. In the present the world of work could provide no such shared ground for most of the population of Tenna. Understanding this fact provides one context for understanding the tangled events of Chapter Three. But this in turn requires more detailed explanation of the shape of economic change in Tenna.

Paddy and Chena

James Brow, working from official figures for the area around Pul Eliya in the late nineteenth century, has demonstrated that successful paddy crops must have been the exception rather than the rule; his point is that paddy cultivation in that part of the northern dry zone may have represented a source of occasional cash income in successful years, but cannot have been the chief source of subsistence for people like the Vedda villagers he studied (Brow 1978: 92–100). He also raises doubts about Leach's claim that a Pul Eliya farmer 'looks upon this shifting cultivation as his main means of earning a cash income in contrast to his ordinary activities as a rice farmer which provide him with a subsistence living' (Leach 1961a: 63–4). Brow suggests that if this was the case in Pul Eliya 'then either it is a recent development or the village is exceptionally well favoured for paddy cultivation' (Brow 1978: 94). Nor was the importance of chena restricted to the less densely populated dry zone; Meyer has argued that chenas provided an essential flexible zone in the ecosystem of the wet zone village in the early colonial period:

> They helped in some cases, to make good the loss of a poor paddy harvest; they could yield a surplus to provide for ceremonial expenses. Moreover they acted as a safety valve: they afforded means of subsistence to marginal individuals (such as young couples not yet settled in village life) or to marginal communities (such as hunters, food gatherers, sugar-palm tappers). (Meyer 1983: 26–7).

Nevertheless, most earlier writers have played down the importance of chena in the rural economy. Leach provides a brief but valuable description of chena (1961a: 289–95); Obeyesekere acknowledges that before 1909 chena 'provided a subsidiary source for paddy and other grains' (Obeyesekere 1967: 209), but otherwise barely mentions it in his description. What for a large section of the rural population over the past 150 years has been the most persistent source of conflict with the State, receives little more than a paragraph in Moore's recent and otherwise comprehensive monograph on State and peasant (Moore 1985: 32).

Brow's evidence suggests that the importance of chena—as the basic source of subsistence in much of the dry zone—has been under-reported in both anthropological and official literature. This must in part be due to a fortuitous collusion between the villagers' propensity to represent themselves as rice farmers (because of those connotations of standing and position that I have suggested are borne by paddy as a 'sociological idiom'), and official disinclination to recognize the economic importance of an activity which was so heartily disliked by virtually all colonial administrators (Leach 1961a: 61–4; Brow 1978: 99).

Eric Meyer has recently argued that the loss of chenas was perhaps the major consequence of plantation expansion for many wet zone villages, and casual employment from the plantations came to fill the economic niche formerly occupied by chena cultivation (Meyer 1983: 36). Following Meyer, we can think of the village economy in terms of two kinds of activity: a fixed and relatively inelastic area of work domin- ated by paddy cultivation, contrasted with a fluid and relatively elastic area dominated in the past by chena. It is in this second area that we can see the major responses to change in Tenna. The huge influx of new settlers in the past twenty years could never be absorbed in the relatively inflexible area of paddy production; instead they have found employment on the margins—in chena, gemming, and cash-cropping.

Both Meyer and Brow have important observations on the social significance of chena cultivation. Chena, Brow argues, is egalitarian, household-based, and oriented to subsistence; paddy, by contrast, is a potential source of inequalities, requiring complex extra-household co-operation, and may be oriented to profit. In particular, control of paddy land is 'a major focus of political action within the village and the means whereby village leaders come to dominate their fellows' (Brow 1978: 105). Meyer's interpretation of the political implications of the two kinds of cultivation during the British period is slightly different:

The villagers viewed the paddy area as the sphere of stability, security and legality; everybody knew the limits, the ownership, the value of each plot. . . By comparison, the highlands were considered as the realm of mobility, of imprecision, of casual activities, of enterprise, and also of illegality (from the point of view of the authorities). There the arbitrary powers of the local leading families (from which the headmen were drawn) had free play, with little interference from the kings or the colonial administration of the early days. One might argue that the headmen as a class derived their wealth from the paddy-fields and their authority from the control they exerted over the margins of the village territory (Meyer 1983: 26; cf. Obeyesekere 1967: 101).

The differences, though, are purely differences of perspective. *Within the village*, paddy cultivation was the dominant idiom of power and hierarchy; *in relations with the wider colonial State*, knowledge of 'marginal' activities like chena, and privileged access to the administration (itself often a product of administrative dependence on landed members of the 'headman class') with that knowledge, were key sources of power and influence. Both perspectives can be seen illustrated in Tenna villagers' accounts of their past.

Paddy stands out from the other kinds of agricultural production in the area by its tangible and fixed nature. It is the very rigidity of its terraced fields and irrigation channels that so commends it to the government, the tax-collector, and those more recent phenomena, the collector of agrarian statistics and the ethnographer. But we should beware of attributing too great an importance to something just because we happen to have relatively detailed evidence on it. Quite apart from any ideological weight carried by this crop in political rhetoric (and it is in fact considerable), its significance in present and past agrarian analysis has been almost certainly overvalued, on the crude grounds that it is something we know about and can measure and assess with a fair degree of apparent precision[4]. It seems reasonable to conclude from the evidence we have that in the past, as in the present, most people in Tenna (like Brow's villagers) did not get most of their income from rice production. Their reasons for participating in paddy production were never simply those of economic necessity. In what follows I will try to present an historical reconstruction of the contrasted types of agricultural production—paddy and swidden—based on a rather ahistorical synthesis of colonial records, local oral memory, and my own first-hand observation in the present.

We have to start with a fundamental contradiction between our first two sources of evidence. For older villagers in Tenna chena was a permanent aspect of the village economy as far back as can be remembered; yet colonial sources are full of bluster about stopping chena, petitions to be allowed to cultivate chena, occasional concessions permitting limited chena in times of urgent distress—reading for all the world as if chena was under strict official control and limitation. Some, at least, of the official hostility to chena must be attributable to its inherent incompatibility with so many aspects of the colonial State. From the start the British were concerned to find owners and chiefs; chena did not require owners and chiefs. The State, like so many forms of power in the modern world, controls in large part by knowing: knowing who is doing what and where. Chena cultivation, drifting across the landscape, often escaped the classifications of power. At the same time my reliance on unofficial sources introduces a different tone into the account. The description of chena is culled from the memories of the old recalling the times of their youth, and is consequently tinged with a romantic nostalgia. In the next chapter I return to these old people's memories and try to set them in a more critical context.

The movement of people across the area is not a particularly modern phenomenon, although it is doubtless more obvious as the affected populations grow. In 1883 the Government Agent described a chena at Udawela 'cleared by squatters who move away as soon as they have finished operations' (SLNA 45/17 17 August 1883); two years later it was reported that many men from villages higher in the hills would come down to the *bintenna* (the dry flatlands beyond Tenna in the east) to cultivate chenas for part of the year before moving back (AR 1885: 139). Similar patterns of seasonal migration continue to the present, although land is only available further east beyond the new colonies, and people come from farther afield and often settle on a more permanent basis at their destination; such indeed is the origin of much of the present population of Tenna.

If chena was so violently opposed by a succession of Government Agents, oral evidence suggests that local representatives of the colonial state took a more pragmatic view of the matter than their masters. Old villagers I spoke to recalled how in their youth they had to apply for a chena permit from the *valavva* (the dwelling-place of the *raṭē mahatmayā* at Mahagasgoda); in return for this the *valavva* would send a representative at the harvest to appropriate one fifth of all the produce, which the villagers themselves would have to deliver to the *valavva*. There is one isolated mention in the records of the practice of taxing chena in the area in the nineteenth century[5], but this is insufficient to suggest that it was long-term official policy. It seems rather to have been a private accommodation organized from the *valavva*. One old man, who was one of the first permanent settlers on the plateau in the 1920s, spoke of the help given at the time by the *raṭē mahatmayā*, not least in paying fines incurred for illegal chena cultivation. Another tellingly recalled how after the defeat of the former *raṭē mahatmayā* in a rancorous by-election in 1943, the newly-elected MP came to the village to tell the men that they would no longer have to pay this 'tax' on their chena plots, thus marking that decisive moment in local affairs when electoral politics first broke through the combination of political and economic power hitherto held by a few families.

So, at least during this century, chena cultivation, whatever its internal position in the village economy, was carried out within the framework of wider relations of power and dominance, specifically those guaranteed by the *radala* monopoly of colonial power. In this, as in paddy, the phrase 'grudging compliance' could best sum up the cultivators' response; I was told how attempts would be made (sometimes successfully) to conceal parts of the harvest in order to avoid paying the owner's share, but that the representative sent from the *valavva* would display a preternatural knowledge of every kind of vegetable grown on each swidden plot and demand the full share of each. Moreover, chena, more than paddy, provided a link with the wider economy; its produce was used in barter for most of the few external resources that were required—dried maize, especially, being exchanged for cloth and salt with roaming Muslim traders.

But within the village chena contrasted with paddy; it was an inclusive and collective activity while paddy was an exclusive if occasionally egalitarian one; indeed, while chena has all but disappeared, paddy cultivation still shows the same combination of hierarchical and egalitarian features, reproducing difference just as it seems to be emphasizing social likeness. In the past, individual ties between landlord and tenant were less socially significant than the collective designation of one of the old villages (Udawela) as a village of tenants and the other (Medawela) as a village of freeholders, a designation which implied a clear superiority of status. All worked the same lands, and some of the 'tenant' villagers owned land while some of the 'free' villagers were tenants, but the notional distinction, based on their ties through paddy to the outside world, continued through the avoidance of marriage and consequent kinship between the two settlements. Eventually the prosperity of the resident *vidānē* (overseer) of the *bandāra idam* ('lord's land,' as *nindagama* was known here) overcame the desire for exclusiveness, and at some indeterminate point around the turn of the century a marriage was contracted between this *vidānē's* family and an important family of the old 'free' village. Effectively, from then on the separate identities of the two villages were lost. In the past they had been separated by their different relations to the soil, and this separation was reproduced in kinship. Now the old difference between the two is all but forgotten by younger people.

If difference was created through relations of tenancy, the egalitarian aspect of paddy production is reflected in the old system of reciprocal labour known as *attam*, described by Knox as early as the seventeenth century (1681 [1911]: 14). One cultivator exchanges one day of his labour (I write 'his' advisedly: *attam* is a male business) for one equivalent day of his partner's labour. If a man needs six men's work to plough his fields in one day, he will have to return a day of similar work to each of his six helpers. The 'host' is responsible for feeding his workers and looking after minor needs like tea, bidis, and betel. The returns are always scrupulously calculated to balance exactly within one cultivation cycle, although it is legitimate for someone to send a proxy, perhaps a son or even a labourer hired for the occasion, to fulfil his outstanding obligations.

At the time of my fieldwork, more than half the work on the old village fields was still organized around *attam*; the proportion was greatest during the early stages of the cultivation cycle on jobs like ploughing and sowing, but decreased with the simultaneous need for labour on different fields during the harvest. Only a couple of plots were cultivated without any *attam* labour—Cyril and his father-in-law preferred to use wage-labour throughout and thus avoid the cumbersome sociability of intermittent returns on their neighbours' fields, and one large family with several adult sons exploited its self-sufficiency—and some of the richer farmers carefully restricted their own obligations to equally well-placed kin and friends, supplementing their labour with a large number of wage-labourers. In contrast to these cases, poorer farmers without the sons to help with their obligations found themselves working day after day to pay off their debts.

In Tenna *attam* ignores caste boundaries, and this greatly increases its appearance of equality. But it is rigid in its exclusion of women, and in practice, and for obvious reasons, the large number of male inhabitants who do not participate in the paddy economy are not involved in *attam* and its finely calculated balances; or if they contribute at all to paddy cultivation it is as day labour *(kuli vāḍa)*, a status avoided by those with pretensions to respectability.[6] Even so, most *kuli vāḍa* is used for the harvest and paid in kind; on the colony lands on the plain below virtually all labour is hired for cash, a situation disparagingly referred to by Tenna's paddy farmers as 'just like *bisnis*'; it is added in mitigation that colony farmers have no other work so must buy all their other food and necessities with cash. But the implication is that paddy cultivation in Tenna is, as it always has been, above *bisnis* and the morality of the market. The *attam* system is under pressure, but still survives, preserving an appearance of egalitarian morality while at the same time excluding most of the population from its moral community of fellow cultivators.

Contrast this with the romantic description of the chena cultivation cycle in the past given to me by older informants. It started with one man, the *vidānē*, getting a permit from the *valavva*. He would collect ten to fifteen men together and they would mark out the area to be cultivated in a circle from a central tree; each cultivator would then be allocated a segment of the resulting 'wheel', building a fence around the circumference, to keep animals out but leaving the internal divisions open (cf. Leach 1961a: 91–5). At the end of the dry months of July and August the jungle would be cut *(val kapanavā)* and left to wither on the ground; after two weeks or so the area would be fired and crowds would gather to watch the spectacle. The rains of October and November were the signal for sowing seeds broadcast on the plots–maize, sesame, chillis, pumpkins, millet (*kurakkan*)—at intervals to allow for the different time required by the crops, and to allow steady cropping of some vegetables. Each man would build a hut (*päla*) on his chena and spend the nights there, from November to July, watching for animals, a cry or clap from one man normally being enough to arouse the other cultivators to chase away the marauder. To pass the time men would sing verses and exchange riddles, often with a Buddhist moral in the answer, from hut to hut. Those without children might be joined by their wives, otherwise the women stayed at home to look after the children.

The women did, however, join in the cleaning of the land before the firing, and everyone who could took part in the cutting of the *kurakkan*. The cultivators would be joined by their wives and children; people from neighbouring villages might also come to participate, and would be paid in *kurakkan* for their labour. The whole crowd would work its way round the wheel, cutting and collecting each plot in turn. The atmosphere was one of celebration (*jaya*) and special verses (*kavi*) would be sung by the cutters.

While *kurakkan*-cutting was a time for pleasure, celebration, and the suspension of social distinction within the cultivating group and their kin and neighbours, the prevailing tone of the paddy harvest has always been somewhat different. The harvest is made up of a sequence of separate tasks, each involving a slightly different combination of labour. The cutting is men's work in Tenna, usually involving teams of *attam* and *kuli* workers crouched in a line across the field. This is followed by the collection of the crop where it has fallen in the field, normally on the day after it has been cut; as many women as men take part, with each household mobilizing wives and children to supplement any outside workers who might have been brought in. The next stage is threshing, which is surrounded with markers of separation from normal life. The threshing-floor (*kamata*) is a bounded area within the paddy-field, the soil flattened and spread with dung (a purifying agent); before the start of the threshing, offerings should be made to the chthonic spirit of the place (*bahirayā*). A special language (*kamata bāsāva*) is employed while working on the floor, supposedly to mislead any jealous spirits who would otherwise overhear details of the farmer's success and be tempted to do him harm. The threshing is done at night by teams of buffaloes, which always work on an auspicious right-hand circuit of the floor (i.e. clockwise). Because of *killa* (pollution), women should not set foot on the threshing-floor. In the past, low-caste (*roḍiya*) beggars would travel from floor to floor, and were paid off in grain by farmers fearful of their legendary curses.[7] In the morning the owner or the owner's representative would come to watch the measurement of the shares of the threshed and winnowed grain.

The tone of the paddy threshing is defensive; the character-istic explanation of any custom is *āraksa* (protection)—protection against spirits, protection against jealousy, protec-tion against the evil tongue—rather than *jaya*, the word used to describe the jubilation of the chena harvest. Both activities are marked by their own specific uses of language, but for paddy these take the form of protective disguises and for chena they are celebratory verses in which all participate. Where chena is inclusive and egalitarian, paddy is in its very nature the stuff of hierarchy, inequality, and exclusion.

Obeyesekere and Leach are both right in their different ways when they insist on the importance of paddy cultivation as a medium of social organization; but it is a particular aspect of social organization—the world of hierarchy and status—which is being expressed. If, as is now clearly the case, many people do not participate in paddy cultivation—or if they do, the participation is on different terms from the past, for cash, perhaps, as owner or labourer—then they are no longer part of the unstated inclusions and exclusions bound up in this activity. This does not mean that they are then necessarily cut free from the village as a moral community; but it does mean that they are far freer of certain important ordering principles. In particular, there is a growing space in social discourse which in the past might have been filled by implicit statements like 'I am a farmer,' 'You are a tenant,' 'He is a lord because he owns the land'. At the same time, the demise of chena removed one activity in which all could participate, working, singing, and joking together. The space left behind in social discourse is that where people could say,

'We are one people because we work together,' or perhaps, 'We are one people because we collude in trying to evade the outsiders' claims on our crop.' In fact similar statements are still possible in Tenna, but they are made in very different ways—most obviously in the competitive idiom of party politics or the unifying process of religious ritual.

Work and Resources

I have summarized the main changes in landholding in Tenna for the period between 1826 and 1982 in the Appendix to this chapter. The overall amount of paddy land has not increased in this period, although an allocation of new land under the rebuilt Udawela tank was still promised on my visit in 1984 (see below p. 160). Outside holdings have fragmented into ever smaller shares while the number of cultivators has remained more or less constant. These cultivators are almost entirely drawn from the Old Tenna families with a few households from the settled *beravā* and *vahumpura* clusters. None of the newer settlers work on these fields except as casual labourers at harvest time. A speculative market in dry land developed in the 1960s and 1970s after much of the village land was declared private by the Land Settlement office. The biggest purchasers have been outside gem-dealers, but as yet very little of the land they have accumulated is under profitable cultivation. All house sites, including Old Tenna and new settlers alike, are on former plots of Crown land, much of it held on license for a nominal rent.

The effect of this is that no one in Tenna is wholly landless: all households have at least a single acre of house-site highland on which to try to support themselves. A longer-term historical trend means that there is as yet no sharp cleavage within Tenna in terms of land ownership; no group of Tennna residents is forced to work, whether as tenants or labourers, for another land-holding group of Tenna residents. The biggest outside landholders in the past, the *radala* owners of the Udawela *nindagama*, were able to expand their resources enormously in the colonial period, but they did this by the acquisition of new resources—paddy land at Gantota, tea estates around Belangala—rather than the appropriation of old resources like the paddy fields of Udawela and Medawela.[8] The recent speculation in private highland, and the accumulation of large blocks of Tenna land by gem-merchants and other outsiders will almost inevitably lead to a situation in the very near future in which a large number of Tenna residents will be forced to work for them in order to gain access to the most basic means of subsistence. But that day has yet to come.

The major change in Tenna is obviously the growth in population. Only a minority of the more settled households can now participate in the shared rhythms and shared meanings of the paddy cultivation cycle. Chena, I was frequently told, is now forbidden. Unlike other forbidden activities (the felling of timber in the remaining patches of jungle, or gemming, for example) this ruling is generally obeyed, if only because chena is of necessity a great deal more visible than the other activities. In a period of ten years, government control and population pressure have combined to end an activity formerly central to economic support. In recent years it had in any case become more frequently a cash-cropping activity, as indeed it is now in those dry zone areas where it is still practised.

In its place I found a diversity of activity. Almost every household in Tenna does some cultivation, though few of the settlers come close to supporting themselves from it. Cash may be earned in a number of ways: casual labouring (in road gangs, on the fields in Tenna and below on the new paddy lands of the Walawe plain, on the gem-dealers' estates); craft-work as carpenters and masons; a small group of men cut and burn lime, which they sell in the town to merchants for re-sale with betel; others collect the bidi leaves which grow wild in the jungle—these are bought by a Muslim merchant, who puts out the job of rolling them into bidis to a number of households on a piecework basis. The two most important activities, though, are gemming and the cash-cropping of vegetables, especially beans. Between them, these activities affect in different ways virtually every household in the village, from the richest to the poorest.

Gemming

In Tenna, gemming is said to have started in the mid 1960s when the newly arrived (and recently married) Mr Ariyaratna and his Old Tenna brother-in-law found a valuable stone, which they promptly sold, provoking the first of a series of local rushes. Everyone in the area, I was told, joined in the first stampede, and the site of that first discovery, near the sixteenth mile-post, is now an overworked wasteland of dried spoil-heaps and quartzy shingle, without an inch of topsoil remaining. At the time, the villagers say, they were quite ignorant about the various stones and their proper values; there was only one buyer in Belangala, a Muslim, and all agree that he bought what they found at a fraction of its true value.

The same pattern of a constant low level of activity, punctuated by a big find and the subsequent rush to the area of the find, continues.[9] But the gemmers consider themselves far more knowledgeable about their activities these days. They are also more knowledgeable about the police, who make intermittent raids on gem-pits in the area from their nearest base fourteen miles away in Belangala. Unless they have a powerful connection to get them off the hook, the few who are caught end up paying a fine (400 rupees—about £12—was the going rate during my stay). But the law has no moral force whatsoever; those caught gemming or forced into undignified flight after a police raid are subject to none of the shame (*lajja*) within the community which would be attached to other illegal activities, like theft or assault, or which can even follow an arrest on the basis of a malicious, false complaint. Indeed, the licensing system seems to be regarded as another inscrutable ploy on the part of the government to give the police an additional source of income.

The trade itself, which attracts many young men in Tenna and the surrounding villages, depends on ignorance on the part of others, and the cultivation of privileged channels of communication and *bisnis* skills. So, for example, while I was in the village, a poor settler working by himself discovered an unusual stone. He took it to a couple of friends of mine, both sometime small dealers (one of whom told me this story).

They were preoccupied with a domestic crisis, trying to arrange transport to hospital for their sick mother, and in any case were short of ready cash in the house. So they sent the finder to another brother, who runs a small tea-shop; he was unsure about the gem, which he suspected might be a worthless piece of what is known as 'earth glass' (*bim viduruwa*). The next day his cross-cousin (*massinā*) from a neighbouring village stopped at the tea-shop on his newly-acquired motorcycle and asked if he knew of any gems going. The tea-shop owner did not realize that his brothers had only been able to have a superficial look and assumed that they too had decided this particular gem was probably worthless; still, he mentioned it to his cross-cousin as a possibility. The cross-cousin and his companion went to see the finder, paid him 300 rupees for the stone, took it to town, and sold it straight away for 70,000 rupees (about £2,000) to one of the town dealers. This dealer is said to have resold it for 20 lakhs (2,000,000 rupees—about £60,000). The town dealer bought a jeep and a new car. The men who took it to him also bought themselves a car; by the time I was told the story the car was rusting next to their house—they had failed to repeat their coup and could not afford the petrol to run it. The finder, who knew of all this, is said to have accepted his 300 rupees philosophically; my informant complained that his brother should at least have got a cut for making the 'connection' for their cousin, but ended the tale with a shrug and the comment, 'That's *bisnis*'.

People speak in paradoxes when they describe the gem business: a rich dealer must be known to be generous (not 'mean'—*lōba*) for people to come to him—his success depends on paying as little as he can for the gems themselves, so he invests heavily in conspicuous philanthropy, as well as the large house and fast car, and is always ready to provide for a village temple or a new Buddha statue. Such investment is doubly worthwhile in a moral environment dominated by fear of the malign effects of *irisiyāva* (jealousy—see Chapter Six). Despite the huge potential profit margins, and the powerful dealers' precipitous rise from dull obscurity to dazzling wealth and fame, few gemmers can be induced to criticize them, even in private; they are good men, I was told, they support the *sangha*, they help 'small people' (*poḍi minissu*) in times of crisis, and moreover they are our people, Sinhala, not Muslim or Tamil like other big local traders in the past.

Production itself is almost never a solo activity. Usually a group of four men will collaborate on a single pit (*patala*); a couple of them may be close kinsmen, but most often they are friends; all finds are divided strictly between the partners. Sometimes they will be sponsored by a rich trader who becomes the 'owner' (*patal ayiti kārayā*) of the team, in which case he pays the team's subsistence (usually a little less than the average casual day-labourer's wage—15 rather than 18 or 20 rupees); whatever is found is split half-and-half between owner and team, before the team divide their half scrupulously among themselves.

Even when there is a sponsor, the relationship between the owner and team tends to be friendly, affable, and informal, at least on the surface; when village traders (*mudalālis*) sponsor fellow villagers (the most common situation) they will often join in the digging from time to time themselves. (Many village *mudalālis* employ the same small number of friendly 'clients' for paddy or other cultivation as well as for gem work.) Within the team all is rigorously egalitarian, in the same way as reciprocal *attam* teams are rigorously egalitarian in paddy work. But whereas *attam* relationships are based on the careful reckoning of a tangible quantity—one day of like labour in return for every day worked—gemming teams are based on an intangible exchange of trust for trust. There is nothing to stop one member of a team from concealing a stone from his fellow members; or the whole team conspiring to conceal a find from the owner. To some extent local knowledge acts as a restraint in these circumstances; if a man sells a stone clandestinely, he has first to be sure the dealer will not talk, and then he has to be sure that no sudden increase in his domestic expenditure is noticed (even if this was paid for from a wholly honourable source, jealousy—*irisiyāva*—will provoke people to think the worst). But most often the members simply have to rely on trust.

Yet the innocent will be told there is no trust (*visvāsa*) whatsoever in the gem business—a son will steal from his own father—although the same word is used frequently in describing the day-to-day operations of the business. The whole organization, from production to sale, is founded on an impossible but necessary trust. *Visvāsa* is a term normally encountered in ethnographic discussions of 'belief' in religious contexts (e.g. Gombrich 1971: 59–60; Southwold 1983: 161 n.65). It is certainly widely used in those situations; I was frequently asked if I 'believed' (*visvāsa karanavā*) in gods, or demons, or this god, or that demonic manifestation. But it is also used to describe vertical social relationships; a *poḍiaya* (small-timer) with a personal tie with a particular big dealer may describe the tie as a 'connection' or 'partnership' (*havula*) and characterize that connection by its 'belief', or, better, 'trust' (*visvāsa*). A similar description is used of relations between a trader and a local supplier; a particular vegetable-dealer will cultivate particular personal relationships with small suppliers over a wide area; each tie is a 'trust.' Similarly a local political boss will cultivate personalized relationships with people who can be trusted to maintain a reliable supply of local information.[10]

Given this, it is striking how little kinship enters into the formation of gemming teams. If it does, it normally involves two brothers working in a bigger team; brothers-in-law are less common, as a rule. Rather, team members describe each other first and foremost as 'friends' (*yāluvō*) rather than 'kin' (*näyō*). It is if the potential strains of the relationship are too heavy a burden to impose on the increasingly delicate structure of kinship; it is safer to risk the loss of a friend than to shatter the universe of kin. Because the moral authority of kinship is feared to be too weak in practice, it becomes all the more necessary to protect it by not using it (an argument made explicitly when discussing marriage strategies—see Chapter Six). Meanwhile, the household is avoided even more than kinship in the social organization of gemming. Women are thought not to be a good thing to have around a gem-pit. I did once or twice come across women gemming, but they were always working in all-female teams. In part this may be because of ideas about women's inherent moral frailty; in practice it is justified in terms similar to those used to justify their exclusion from the threshing-floor. To these tensions, we should add the enormous strains generated throughout a gemmer's kinship network when he does strike lucky in a big way. The area abounds in comforting tales of men made wealthy overnight who cracked under the social pressure that followed.

Success in gemming requires the correct circumstances, and gemmers are eager observers of auspicious signs (*subha lakuna*). As in threshing-floor rituals, offerings of incense may be made at a pit to placate the *bahiraya*, the protectors of the earth's riches, before starting work; water is swirled through the baskets of *illam* (the gem-bearing soil) an auspicious (odd) number of times before the cleaned diggings are inspected for gems; in general, success comes to those who approach it in a good clean way (*hondin pirisiduvin*), there is even, I was often told, although no one locally knew any examples, a gem-pit language (*patal bāsāva*) used in the Ratnapura pits parallel to the special language of the threshing-floor. Many gemmers made vows to the local deity Mangara for help in finding gems.

Like threshing-floor rites, gem-pit practices emphasize the division between the ritually pure and morally correct men inside the pit and the impure and morally suspect world outside. Also, like threshing-floor rites, they may be as often ignored as observed; everyone seemed to observe some of them some of the time, no one observed all of the time. But while threshing-floor rites are generally held (by villagers) to be fading fragments of a once unitary and unanimous ritual order, the ritual trappings of gemming are recent borrowings from, or innovations within, other ritual orders—they are increasing and coalescing rather than fragmenting and disappearing. A ritual context has, in twenty years, been borrowed or produced for a new economic activity, just as a ritual context—the *pansala*-based ceremonies described earlier—has, in the same period, been created for the new social order of Tenna. Gemming creates a partial re-enchantment of the landscape, just as it creates the possibility of new forms of solidarity. Again we must remember that the changes in work patterns are not simply imposed on people; people in Tenna are the active producers and reproducers of their own circumstances, and new kinds of activity may bring people together—as well as divide them—in new ways.

Beans

The obvious common element between gemming and cash-cropping is the possibility of large financial rewards at the end; before that much is different. Trade and some use of cash have no claim to novelty in themselves; farmers from time to time plough up old Dutch coins, suggesting a long familiarity with specie, and, in addition to describing the bartering of chena crops for salt and cloth, nineteenth-century sources make intermittent reference to the cultivation of cash-crops like cotton, tobacco, and coffee in this area. There is no evidence, however, to suggest that until recently these accounted for more than a fraction of local economic activity.

This has changed rapidly with improved access to markets. The wartime chena farm (below p. 158) was the first large-scale exploitation of the newly completed Gantota road. After the Second World War an increasing proportion of chena crops was sold for cash. From the late 1960s onwards, 'garden' crops (i.e. based on permanent dry-land plots) were encouraged: first tobacco, then tomatoes, then most recently green beans (*bōnci*). In all three cases there has been a pattern of initial success by a few farmers, quickly copied by an army of imitators, resulting in an eventual glut, a depressed price, and an equally swift decline in the crop. But each crop has been oriented to a wider market than its predecessor. Tobacco cultivation on a big scale (which has established itself successfully around Kandy and to the north) was focused on a few local men, owners of drying-barns, who provided both capital for cultivation and purchasers of the crop. Tomatoes were trucked for sale in Belangala. Green beans are a far more sturdy commodity, and from the first their cultivation has been directed at the vegetable markets of the Pettah in Colombo.

As a crop, beans are well suited to the conditions of a place like Tenna. They are easily damaged by heavy monsoonal rains but grow quickly—six weeks from sowing to cropping—in the long dry seasons. During maturation they need daily light watering; this is done by hand with water gathered from the small streams that feed the Tenna fields and flow right through the year. As well as water they need frequent spraying with pesticide, and other capital inputs. In 1983 the cost on a half-acre plot would be about 300 rupees for pesticide, almost 1000 for fertilizer; in six weeks or so this would produce 300 to 400 kilos of beans, which at the time could be sold at ten rupees per kilo, representing a potential profit of more than 2000 rupees (£60) on one crop. By 1984 the price had dropped to seven rupees or less, leaving the crop profitable but less spectacularly so. The crop is suitable for any land with easy access to a small stream, and most of it in Tenna is found on fallow paddy-fields, or unused Crown land; very few cultivators pay any share on the crop to a non-cultivating landowner. Otherwise it requires a great deal of steady, light labour, and a heavy initial cash investment; in addition it must be transported the one hundred miles to the Colombo market.

Bean cultivation in Tenna started about 1978; for most of the first five years of its growing success most of the capital and most of the transport were controlled by the same man. He was a lorry-owner from a village just outside Belangala, whose elder sister had married into one of the Old Tenna families. Early in 1982 his brother opened a store in the centre of the village and moved in. Their sister's house served as the centre of operations for the bean business, and one of her adult sons acted as the *mudalāli*'s agent in the village, supplying the fertilizer, pesticide, and spraying equipment, and organizing the picking and packing of the crops. At the height of the harvest the *mudalāli*'s truck would collect the beans nightly from pre-arranged pick-ups along the road, delivering the beans early the next morning to the Colombo market. As well as buying virtually all the crop, this man advanced the pesticide and fertilizer on credit, buying all of the cultivator's crop at a previously agreed price which, needless to say, was well below even the local market price, let alone that in Colombo.

By the time of my arrival in 1982, other truck-owners were competing to buy beans in the village and run them to Colombo, which finally forced up the price enjoyed by village cultivators. Even so, at least half of the cultivators were dependent on the original *mudalāli*'s advances for 'expenses' (*viyadam*), and they still had to dispose of their eventual crop to him at the price settled with the agreement to provide the various sprays. Other richer villagers—gem-dealers, traders, and successful farmers from the Old Tenna families—had also set themselves up as *viyadam kārayō* ('expenses people,' although 'capitalists' would be a close-enough translation), providing the capital for the cultivation to poorer villagers who put in the labour, the produce being either shared half-and-half with the provider of expenses or sold to him or her at an agreed price before being resold for shipment to Colombo. Only the richer of the Old Tenna families could raise the cash to grow a crop for themselves. The vast majority of the cash-croppers, while making a healthy enough sum for themselves, still saw up to half of it creamed off as effective repayment for credit. The effect, moreover, was clearly cumulative; those who had profited by advancing credit for one harvest were able to advance more the next. Even if earlier credit-tenants kept their own profit and became self-financing the next time, there was no shortage of willing labour to step into the gap and accept the terms of an advance in their stead. The local economy was caught up in a frantic cycle of capital accumulation, with an ever-wider gulf opening between those of the Old Tenna families who had started with capital to spare and those—the great majority—mostly newer settlers who were dependent on credit for their cultivation. Credit, not land ownership or wage labour, was the essential medium of this process.

The plots themselves were usually a quarter to half an acre each. Poorer families, especially young couples, cultivated these as households. Richer households, able to provide their own capital, left the cultivation to teenage boys and young unmarried women, with the adult males concentrating on paddy or else on their own role as advancers of credit for others' cultivation. These individual plots represented individual earnings for their young workers; some of the money would be contributed to their households, but most of it they could spend on themselves. There were many new bicycles, sewing-machines, and clothes amongst this group during my fieldwork.

Unlike the three other kinds of work—paddy, chena, and gemming—bean cash-cropping was not accompanied by any

distinctive ritual; no one spoke to me of earth spirits to be
placated, or songs to be sung for the harvest. And, perhaps
fittingly for such a cash- and market-oriented activity, its work
pattern did not produce the solidarities and divisions of the
moral universe associated, in their different ways, with the
other kinds of work; rather, it reproduced the units of the
population at their most atomistic, first as households, then as
individuals. The difference it emphasized was the growing one
between those with and those without. Out of it was emerging
a stratum of far more prosperous villagers. Most of these had
begun as small tenants or owners from the old villages; their
sons had often done well in the gem trade and started up in
some kind of petty *bisnis*, and their rewards from politics had
been land or jobs for one of the family, which had further consolidated their position. They were not particularly secure;
two of the most prosperous of these families had risen from relative poverty very recently, and a few bad business breaks
could easily despatch them back there.

The Moral Implications of Material Change

The picture of the past provided by my older informants was
dominated by two economically and sociologically complementary activities: paddy and chena. Paddy was exclusive
in its organization: differences between men and women,
owners and tenants, members of different castes and villages,
were all bound into the rhythms of paddy work. The use of
cash was, and still is for many, avoided; necessary payments
are largely made in kind, and a great deal of labour is still
organized in terms of precisely reckonable reciprocity. The
effect is to emphasize a bounded moral community of
co-cultivators, which is now contrasted with the world of *bisnis*
outside the village paddy fields. New settlers, like women, are
excluded from this moral community, except as casual
labourers, a role which carries no standing or lasting social
obligation. Paddy cultivation in Tenna, for those few who
practise it, is probably more profitable than it has ever been
before, but it now stands as an enclave of order in a world
dominated by different values.

Chena was an inclusive activity. All could participate and men and women, young and old, kin and neighbours co-operated in the harvest. It was not completely open, though. Official disapproval meant that local representatives of the state (within the village the *vidānē*, in the wider area the *ratē mahatmayā* and his fellows) were able to demand a share of the crop in return for their complicitous silence. Chena products have long been bartered, and in the course of time chena became an area of cash rather than subsistence activity. Chena is also more flexible than paddy, and new settlers were more often economically absorbed through their participation in chena, a participation which allowed them some equivalence with their more settled neighbours; for most of them the only paddy work available was as wage labourers, a role which lowered their standing in the eyes of others.

The solidarities of chena work were, I suspect, flimsier and more temporary than the rapturous descriptions of the harvest might suggest. The kind of dry-land cash-cropping that was so dominant in Tenna during my stay has evolved seamlessly out of the older patterns of chena production. Plots shifted less and less; choice of crops became more market-oriented and demanded higher inputs of labour and capital; production became organized on an increasingly individualistic basis. And, with the possibility of systematic capital accumulation for those who can support their own production without recourse to credit, this is the area where a deepening class division within the Tenna population looks most likely, not least because almost all the providers of credit are identified as Old Tenna *goyigama*, and the majority of indebted cultivators are settlers. This was a division that no one cared to acknowledge explicitly during my stay; relations between providers of credit and cultivators still tend to be conceptualized by the cultivators in terms of 'help' (*udavva*) rather than exploitation.

Further away on the horizon is the possibility of the exhaustion of existing Crown land in Tenna. In this case more and more of the population would have the alternatives before them of seeking work from those outsiders who have bought up so much of the former Settlement land—a pattern quite common in areas where the highlands were settled and sold a generation or more earlier (cf. Meyer 1982, 1983)—or moving on again from Tenna into some less populous part of the dry zone. In the longer term, even this prospect will be closed as the finite amount of Crown land becomes overwhelmed by migration and population growth. How far away we are from such a prospect is unclear, but it is worth remembering that much of the worst inter-communal violence in recent years has taken place in heavily squatted areas of the northern dry zone, particularly around Vavuniya and Trincomalee.

Gemming also seems to privilege those with access to capital and cunning, but the possibilities for rational accumulation seem more restricted. Chance plays a far greater part in finding gems, although skill and judgement are necessary to turn a lucky break into a successful career as a gem-dealer. The technology of gemming requires more co-operation than cash-cropping, and the dominant idiom invokes 'trust' (rather than the calculated repayment of credit or reciprocal labour) as the bond between workers and their employers. 'Trust' is also invoked, even less probably, as a key value in relations between buyers and sellers. Not surprisingly, gemmers, like earlier generations of paddy producers (but unlike cash-croppers), inhabit an enchanted landscape, and subject as they are to extremes of fortune, devote a great deal of attention to technologies of supernatural control. The dealer's career seems to require particular attention to social investment—flamboyant donations to a temple, support for particular clients at times of crisis—partly to offset the hostility and jealousy riches are known to attract, partly to remind suppliers of the dealer's generosity so as to attract yet more riches.

The old villages were based on a complementary pattern of common activity. The huge increase in population in recent years has been almost entirely absorbed and occupied in the non-paddy area of the village economy, and now mostly in activities which separate different areas of experience: the newcomers were first of all involved in chena farming, but now they are to be found in gemming, cash-cropping, and the myriad other crowded economic niches available. We should not, therefore, be too surprised that the poor fail to conceptualize their poverty in class terms. 'Class' is a way of talking about material relationships based on shared experience:

Class happens when some men, as a result of comman experiences (inherited or shared), feel and articulate the identity of their interests as between themselves, and as against other men whose interests are different from (and usually opposed to) theirs. The class experience is largely determined by the productive relations into which men are born—or enter involuntarily. Class-consciousness is the way in which these experiences are handled in cultural terms: embodied in traditions, value-systems, ideas, and institutional forms. (Thompson 1968: 9–10)

What is lacking in Tenna (or was lacking during my stay) was that grounding of common experience in which men and women might see a common interest and identity in common activity, and might also see that interest as being contested by some other similarly constituted group.[11] No such group had clearly emerged in the village (although the more enterprising Old Tenna families might very soon start to seem like that to the poorest settlers), while the groups outside the village—the *radala* landlords or the town gem-merchants—had a very uneven impact on the lives of different households. If we want to talk of class in this part of rural Sri Lanka, then we must compare the experience of the population of Tenna as a whole with that of the urban 'sophisticates' who still control so much of local politics and economics. 'Urban' (*tavumbada*) and 'rural' (*gambada* or *piṭisara*) are key diacriticals in the language of local class relations (Spencer 1984), and, as I shall argue in Chapter Seven, access to the State has been the crucial relationship in local material advancement since the coming of the British.

There are, of course, other aspects of economic change: there are far, far more people living longer and in greater comfort; and the State has taken an ever greater role in local economic matters. But the point I wish to close with is the volatility and diversity of economic activity in Tenna. In the past common areas of work provided shared understandings which in turn informed more general social classifications. Again it must be stressed that these shared understandings were themeselves the arena for often bitter disputes; assertions of position and standing were frequently made and equally frequently challenged in terms of landholding, tenancy, and the right to belong to a particular village (cf. Selvadurai 1976). It is interesting that the kind of land dispute mentioned by earlier writers had all but died out in Tenna, just as party politics had assumed a much more prominent part in village life.

Without the common areas of everyday work there are no obvious shared understandings based on productive relations which are equally meaningful for all the people who now live in Tenna. At some time in the future people may start to understand their situation in terms of access to land and capital, and the population may define its own social boundaries and interests in those terms. But this has yet to happen. Economic change in Tenna has presented major problems for a local social idiom which in the recent past linked work, birth, and belonging. That idiom no longer stretches to cover more than a portion of the population, while sudden changes in fortune constantly threaten the expectations of kinship and neighbourliness. To find answers to those problems people have had to look elsewhere for the necessary common experience needed to define themselves and their collective and individual identities. In the absence of common experience they have had, in the last analysis, to create it for themselves. That is one thing that was happening at the *pansala* when the fight broke out.

Appendix

Landholding in Tenna
1826–1982[12]

Paddy

There are between thirty and forty-five acres of paddy land in the old villages of Udawela and Medawela.[13] About two-thirds of these form a cluster on the hillside near the old Udawela house sites and are fed by streams which feed into the restored tank. They are referred to now as the Udawela fields; in fact, in the past they were divided between the two villages. A second group of fields lies about a mile away and is fed from other streams; these are now usually referred to as the Medawela fields. Some new settlers have also cleared and terraced (asweddumized in Anglo-Sinhala) small paddy plots on government land; these are largely unrecorded and too small and recent to be of great significance in the local economy.

The clearest picture of tenure and cultivation on the old village fields in the past is provided by the villagers' memories. A conflated version of many conversations would suggest the following picture. In the old days there were two villages (*gam*) here—Udawela and Medawela. Udawela was a lord's village (*nindagama*) belonging to the people from the *valavva* ('manor,' i.e. the *ratē mahatmayā* and his *radala* kin). As well as their own fields, the villagers worked the lord's fields as sharecroppers (on *andē*) as well as providing free labour on a section of the fields (*muttettu*). The inhabitants of the adjacent village of Medawela were freeholders, owing no labour to superiors of any sort. Although both villages, apart from a handful of drummer caste (*beravā*) houses, were of *goyigama* caste, the freeholders considered themselves of higher status than the tenants, and the two villages did not intermarry. The original owner (*mulinma ayiti kārayā*) of the Medawela fields was the *māha gamarālā* (great village lord), whose name was Dingirihami; existing holdings have devolved from him through the generations.

The fields were until recently cultivated for only one harvest a year. Moreover, the hill streams do not provide enough water to cultivate all the land in the large block of fields nearest to Udawela. This block is made up of five separate fields (four since the loss of one under the new tank) fed from the same hillside streams. Cultivation alternates (as I was told it always has) between the higher and lower of these fields on a season-by-season basis. But the higher and lower fields, although contiguous, in fact have always been split between the two old villages. The point is that while Udawela and Medawela were sociologically quite distinct in the past, their fields were cultivated as a single unit; successful cultivation required co-ordination and co-operation across the village boundaries.

A detailed comparison of the earliest colonial records with field data suggests there has been limited change in the broad pattern of paddy landholding. There has been an increase in the proportion of land held by non-residents in Medawela (from 13 per cent to 50 per cent), with the ratio of resident (36 per cent in the 1820s, 40 per cent in the 1980s) to non-resident ownership in Udawela staying more or less constant during this period (cf. Spencer 1986: 138, 149). What these figures do not reveal, of course, is a predictable stability in the number of cultivators actually working the fields, and a massive (but unchartable) increase in the number of holders of tiny shares in the land. A second important consideration which cannot be discerned from these figures alone is the growth in landholding outside Tenna in the late nineteenth century. The *radala* owner of the Udawela fields at that time had gained at least 2000 acres of tea land as the result of a successful battle over an old royal land grant, and was also the holder of just under half of the hundreds of acres of new irrigated land under cultivation at Gantota in the first decade of this century (see Spencer 1986: 48–123). The Gantota scheme in particular provided a surfeit of good paddy land for would-be investors from the 1890s onward, so it is hardly surprising that relatively little of the less attractive land in Udawela and Medawela passed out of the village at this time. The single biggest block of land held by outsiders is the old *nindagama* holding which remains much as it was in the early nineteenth century, except that now it has fragmented into shares of between one-twentieth and one-eightieth and the holders are dispersed throughout the island, most of them in Colombo but some of them abroad. No single outside owner controls more than two or three acres in any season at Udawela and Medawela.

Although there are a few prosperous paddy farmers (prosperous by Tenna standards), no single villager owns more than about four acres of paddy, while only two or three of the richer villagers rely upon paddy farming for their main income. Of the few who do, one owns no land at all, his prosperity being entirely based on successful sharecropping; other villagers with more paddy land on paper are in fact much poorer. The reason lies in the combined effects of the 1958 Paddy Lands Act (that 'astonishing piece of Marxist legislation,' as Leach memorably described it [1961a: 242 n.1]), and the introduction of new high-yield ('green revolution') strains of rice in recent years, which has increased both yield and capital costs for the cultivator. The 1958 Act was designed to protect the poor sharecropping tenant from the depredations of the rich and powerful landlord, and was one of the lasting contributions of the leftist element within S. W. R. D. Bandaranaike's populist coalition of the late 1950s. In place of the half-and-half division of the harvest under prevailing sharecropping arrangements (known as *andē*), the tenant was to pay either a much lower proportion of the harvest or else a fixed rent of eight bushels per acre, whichever was more advantageous. It is generally agreed that the Act was a disaster—tenants were evicted and replaced by (unprotected) wage-labour on a vast scale—which makes its apparent success here all the harder to explain.[14]

On many of the old village fields in Tenna, and on many of the Gantota fields cultivated from Tenna, the tenant cultivates on what is known as *panata* 'by the rule'—the rule in question being the 1958 Act. The Act has not been uniformly implemented. In fact the old village lands are cultivated under a confusing combination of customary and reformed share-cropping agreements; I know of at least one case where the same tenant, cultivating for the same landlord, pays half of the harvest on one field and the smaller legal minimum on the other. But despite such oddities, certain general patterns emerge. Most absentee landlords receive the legal minimum (*panata*); this is true of virtually all the *bandāra idam*. Exceptions like that just quoted were explained by tenants in terms of the different divisions of the cost under the two systems. Under customary *andē*, landlord and tenant divide the costs of seed, ploughing, and fertilizer; under the *panata* system, the tenant bears the brunt of the capital cost. On marginal land with a high risk of crop failure tenants prefer to spread the capital risk by cultivating on *andē*, even at the expense of a smaller share of the harvest. Within the village, when both owner and tenant are resident, almost all tenancy is *andē*, and owners prefer to engage new tenants on a harvest-by-harvest basis (presumably to avoid the danger of sitting tenants insisting on their legal security of tenure). The main exceptions are cases where tenants have recovered abandoned fields and established themselves as secure *panata* tenants on co-villagers' land.

Improved strains and better production techniques have greatly increased the potential surplus on any plot since the 1958 Act became law; but the use of HYV (high yield variety) strains has also increased the capital cost of paddy production, as it has done elsewhere in the region, especially since the oil-price boom of the 1970s forced up the price of chemical fertilizer. A result of this within Tenna is that paddy production is most profitable for those who can combine the required capital with local participation in cultivation: a rich village tenant is better placed than an absentee owner. In some cases, those tenants with an established tenancy, who are paying the *panata* minimum, sub-let their tenancy on *andē*, paying the (absentee) owners from the half share of the harvest they receive from their sub-tenants.[15]

Participation in paddy production is almost entirely the preserve of Old Tenna families and more established members of the *beravā* and *vahumpura* clusters of households. The few newer settlers who cultivate paddy do so either on small plots along stream-beds which they have terraced themselves, or else they tend to be tenants of other villagers, working on the least advantageous terms. The most successful paddy farmer is Mohottihami, the old *vidanē*'s son; he works various plots of his mother's ancestral land, as well as land bought by himself and his father, but also works as much land again as a tenant of various outside owners, both here and on the Gantota fields. He acts as the local agent for the holders of *banḍāra iḍam*, taking his own cut from their share in return for overseeing the cultivation. He also owns all the village buffaloes, used in ploughing most fields and essential to the threshing, for which he gets paid in kind from the harvest. At harvest time he is a familiar figure, going from threshing-floor to threshing-floor, totting up figures on the back of an old envelope (his buffaloes guarantee him some share of virtually all the paddy in the village, but in addition to his own calculations he prepares the cultivation list for the Cultivation Officer), and calculating his various cuts.

Settlement Land

Recent land transactions in Tenna have been less and less involved with the village's relatively small area of paddy land, and more and more with the category of land officially known as 'highland.' Between 1954 and 1962 the Land Settlement Office reported on the highland of the villages of Udawela, Medawela, and Tenna, allocating and demarcating areas of dry land as Crown and as private. Individual plots of private land were granted to claimants with holdings in the old village lands, and some of the land deemed to belong to the Crown was sold in small blocks of between one and five acres. A total of 234 acres of new uncultivated land was declared private; by 1982 at least 187 acres of this had changed hands at least once, and some plots had been sold and resold many times. The price had escalated sharply in the same period. The Crown sale price was five rupees an acre in 1960; Appuhami *mudalāli* and his brother paid 18,000 rupees in 1981 for the central plot on which Appuhami had built his shop. At the time the day-wage for a village labourer was eighteen rupees.

This was the most expensive land ever sold in Tenna. But the price of much of the other ex-Settlement land has climbed steadily. The biggest buyers have been gem-dealers from Belangala and beyond, some of whom have accumulated very large blocks. Because of the 1973 land ceiling, much of this land was registered in the names of the dealer's children, thus obscuring the size of the real holding, but the biggest holdings seemed to be between twenty and perhaps fifty acres.[16] Even so it is remarkable how little of even the most frequently sold and resold land is under any cultivation at all, and how unproductive much of that limited cultivation actually is. It would seem that a great deal of the investment in this land is purely speculative; testimony to the large amounts of ready money brought into the area by gemming in the 1970s, when restrictive government policies prevented the purchase of desirable investment like minibuses and trucks (both popular with the gem-dealing class now). It is interesting, though, that very little of this money went into paddy land, possibly because such land was only available, if at all, in small, burdensome shares. In contrast, the purchase of several acres of land at a time at least permitted the illusion of being an estate owner. The ideological attractions of landed property, or the style of life associated with landed property, still persist in rural Sri Lanka, and the *arriviste* Sinhala gem-dealers (many of whom have acquired all their considerable wealth in the last ten or fifteen years) occupy much of the social space vacated by the now largely departed *radala*: they are treated with the same deference by villagers (the honorific suffix *appu* to a name is now used just as commonly for *radala* men and prominent gem-dealers), they act as intermediaries with the government, police, and local politicians, and they provide favours for those who profess a personal 'connection'—the loan of a car for a wedding in the family or to rush a sick relative to hospital.

Since the Settlement of highland in Tenna, a new stratum of rich men has been quick to snatch up newly-available resources rather than attempt to control old resources and the people dependent on the old resources. A few families, it is true, are wholly dependent on the new estate-owners, and act as watchers or farmers on their land, but very few are dependent on access to this land for the bulk of their income. Far more valuable is access to the landowner in times emergency. And for the landowners themselves the investment in these lands seems to be but one of a range of essentially social investments they have made in order to cultivate their standing in the area; an example of the blend of self-interest (because good gems come to those known to be rich and generous, and buying land, like building new temples, is a good advertisement of these facts) and philanthropy so characteristic of the gem business in this part of Sri Lanka.

Crown Land

The final category of land in Tenna is Crown land. Between 1935 and 1970 the then government of Ceylon allotted 777,000 acres of Crown land to 580,000 allottees under the terms of the Land Development Ordinance (LDO; see Moore 1985: 40). Most of the former residents of Medawela and Udawela have received allocations of LDO land in Tenna, although little of it is under productive cultivation. In addition, post-Independence governments have adopted ever more lenient attitudes toward encroachment on Crown land; a 1978 survey estimated that 'almost a million acres of Crown land were being illegally occupied by over half a million persons/households' (Moore 1985: 42). Virtually all the settlers and all but a handful of the Old Tenna households now live on one-acre plots of Crown land for which they hold a license in return for a nominal rent. These plots are mostly used for house-sites and small gardens, but illegal gemming and most of the cash-cropping also take place on Crown land.

NOTES

[1] One trader had owned 7½ acres of the Pul Eliya field in 1890 while the only outside holder owned 3½ acres in 1954 (Leach 1961a: 173).

[2] Leach implies the existence of widespread landlessness in the area around Pul Eliya (many Pul Eliya landholders employ outside hired labourers on their fields) without discussing its implications for his study (Leach 1961a: 35; cf. Obeyesekere 1967: 210).

[3] The experience is commonly reported in the folklore of Sri Lankan rural research (Colin Kirk, Richard Slater: personal communications).

[4] I am grateful to Piers Vitebsky for first drawing my attention to the 'rizocentric' bias in Sri Lankan agrarian studies.

[5] SLNA 45/24 9 September 1890. The practice seems to have started in the 1860s and stopped on the Governor's orders at some time in the 1870s.

[6] The Sinhala aversion to wage labour, with its *déclassé* connotations, has been widely reported in the literature on *attam* labour (e.g. Robinson 1975: 62–80); this aversion does not, however, extend to salaried government work, which is highly valued.

[7] Not all of these customs are followed by all farmers, nor all the explanations known; the version presented here is something of an 'expert' view gleaned from those thought to be especially knowledgeable. It was generally agreed that these customs were more assiduously followed in the past, but most are still practised. I was told that the threshing is done at night because the buffaloes could not work in the heat of the day; this did not explain why tractors, when they were brought in to replace buffaloes on a couple of fields, also worked at night. When I asked why the buffaloes always circled the floor in the same direction it was suggested that as this was the way they had always worked in the past a change might cause them to fall over. Amongst the *bisnis*-oriented farmers of the colonies, I was told, very few if any of these customs are practised.

[8] The fortunes of the *radala* in the late nineteenth and early twentieth centuries are documented in more detail in Spencer (1986: 48–85).

[9] Joe Weeramunda of Colombo University, in so far unpublished research, has found a similar pattern of finds and 'rushes' around Monaragala.

[10] I owe these two points to Evan Due and Tamara O' Grady respectively.

[11] The importance of *shared* experience is highlighted by Scott's excellent ethnography of rural class relations in a village in Malaysia (Scott 1985); not only was the village concerned based on paddy monoculture, but it was observed at a moment when, because of technological change, many former labourers were being squeezed out of the production process itself.

[12] This account is based on the following sources: Grain Tax Register, Meda Korale Helaudapalata, 1826–30 (SLNA 45/2737); Ratnapura Land Registry Records 1867–1982; Cultivation Officer's harvest records 1977–82; author's survey of Maha and Yala paddy harvests 1982–3. Pre-colonial evidence for this area can be found in Perera (1938) and Nyanawimala (1967).

[13] The figure varies over time—some lands listed in official documents have hardly ever been cultivated, while one whole field has now been flooded by the restored village tank.

[14] For further discussion of the 1958 Act and its consequences see Herring (1983: 50–84) and Moore (1985: 50–65); Herring gives a figure of 40,069 reported evictions under the Act by 1970 (Herring 1983: 73). Clearly, in this, as in other tenurial matters, there is considerable regional variation and the Tenna evidence should certainly not be taken as typical; my general impression is that large-scale paddy landlordism, reliant solely on (often migrant) wage-labour, is especially characteristic of the large tank- and canal-fed paddy tracts of the eastern and northern dry zone (especially Hambantota, Batticaloa, and Anuradhapura Districts; see Harriss 1977 and Moore 1985: 182–4; cf. Brow 1981).

[15] In such a case the established tenant is known as a *panata ayiti*, literally 'owner of the rule.'

[16] Tracing the career of particular individuals through the registration of land transactions is revealing even in its difficulties: it is possible to develop an eye for the upwardly mobile gem-dealer, acquiring ever more fanciful honorific flourishes (*nilamē, mudiyansē, basnāyaka*) to what, in earlier deals, had been a depressingly mundane personal name; or one can spot the sudden rash of gifts of land to co-residents at the same address (sons and daughters, I would guess) that followed the imposition of the ceiling in the 1973 land reform.

Chapter Five

Pastoral and Counter-Pastoral

Pastoral

At least some of the changes in material circumstances in
Tenna, most obviously the growth in population in the past
half century, are sufficiently large and well documented to
allow a relatively clear and straightforward description. It
should also be obvious that change on such a scale must of
necessity provoke strains and tensions in the way in which
people understand their own social positions. In this chapter
and the next chapter I attempt the more difficult task of
describing some of the ways in which local understandings
have changed, and some of the consequent conflict and
muddle. In this chapter I concentrate on the understanding of
rural change, and trace some of the major models of change
available to the people of Tenna. In the next chapter I turn to
the description of tensions in the texture of everyday social
relations.

Models of change are, of course, crucial models *for* change,
so that the interpretation of colonial perceptions of Tenna and
its neighbours necessarily involves a parallel account of the
way in which those perceptions affected the policies of the
State in the area. One theme, summed up in the rhetoric of
'distress' and 'improvement' employed by colonial administrators, was swiftly taken up by nationalist politicians and can
be heard in the talk of village political leaders like Cyril. But
'improvement' is also a cultural process, and the establish-
ment of new institutions for the transmission of new cultural
understandings, the school and the *pansala*, is another
necessary component in the often difficult process of reimagin-
ing and remaking Tenna in the borrowed imagery of Sri
Lankan pastoral.

In Europe, the idea of the rural has played a central part in the history of the moral imagination. From the poetry of Wordsworth or the paintings of Constable to the banalities of contemporary advertising, the rural has been used as a vehicle for differing powerful ideas and evaluations. Rural may be opposed to urban as poor, backward, ignorant, or—just as likely—traditional, natural, unchanging. Similar evaluations have been employed in South Asia, where the complexity of the rural as a bundle of signs—a 'structure of feeling' in Raymond Williams's vocabulary (Williams 1977: 128–35)— is further accentuated by the experience of colonialism. Class divisions in colonial society refracted through the experience of colonial education to produce new divisions within society and new ways of talking about them, of which 'the rural' was one. Colonial administrators had preconceived ideas about the countryside and its inhabitants; these ideas were themselves adopted by sections of the colonized population, often reappearing in nationalist criticisms of colonial rule. And, as we shall see, in Sri Lanka these criticisms have provided the dominant framework for much subsequent academic work on change in the countryside.[1]

One theme, commonly expressed by academics, politicians, and administrators, is of rural decline. So, for example, the Kandyan Peasantry Commission, reporting in the early 1950s, observed that, 'the village community, with its communalities and obligations, has in a great measure disappeared and so also the old conceptions of community effort' (Sessional Paper XVIII 1951: 12). A few years later, a survey report from the then University of Ceylon substantiated many of the points made by the Commission, not least the idea of a crisis in the countryside: 'What we wish to emphasise is that the rural society in the Kandyan areas, and perhaps in other areas too, under the dual pressure of population rise and a stagnant and exploitative economy, is fast disintegrating and approaching a critical stage' (Sarkar and Tambiah 1957: xiii). This survey was published as *The Disintegrating Village*. Twenty years later, in the late 1970s, the same title (but couched as a question) was used for another collection of village studies. And while the editors of this later collection were rightly critical of some earlier assumptions about rural change, similar broad apprehensions are endorsed in one passage in their introduction: 'Poverty shows no sign of fading away; inequality is often alleged to be worsening, and the sense of mutual interest and mutual responsibility which formerly characterised relationships between villagers is on the wane' (Morrison *et al.* 1979: 5). So, the 'village community' and 'community effort' are disappearing, 'rural society' is 'disintegrating,' and a past in which villagers considered each other in terms of 'mutual interest and mutual responsibility' is contrasted with an impoverished present. In all of these generalizations the rural is presented, implicitly or explicitly, in terms of loss—loss of community, loss of harmony. The countryside never simply changes, it *decays*.

This sort of valuation of rural change is by no means confined to Sri Lanka. English agriculture and the English countryside have been subject to a very long process of social and economic change, stretching back over many centuries. Yet in the 1960s it was still possible for one writer to present a similar contrast between a recent past of rural harmony and a present of loss: 'A way of life that has come down to us from the days of Virgil has suddenly ended'; and 'A whole culture that had preserved its continuity from earliest times had now received its quietus' (Ewart Evans in Williams 1973: 9). These judgements are quoted by Raymond Williams in his important study of ideas about town and country in English literature, *The Country and the City*. As he shows, they merely echo a host of earlier judgements: thus Leavis and Thompson in the 1930s—'The "organic community" of "Old England" had disappeared; "the change is very recent indeed" ' (in Williams 1973:9); Hardly in his novels of the 1870s to 1890s harking back, like George Eliot before him, to the lost world of the 1830s; Cobbett in the 1820s lamenting the passing of the rural order of his own childhood in the 1770s and 1780s, a time when Crabbe and Goldsmith wrote their verse laments on an even earlier decline of the village. Williams likens his literary pursuit of the old rural order to stepping on an escalator: as we move back in time so too the laments for the loss of the old, timeless order always situate it 'just back, we can see, over the last hill.' And the hills go back a long way: in Virgil's *Eclogues*, written two millennia ago and supposedly the source of that 'way of life' invoked at the start of the pursuit, we find an explicit contrast between a remembered rural harmony and threats to that harmony in the form of wars and evictions.

It almost goes without saying that, in the past, anthropologists have also framed their understanding of rural society in similar terms. The search for the 'disappearing primitive,' 'rescue ethnography', the siting of ethnographic accounts one or two generations back in the time of pristine tradition—these are all familiar enough devices in the genre which James Clifford has described, after Williams, as 'ethnographic pastoral' (Clifford 1986: 110). In this the distance from the town becomes a distance back in time:

Ceylon is a highly sophisticated and complex island. The intellectual life of Colombo and Peradeniya is lively and important; its political repercussions can be felt around the world. But in this volume we leave all that aside, and concern ourselves almost entirely with the small, relatively isolated, traditional communities far from sophisticated centers. (Yalman 1967: 3)

The relative isolation of Hinidum Pattu and its absence of 'progress' makes it an excellent region for anthropological field work, specially as a 'baseline' for ascertaining traditional modes of behaviour and culture and an assessment of change. Such a task is practically impossible in most other Divisions of the low country owing to radical changes they have experienced. (Obeyesekere 1967: 6).

On the one hand sophistication, complexity, intellectual liveliness, politics; on the other isolation, smallness, tradition, distance. Yalman's work, in which history and change are not so much denied as ignored, is less relevant here than Obeyesekere's study, which provides the fullest academic working of an argument already encountered.

Let me again invoke Williams's image of the backward-moving escalator. We can, I think, step on board a similar escalator in Sri Lanka. In a public lecture in Colombo in the early 1980s, Obeyesekere offered a picture of social devastation in the countryside wrought by demographic pressure and consequent inter-village migration:

In the sixties and after things had changed; the population explosion produced a generation of children of migrants, and there was increasing competition for village resources. Moreover outsiders, who had no kin ties with the village also began to move in, for a variety of social and economic reasons. The effect of these social conditions was to radically alter the pattern of traditional village society, and produce division, social conflict and economic crime in village society. (Obeyesekere 1983: 18–19)[2]

What was destroyed was 'the kin-based homogeneous nature of traditional village society,' something which had managed to survive, albeit under pressure, until these changes of the last twenty years. But what of the 'The Disappearing Village'? Morrison and his co-editors in 1979 claim the need for some siting of the traditional, if only as a benchmark for the assessment of change:

For our purposes 'traditional' refers to the period around the end of colonial rule, and especially to the time before the dramatic explosion of the Island's population which began in the late 1940s as a consequence of improvements in health services and control over malaria (Morrison *et al.* 1979: 15).

The 1940s as the period of tradition? Wasn't this the time when the Kandyan Peasantry Commission was carrying out its investigations into the rural crisis? And didn't these investigations themselves spring from political anxieties in the 1930s about the condition of the countryside?

The 1920s and 1930s were the period when nationalist politicians 'discovered' the rural crisis (Samaraweera 1981; Meyer 1980), but in this they depended on earlier views like Leonard Woolf's fictional portrait of the death of a village, *Village in the Jungle* (Samaraweera 1981: 135). Even earlier than that, in the 1890s, we find a colonial official discussing the effects of the Grain Tax and concluding, 'In brief the old Kandyan Feudal system and village life have broken up and are rapidly disappearing' (Fisher in Sessional Paper IV 1891; cited in Obeyesekere 1967: 288). And, before that, in the 1850s we find civil servants already expressing fears about rural decline and initiating new measures in irrigation policy as a result. But

[Governor Sir Henry] Ward and his advisors quickly realised that the mere provision of water was inadequate; 'the spirit and practice of mutual obligation which was so important a feature of peasant agriculture' had either died out or become moribund because of new forces—such as individualism—which had come to the fore with British rule. (Samaraweera 1978a: 71).

The sense of 'mutual interest and mutual responsibility' said
to be merely 'on the wane' in the 1970s appears in fact to have
'died out or become moribund' by the 1850s. The escalator
moves us back; the view remains the same.

Counter-Pastoral

All of the voices heard so far in this chapter are at some
remove—academic, political, or administrative—from rural
life. One easy way to assess these various versions of the rural,
in which 'community' and 'harmony' are to be encountered
only in their absence, is to compare them with the memories of
those old enough to remember the past. Here are some
versions of the past I collected in Tenna. First from Appuhami
mudalāli's father, an old *goyigama* man whose own father had
moved to the village to marry in *binna* (uxorilocally) around the
turn of the century but whose sons had prospered in the gem
trade in the 1970s:

Q: Is there a great difference between the past and the present?
A: In Udawela in those days there were very few people. . . . On this side of
the fields there were five houses, and on the other side there were five
houses.
Q: How many houses were there in Gantota?
A: In those days there were very few people in Gantota. The children did
not grow; they suffered from fever—stomachs were like this, so big. . . .
Q: This was malaria?
A: Yes! It was malaria. Fever, everywhere fever. People were dying, they
died and died. There were very, very few people at Gantota. Later when
they began to spray the houses for malaria, the fever went down and the
population increased, the children began to grow. At that time it was almost
impossible to get a little breast-milk for medicine. None of the children grew
at all—their limbs were very thin, they suffered from fever, stomachs
contracted. There were very few men and they were outsiders. None of the
old inhabitants of that village survived. The men who lived at Udawela in
those days came from various places to cultivate the *bandāra* fields. Now it
has prospered (*diyunuyi*) and the population increased. It's the same here. In
Udawela there were five houses, each with four or five people. . . . But all
the men of my age died young. In my lot all the young died. No medicine.
Then this increase in population, decrease in illness—all due to spraying
insecticide for malaria. In those days there was fever everywhere.

Afterwards hospitals were built, temples were built. Before there was
nothing like that: no temple, no school. Mere subsistence (*hamba karagen
vitarayi*). People suffered (*minissu bohoma dukayi*).

Fever, suffering; as the old man started to tell me of his
contemporaries who died in their youth his eyes filled with
tears.

Yet the same man on another occasion provided me with a
vivid and rapturous description of the lost joys of swidden
cultivation in his youth. And it was clear that he was unhappy
with many of the changes in daily life; his sons now insisted he
should no longer work in the fields and this left him idle at
home; they claimed he could not and would not understand
the world of *bisnis* in which they hustled a living. At one stage
the differences grew so acute that he walked out of his own
house (which he shared with a married gem-dealing son) and
stayed in the house of his eldest son—the poorest of his
children and the only one who tried to make a living as a
cultivator in his father's way. The role in which this old man
seemed happiest was that of the *upāsakā*, the pious layman. On
poya days he would invariably dress in white and spend most
of his day at the *pansala*, reading his copy of a popular collection
of Buddhist texts. In the evenings he would often stop at the
pansala to talk with the priest and listen to his discussions of
politics and the world with the younger visitors.

I mention this because the three most frequently invoked
institutional changes in the village's past were the school, the
temple, and access to health care. This is a *vahumpura*
immigrant from the 1930s describing the way of life found
when he arrived:

People in this village were like Veddas. They would group together, go to
the jungle, kill the animals and eat. That was their work. In Udawela that
was how they lived. Each day they would go hunting, kill animals and eat
them, and then the next day they would do the same. A little paddy
cultivation, a little chena—that was how they lived.

This man was from a village fifteen miles away beyond the
town. The comparison with the way of life of Veddas is
especially evocative. The category of Vedda—the supposed
primitive aboriginals of nineteenth-century ethnological
fancy—is frequently invoked in Sinhala as the sign of the

uncivilized; they are the people of the forest, hunters, or, more loosely, simply the isolated and uneducated rural poor (Brow 1978: 26–39). For this lower-caste immigrant to the village a remembered scorn for the unsophisticated ways of the inhabitants may serve as compensation for the vividly remembered injuries of caste from the same time. Others remembered the pleasures of hunting with less reserve: 'In those days there would be meat cooking in every house,' one man recalled with evident pleasure. But now, with so much of the jungle cleared and game severely depleted, hunting has been reduced to the status of an occasional entertainment for some of the young men, frowned upon by many of the more assiduous Buddhists in the village.

Another low-caste man, this time a *berava* (drummer) who was one of the first chena-cultivating settlers in Tenna in the 1920s:

Q: How does caste custom (*jāti sirit*) compare with the past?
A: Now all the customs are good. In the past it was very severe (*sära*). Terrible. Could not enter a house, could not go to a house wearing a new shirt like this. Now it's not like that. When you go to a house everyone will be treated alike.
Q: When did it change? Did it change gradually?
A: It changed little by little. When the first priest came here he changed everything. He preached to all of them and reformed them. Now there's no difference between them. All the castes live together without any difference. . . . Now everyone lives like children of one person. There is no attention to caste whatsoever.

Again, this account needs to be read in context: as I shall show later, caste remains a more active force than this might suggest. But there was consensus among all who were old enough to remember that caste was far less muted in the past than it had become in the present. And consider the last part of the old man's account: it was the teaching of the first priest to come to the new temple in the late 1930s which changed the attitudes of the old villagers; and the effect of this preaching, tellingly, is that 'Now everyone lives like children of one person'. For this man, the coming of the temple was part of a process which created a kind of kinship among all the inhabitants, regardless of their particular origins and circumstances.

I will return to the old and their memories from time to time in what follows. It should be borne in mind that these passages are taken from relatively formal tape-recorded interviews and represent more or less considered representations of past and present. In this context I found the general contrast to be between a past of ignorance, poverty and disease, of foolish and un-Buddhist attentions to the niceties of caste, and a present which could be summed up in the word *diyunu*—'improved.' But in many other contexts, memories of the past were far less bleak. I mentioned hunting and the chena harvest as lost areas of life remembered with pleasure by the old. The *beravā* man who described caste in such acerbic tones, nevertheless in the same interview described the arrival of so many settlers on the plateau in terms of 'uncleanness' and 'pollution.' We were talking of the territory of the deity Mangara, and he told me how in his youth the people might hear the sound of the god's flute from their chenas:

Tenna means a place of buffaloes. In the past it all belonged to the gods. You could not cross the stream to come here in an unclean state (*apirisiduven*). You had to wash and make an offering of coins (*panduru*) and then cross to this side. . . . That was how Tenna was. Because people no longer pay regard as they did, the gods have left this area and gone to other parts of the country. They are not here now; they merely show their power but they have left this place. They do not live in places where people live because such places are unclean.

Here the influx of people is equated with a literal disenchantment of the landscape. Materially and socially things may have 'improved,' as he so eagerly asserted at other points in the interview, but there have also been losses.

These conflicting assessments of their own past are partly the product of the striking material changes they have seen in their lifetimes: the eradication of malaria and consequent population explosion; the building of the school and the temple; the expansion of state employment; the waves of new settlers; improved and far more profitable cultivation practices; gemming; access to newspapers and radios. But they also reflect crucial cultural changes. The school, the temple, the radio, the press, are all new cultural resources. They ensure that the children growing up in Tenna have immediate access to much of the same culture as children growing up in all Sinhala-speaking parts of the island. But this also serves to separate them from parts of their own past and the experience of their parents and grandparents; and the old have to live amongst surroundings which are both familiar and unfamiliar. The physical landscape has changed enormously, but so has the intellectual landscape; the rural past has become a central theme in national political ideology (Moore 1985; Tennekoon 1988; Brow 1988). The memories of the old are now constantly jostled by new values and emphases, and, implicitly at least, compete with other, more public descriptions of rural order.

Relief, Distress, Improvement

I have started with representations of rural change and have contrasted urban laments on the loss of rural community with rural voices at once celebrating improvements of all sorts—moral and material—and yet occasionally allowing nostalgia to touch their accounts of the past. Another view—occasionally encountered—is of a past even further back, in the time of the kings, when the land was a land of plenty. I now want to discuss a third way of talking about rural life—that of the British administrators of the area—as a means of leading into a summary of the main areas of 'improvement' in Tenna over the last hundred years.

Not surprisingly, in the kachcheri records now stored at the Department of National Archives in Colombo evidence of local conditions grows more detailed and specific with the passing of time. The main exceptions to this are the registers of the Grain Tax, the earliest of which (from the late 1820s) provide remarkably detailed accounts of village-level agricultural arrangements; apart from these, the records tell us little of the period from 1820 to 1850. In 1864 the AGA visited Gonagala, the Muslim shrine adjacent to Tenna. The following year his successor visited Malgoda, making a detailed record of landholdings there and in neighbouring Udawela and Medawela. At Malgoda he noted, 'It is about thirty years since any agent visited this village.'[3]

The area as a whole—the *bintenna* (low-lying plain) of the Province—seems to have become the object of official concern at some point in the 1850s. In 1877 the Assistant Government Agent (AGA) summed up his predecessors' views:

The people of the Bintenna of the Meda, Atakalon, and Kolonna Korales are in a state no less pitiable than that of of the most distressed inhabitants of other Provinces, and, like them, for want of food which a waterless soil cannot yield. As long ago as 1857 I find that Mr. Mitford pleaded earnestly on behalf of this part of the district, since when Messrs. Birch, Russell, and Saunders have all in turn recognized its need, and made their observations known to the Government. (AR 1877: 87)

Eight years later, a new Government Agent (GA), Herbert Wace, in his first report, provided an equally bleak picture, supplemented with rather more detail:

It is in the Kolonná Kóralé and in the Bintenna of the Atakalan and Meda Kóralés that the food-supply is meagre, often inadequate, and generally of a very poor quality. The main food-supply is kurakkan and dried elk-flesh, Indian corn, and tenna [sesame]. . . . The dry grain thus raised on hén [chena] is largely bartered by the cultivators for salt and dry fish with the Moor traders from Hambantota District, who bring up large tavalam [caravan] droves every harvest. . . . The people are too poor to import rice or other food, and are entirely dependent on the chena cultivation and the occasional yield of their paddy lands. The consequence is that distress and sickness are very prevalent in the Bintenna, and at the close of the year it was necessary to apply to Government for relief to some of the villagers, which was given in the supply of kurakkan, till the chena crops were ready for reaping. (AR 1885: 139)

There is evidence to suggest that the economy described by Wace remained largely unchanged throughout the colonial period. One of the earliest descriptions of the Province—from 1818—mentions the monopoly on trade of itinerant Muslims who would barter cloth and salt for crops yet to be harvested in the field; their salt route from the pans of Hambantota into the Kandyan Provinces long pre-dated the British conquest.[4] This is another aspect of life that evoked fond memories from older villagers, who told me of the time when they could grow almost all they needed, except cloth and salt, for which they had to barter with roving traders, and when cash was almost never used.

The colonial administration was less interested in the

details of rural barter than in the conditions summed up in the concept of 'distress.' The word recurs again and again in official descriptions of the area in the second half of the nineteenth century. If we can speak of an 'official mind' in this part of the colonial era, then 'distress' was the prerequisite for any active intervention by government in the local economy (cf. Moore 1985; 298–9 n.122). Two kinds of short-term measure were employed. The first of these was the granting of government licenses for extra chena cultivation, a move which required considerable warning in order to have any effect and which in any case was of no use when it was the chena crops themselves that had failed. The threat of distress seems to have been a constant rhetorical device in local representations to a government which, to local interests, seemed to suffer from an irrational distaste for traditional swidden agriculture. The second option was 'relief,' usually in the form of labouring work on roads or other public works in return for grain or other foodstuffs. Such works were frequently instituted in the late nineteenth and early twentieth centuries; they were still common in the time of my fieldwork as a response to drought or other natural difficulty. It seems, therefore, that from the 1880s (and possibly earlier) large-scale crop failure and consequent starvation were regularly ameliorated by recourse to government. A limited but essential trade with the outside world which pre-dated the colonial era was gradually supplemented by a very real dependence on the emergency support of the State.

Even as they were being employed, these responses were felt to be inadequate. In particular, official prejudice against chena cultivation was such that every possible effort was made to persuade the villagers to turn to other kinds of agriculture. In 1911 the GA committed the following gloomy description to his diary; after commenting on the recurrent droughts that had blighted the agriculture of the area ('the last good rainfall was in 1899') and dismissing the 'cry for chena' ('not a remedy but an anodyne'), he mused on the way the inhabitants clung to their villages despite the availability of work in the wet-zone rubber plantations then opening up to the west and on the newly irrigated lands under the Gantota scheme to the east:

The people would rather die among old surroundings than migrate in either direction. These Kandyan villages or rather parishes consisting of a few scattered houses among many square miles of sun-dried hills, belong to a primitive order of things which cannot be maintained on any modern principles of rural economy, in other words life in them cannot go on for long without chena cultivation, and chena cultivation in the long run makes poverty permanent. (SLNA 45/333: 15 February 1911)

Needless to say, this assessment of their plight was not shared by the villagers; even now, chena cultivation is remembered as a fundamentally joyful activity (see Chapter Four above). But to administrator after administrator it seemed to be a positive evil, sapping the cultivators' moral fibre; that it involved even more than usually sporadic patterns of activity and inactivity can hardly have helped. Paddy, by contrast, was viewed as the stuff of which a sturdy yeomanry might be made. Immediately before the passage just quoted, the GA writes of the 'broad expanse of good paddy land' at Gantota, to which the villagers showed an inexplicable reluctance to move; only sentences later he mentions the high death toll from disease there, without actually making the all too obvious connection.

This expansion of irrigated land two miles from Tenna along the banks of the Walawe Ganga at Gantota, was the major colonial effort in this area. Under this scheme more than 600 acres of newly irrigated land were leased out in the 1890s; the single biggest holder (with nearly half of the total under cultivation in 1905) was the highest 'native' official in the area, the *raṭē mahatmayā* who also owned the bulk of the lands in Udawela.[5] The rest of the lands were leased mostly to merchants from the town of Belangala, but the scheme was plagued by a shortage of labour. The villagers in Tenna, Udawela, and Medawela were well placed to benefit from the increase in land available to would-be sharecroppers.

In 1911 a visiting GA had listed the 'manifold obstacles' to the Gantota scheme's success; the language is only a little different but the physical details are almost identical with the old man's memory of Gantota with which I started the preceding section:

(1) A very small resident population.
(2) Physical degeneracy of those who live here: the women all get flat-breasted and lose, so I am told, their lacteal glands.

(3) Prevalence of venereal disease due to influx of low-countrymen and the loose morals of the Durayas [a low-caste group].
(4) No dispensary. If a man falls ill he has to climb a hill, which would tax the strength of a man in sound health, in order to get medicine.
(5) Want of a cart road.
(6) The bad reputation of the place, and the considerable number of pioneers who fell sick and died here.[6]

In an effort to encourage population growth, a bounty of five rupees for every child born in Gantota was introduced in 1919. After a visit in 1934 the GA spoke of the reputation of the village's women for sterility and described three children proudly produced for his inspection: 'most charming grave faced mites; chances of growing to maturity said to be somewhat slight and the little victims seemed almost "mindful of their doom".'[7]

If health presented the most serious problem for the administration's efforts in the area, the economic effect of the lack of good transport might have seemed more open to swift amelioration. The government had a good supply of cheap, or even free labour: under the Roads Ordinance all able-bodied men were required to give several day's free labour a year (with the option of a cash commutation) for the maintenance and improvement of local roads. In addition, recurrent relief works in time of crop failure and distress almost invariably took the form of work on road improvements in return for payments of dry grain. What was needed was a link with the bazaar town of Belangala, which was on the main road from Colombo to the southern towns of the tea-growing area and had been a centre of local trade since the earliest days of British rule.

The road was started in 1887 (AR 1887: 29) but despite constant calls for support and aid from the provincial administration it was not open to wheeled vehicles all the way to Gantota until the 1940s. In the intervening years the road was extended in instalments, and cart-based trade grew up along it. The *vahumpura* population in Tenna started with one couple who built up a successful carting business transporting rice and other goods between Gantota and the town. An even more successful carter bought up large areas of land in the villages along the road, and became the major holder of land in Gantota itself in the 1930s.

Meanwhile a dispensary was established in 1919 in Gantota, and in the 1920s this was extended to become a small rural hospital. Even so, the area suffered a particularly severe malaria epidemic in 1929 and 1930. The hospital was never more than a limited success, rarely adequately staffed or supplied. Not surprisingly, my informants remember depending instead on the medical facilities provided by the newly-opened tea estate at Galpitiya eight miles over the hills toward Belangala. Gantota itself was to prove habitable only with the introduction of spraying with DDT (and more recently Malathion) in the 1940s. The control thus established over the worst enemy of the population completely changed the material conditions of life here, as elsewhere in the dry zone. But, as with the road, this second major change induced by the colonial government took effect only in the last years of colonial rule.

In the years immediately before Independence, the administration was increasingly subject to political pressure from a new and ambitious generation of local politicians. Even before the introduction of universal suffrage in the 1931 Donoughmore Constitution administrative attitudes were increasingly affected, one way or another, by nationalist rhetoric. This sometimes took the form of a self-conscious official championing of a mute peasantry against what was seen to be a strident but unrepresentative Ceylonese political elite. Meanwhile that same elite needed policies, ideas, and explanations of what had happened and what should happen in the rural sector. Earlier agitation on Crown and waste lands and the effect of the Grain Tax evictions of the 1880s (much of it the work of metropolitan political economists) was pressed into new service. The 'disintegrating villages' of the 1950s and 1960s, as a description of rural change, have their intellectual roots in earlier elite politics. As Samaraweera (1981) has pointed out in an excellent essay, the interpretation of the rural problem offered by nationalist thinkers in the 1920s and 1930s rather carefully avoided large areas of agricultural change—the huge increase in local elite landholding documented by Peebles (1973: 216–67) for example. Their interpretation of the rural problem, and the corresponding policies proposed for its alleviation, represented a compromise between the new need for political rhetoric with mass appeal and the sectional interests of a political class many of whom were themselves large landlords. In this, rural decay was blamed on the effects of European investment, and the role of local capital either ignored or played down.

The first immediate manifestation of the changing balance of interest within the colonial state was the appointment of the Land Commission, a body set up in 1927 to investigate and make policy recommendations. The Commission made two central recommendations for future policy: that 'Crown land is held in trust for the whole community inhabiting this island' and 'that the "preservation of the peasantry as a social group" should govern the formulation of future land policy' (Samaraweera 1981: 145; cf. Samaraweera 1973). These intentions were embodied in two important pieces of legislation: the Land Settlement Ordinance of 1931 and the Land Development Ordinance of 1935. The first of these provided for a planned framework of mapping and allotting existing village lands; the second for the controlled expansion of peasant holdings, both on the edges of existing settlements and in increased colonization efforts in the dry zone.

The small hill-villages around Gantota had of course long provided a source of labour for the vast but unhealthy lands along the river on the plain. Many farmers still walk from Tenna to their fields in Gantota every morning. Eventually, the healthier air of the higher land above Gantota attracted the attention of the administration, and about the time of the 1929 malaria epidemic in the area, new colonization, in the form of one of the first of the new Village Expansion Schemes, was planned on the plateau below the old villages of Udawela and Medawela. The idea was that this would provide a healthy environment in which to settle much-needed cultivators for the Gantota lands. A planned water-supply system in Tenna was never really successful (a reliable piped source was finally set up in 1981) and the initial flow of settlers was unimpressive, really gathering force only in the post-war, post-malaria years. But new resources and new encouragement had been given to the existing population. The new resources were the grants of long-term leasehold land in Tenna, as well as the road which now extended this far but no further. The official interest and encouragement embodied in the water pipes and a new village-council building were a far cry from that GA's description twenty years earlier of these villages as part of an unjustifiable and doomed 'primitive order of things'.[8] By the end of the 1930s the area was being visited by a Sinhala Minister for Agriculture and Lands interested in the scope for development; seventy years earlier a visit from the Government Agent might be a once-in-a-lifetime experience for a villager. In the intervening years there had been a remarkable change in the relationship between the peasants of the area and the State.

There is now in Tenna a high degree of both direct and indirect dependence on the State. Direct dependence comes in a number of forms. Before the 1960s the only State employees in the area were the *āracci* (headman), whose jurisdiction extended over a number of villages in the area and who was usually based some distance away at Gantota or Malgoda, and the *vel vidānē* (irrigation headman), who supervised agricultural arrangements in each settlement and acted as spokesman and representative in dealings with officialdom. In 1982 Tenna had twenty-three holders of full-time jobs: six schoolteachers, ten holders of government posts (the *grāma-sēvaka*, Cyril, the postmistress, a bus-conductor, and so on), and seven employees at the new wall-tile factory on the Belangala road. Virtually all the other households received food stamps under a recent scheme which the 1977 government had introduced to replace the earlier rice ration under which all households received a free weekly allowance of the staple. And, as well as these regular contributions to subsistence, there were still periodic relief works—usually involving work-parties clearing local paths in return for 'dry rations' of lentils and tinned goods and the like—in which all but the richest villagers would participate.

A degree of indirect dependence was typical of almost all local economic activities. House sites and gardens were almost all on Crown land, for which the holder only had temporary title, if any. Gemming without a license was illegal and subject to periodic police raids and consequent fines or bribes. A number of people were involved in illegal timber-felling in what remained of the old forest cover. Even collecting firewood from the surrounding scrub could count as illegal (or so I was assured by my friend who ran the bakery which depended on local wood for its fuel). Ever since the colonial State's efforts to stamp out chena cultivation, Tenna's economic survival has depended on activities carried out in a penumbra of dubious legality. The effect has been to bolster the power of those with local knowledge and privileged access to the machinery of government—the 'headman class' of the colonial period (*āraccis* and higher officials like the *raṭē mahatmayā* and *kōralē*) who were able to demand informal tithes from illegal chenas and free labour on their own fields (cf. Meyer 1983: 26), and the local 'political class' of the present day, who, it was generally acknowledged, could easily make their opponents' lives impossible through petty official harassment.

Direct and indirect dependence on the State, and the long history of slowly growing state interest in 'improvement' are important ingredients in the growth and shape of village politics (see below Chapter Seven). But this interest and intervention has been shaped and channelled by particular images of the rural good life, images which have changed over time and gradually grown closer to the aspirations of rural people themselves, but which nevertheless have their roots outside the experience of rural life.

Temple and School

In the 1930s and 1940s, as the State was involving itself ever more actively in hitherto isolated settlements like Tenna, these settlements were provided with (or provided for themselves) two institutions which supplied new intellectual resources with which people might understand the changing circumstances of local life. These were the temple and the school. Their introduction into the area was an indication of the passing of a predominantly oral and local culture and its replacement by a national culture reproduced in print and, more recently, through radio and television, and instilled in the peculiar rituals of the schoolroom.

The history of the Tenna temple is part of the larger history of the *sangha* in this part of Sri Lanka. In the early years of the nineteenth century, members of low country castes, barred from ordination as non-*goyigama*, successfully established their own orders with help from Burma. The first and largest of these was the Amarapura Nikāya, which quickly fragmented into a number of separate parallel *nikāya*, followed by the Ramanna Nikāya, which is the smallest of the three primary divisions of the *sangha* in contemporary Sri Lanka. The low country sects gradually established themselves in Sabaragamuva, and by 1847 a native Christian observer was able to report a considerable change in the religious life of the area:

The object of the Amarapoora priests is to bring back the doctrines of Budhism [sic] to their pristine purity, by disentangling them from caste, polytheism, and other corruptions to which they have been subject for ages, and these priests, how difficult soever the task maybe, have made considerable progress in this reformation in the low countries, but especially in Saffragam which may at present be regarded as the chief seat of this reformation, and where the difference in the tenets and principles of the two sects is wider and greater than anywhere else, though the Amarapoora sect originated with the Chalia priests of Amblangode and Galle about 40 years ago. (De Silva 1847: 276)

Writing elsewhere, the same author attributes this unexpected development to the influence of 'the respectable families' of the province who had welcomed the reformist sect to the area in the 1830s (Malalgoda 1976: 140–1). The reasons for this elite support of what elsewhere was a non-*goyigama* movement are not wholly clear. Malalgoda mentions Sabaragamuva's long tradition of autonomy from Kandy, and there is no doubt that there might be political advantages for the local *radala* in supporting a break from the control of the central Kandyan elite who controlled the dominant Siyam Nikāya temples at Asgiriya and Malwatte in Kandy.

In the twentieth century one particular division of the Amarapura Nikāya has come to predominate in the area. Its most famous member has spent much of his time in recent years lecturing in Europe. His father was a wealthy Belangala merchant who endowed a temple just outside the town where his son was ordained. Other members of the *nikāya* in the area are *goyigama*, the sons of slightly wealthier villagers. In addition there are a number of European members. The result of this diversity is a rather odd style; the local monks are considerably more down-to-earth than the occasional European Buddhist, but still, I suspect, a great deal less worldly than the average Sri Lankan monk. At more or less the same time as the founding of Tenna *pansala*, new temples were build in two neighbouring villages, again by the same branch of the *sangha*.

The *pansala* at Tenna was founded in 1936 by Kiriyansa, a *vahumpura* immigrant from Mahagasgoda, who had worked intermittently for the *raṭē mahatmayā* and his family at Gantota before settling at Tenna, where his wife ran a carting business. His brother, who settled with him, had spent six years as a monk before disrobing, and had taught at least one of my older informants to read and write. Kiriyansa is said to have been inspired to build a *pansala* by a dream he had after falling asleep at the foot of the old bo tree in what is now the centre of the village. He donated his own land and organized the construction, with voluntary help from the old villagers and some support from the *raṭē mahatmayā*. The first priest to come to the *pansala*, from the temple at Galpitiya eight miles away, at first only stayed for the three months of the *vas* rainy-season retreat; he has now succeeded to the position of *nāyaka* (head) of the *nikāya* and incumbent at the big *pansala*, but he has retained his interest in the village. His successor stayed for eighteen years and did much to extend the fabric of the *pansala*, adding a shrine-room, a preaching-hall, and a *sīmāgē* ('boundary-house' for certain monastic meetings). For a number of years after that the incumbent was a Tamil convert from Jaffna (reflecting the fame of the then *nāyaka*). After his death, the present incumbent arrived.

The foundation of the Tenna *pansala* seems to have been part of a conscious effort by this branch of the *sangha* to 'colonize' the area. Earlier, the nearest *pansala* was a difficult journey of at least eight miles, and the inhabitants' involvement with institutional Buddhism could best be described as minimal. I was told, at first, that efforts would be made to fetch a priest to conduct funeral rites in the event of a death, but in fact many were simply buried with little or no ceremony. Similarly, some said that in the old days efforts might be made to visit a *pansala* on a major day such as Vesak *poya*; but the general feeling was summed up in one man's statement that 'we knew nothing of the *dharma* then.'

The second element in Tenna's cultural transformation was the founding of a village school. The incidence of literacy in Tenna now, as elsewhere in Sri Lanka, is very high; all but a few old women can at least read and cope with the signatures necessary for any dealings with officialdom. A few of the old men had learnt to read at a school in Malgoda, which was founded in the 1880s by a rich family of that village and subsequently taken over by the colonial government. Others had learnt by staying with relatives nearer to schools, or had been taught the rudiments by their fathers. But until the 1940s the nearest school was several hours' walk away, and the distance involved made it impossible for children resident in Tenna to attend.

In 1940, as part of the war effort, a commercial company was granted permission to use a large area of the Tenna plateau for chena farming. All the existing population were provided with work, and additional wage-labourers were drafted in (although many are said to have fallen victim to the still notoriously unhealthy air). In addition, men from the 'respectable families' of the area were employed on the scheme in a supervisory capacity. The scheme lasted for three years, during which time the workers began to take an interest in the new village *pansala*, and funds were collected to pay a teacher to teach the children in the *pansala*'s ramshackle preaching-hall. The priest was an enthusiastic supporter and tirelessly petitioned the government for aid. After the war the government agreed to take over the school and gave the old village-council building (part of the abortive village expansion of the 1930s) as a schoolhouse.[9] Various teachers came and went as the roll gradually grew; in 1964 the new schoolmaster married the daughter of one of the village families, thus becoming the first villager with a salaried job. The UNP government elected in 1977 built a new and bigger school; in 1984 it had 194 pupils and a staff of eight. By then three village boys had made their way to university.

The school and the *pansala* are the two key institutions which link Tenna with a wider national culture. Both came to Tenna in the decade before Independence, arriving just ahead of the tide of new immigration into the village. And both were a mixed product of local initiative and outside support: a new settler managed to persuade the other villagers to co-operate in building the *pansala* (given to an actively reformist branch of the *sangha* which had been building support in the area over the previous century) and the school was a joint product of the overseers on the chena farm (many of whom were sons and grandsons of the earlier *radala* patrons of Buddhist revival in the area) and the new priest, before the government was persuaded to take over the running of it. Most important of all for our purposes, the school and the *pansala* both provided access to new ways of understanding the changes that have subsequently swept over Tenna.

A New Rural Order

Village politics in 1982, like national politics at the same time, were dominated by the rhetoric of development and improvement. On one occasion, carried away by the force of his own oratory, Cyril the UNP leader told a crowd that he had received a letter from the Prime Minister promising to build a model village for the poor of Tenna. This was an allusion to a scheme, championed by the Prime Minister amid much publicity (and at considerable expense), in which such model communities were being built all over the island. In contrast to the higgledy-piggledy sprawl of most Sinhala rural settlement, the model villages boasted serried rows of disciplined identical houses. The Prime Minister was himself an urban politician with a power base in the slums of Colombo;[10] Cyril was the son of a Belangala merchant and seemed to share, at least on this occasion, something of the Prime Minister's vision of a new and ordered style of rural life. When I visited him on my return in 1984, Cyril reeled off a list of impending improvements he was 'bringing' to the village (the promised model village was by now long forgotten)—these included a health centre and, ultimate shrine of suburban order, a public toilet by the bus-stand at the Gonagala junction. The idiom of improvement is now firmly established at the heart of village politics.

Meanwhile, other changes have been effected through the combination of local initiative and State support which brought the school to Tenna in the 1940s. Remains of an old pre-colonial irrigation tank used to lie immediately below the two old villages, the *bund* (dam) badly broken. In the late 1960s a group of men from various villages in the vicinity who had formed themselves into a now defunct body called the Mangara Youth League,[11] petitioned the government through various local worthies for help in restoring the dam. The then SLFP MP promised help during her victorious campaign in the 1970 election, while the original incumbent of the Tenna *pansala* gave vigorous support. In the event, the 1970–7 government provided earth-movers and other heavy equipment while gangs of locally organized volunteers cleared the scrub and performed the lighter tasks. A new tank, intended to provide water for many acres of new paddy land, was finally opened, albeit too late in the career of the SLFP government for any progress to be made with the clearing of the new land and its allotment to tenants.

The government was in fact voted out, and the irrigation channels were allowed to dry up unused. From time to time land tribunals (*iḍam kachcheri*s (would be held to decide on the allocation of the new land; each time a decision woud be reached, only to be subsequently annulled by political intervention (by the MP, said the MP's enemies; by the MP's enemies, said his friends) as the list of claimants grew longer and longer and re-surveys suggested that an ever smaller quantity of land could be realistically irrigated. At the end of my final visit in 1984, the village was going through an outbreak of generalized outrage at the issuing of a 'final' list of allottees; inevitably, the disappointed far outnumbered the satisfied, and the usual political brokers were competing vigorously to disown any personal responsibility for this piece of patronage. Before I left I learnt that the latest list had been scrapped; the MP had called for a new list with the size of the allotments halved, so that twice as many people would receive a share of the new land. Meanwhile the tank stood as a complex but tangible symbol of many of the different threads that make up the experience of rural change in Tenna: local initiative and central power, politics and patronage, the past and the future.

The village tank which would at last symbolize Tenna's identity as a village of sturdy rice-farmers (even if the land promised could never go round those who felt themselves entitled to a share) also serves to place Tenna squarely within a new vision of rural order. Anyone who spends any time at all reading the reports of government politicians' speeches which fill so many of the pages of the Sri Lankan press will notice certain recurrent motifs. When speaking of the countryside and its inhabitants—whether in an imagined glorious past or a promised glorious future—all that is good is often summed up in the triple image of *väva, yäya,* and *dägäba*: tank, paddy fields, and stupa (the last standing metonymically for *pansala, sangha,* and the full panoply of the Sinhala Buddhist historical mission). So, in commissioning a new reservoir as part of the vast Māhaväli project, a government minister used this image to link past to future: 'The soul of the new Māhaväli society . . . will be the cherished values of the ancient society which was inspired and nourished by the Tank, the Temple and the Paddy field' (Dissanayake in Tennekoon 1988: 297). In fact this triple image of rural harmony is said to have been invented by Martin Wickramasinghe, a twentieth-century novelist of nationalist inclinations (Goonatilaka 1984: xix); as one astute analyst has recently pointed out, the symbolism of temple and tank is at once retrospective and prospective in intent, signifying 'a particular type of past as well as the (desired) shape of the present and future' (Tennekoon 1988: 297). The Tenna tank is a good example of this: rebuilding for the future in the image of an imputed past, it draws on the same nationalist historiography as the major dry zone colonization projects which are explicitly intended to echo the supposed agrarian civilization of the time of the Sinhala kings.

On my return trip in 1984 I organized a competition at the village school: older children were to write on the topic *apē gama* (our village), the younger children were to do drawings on the same theme. All the drawings from the youngest class featured the same three salient features, iconic amidst the childish scrawl: a tank, a temple (almost always represented by a stylized *dägäba*, although this is lacking at the Tenna *pansala*), and a stretch of paddy-field. The drawings had been done in class and the teacher had obviously, and tellingly, told the children what to include. The children, asked to represent *their* village, had faithfully reproduced an imagined image of rural order.

In Tenna these essentials of the rural vision, shared by politicians and schoolteachers, are creations of the very recent past, only now becoming tangible through the combined efforts of outsiders, villagers, and the State. The tank was rebuilt in the 1970s. The paddy-fields have always been there, but as was clear in the last chapter, few of these children could ever expect to work in them except possibly as casual day-labourers. And the *pansala* was built after a settler's dream half a century earlier. The *dāgäba* in the drawings is as yet unbuilt, but I am confident that before long this essential icon of Sinhala pastoral will also become a tangible feature of the remade landscape.

My point in this chapter is twofold. First, Tenna has changed and continues to change, and much of the change has been exogenous: the State has involved itself more and more in local life, and newcomers—settlers, teachers, priests, politicians—have been important agents of change. But secondly, and crucially, these newcomers have brought with them new images of rural life—models of the past which serve as models for the future. Nor can these imaginings be simply dismissed as the empty rhetoric of politicians. They are crucial factors in political decisions: for example, the decision to invest so heavily in new irrigation and settlement schemes in the dry zone—of which the accelerated Māhavāli Project which dominated the headlines at the time of my stay is the most recent and biggest—involves conscious emulation of a glorious past before colonial rule, even before the ideal of national homogeneity was supposedly corrupted by the presence of non-Sinhala non-Buddhists. And so it is that the privileged tropes in the rhetoric of rural change serve to exclude whole sections of the population, deepening the divisions in society even as they invoke a world of halcyon order and community. The old in Tenna have now to reconcile their own memories of the past with a present in which another, more powerfully articulated version of the past is gradually taking shape and substance in the transformed landscape in which they grew up. The result is a kind of double dislocation: a dislocation of everyday experience, as their familiar surroundings are rendered new and unfamiliar; and a dislocation of their past, as their memories have to measure up against the rhetoric of politicians, schoolteachers, and priests.

Meanwhile their children and grandchildren are moving away from the world they used to know. In 1984 three enthusiastic young graduate teachers were appointed to the school in Tenna. While they were popular among many of the younger people in the village, I felt that the school principal (locally educated and firmly set in his ways) was as unenthusiastic as politeness would allow about many of their innovations. I remember one of my many conversations with the young teachers about the possibilities for improvement and development in the school and in the village. They quickly started to compete with each other to offer me examples of the kind of things they felt they were up against at the school. The examples they quoted were all of what they called 'rural' (*piṭisara*) speech: children using demeaning second-person pronouns in addressing each other, or unthinkingly employing coarse or 'bad' words which had to be corrected by the teachers. Some of these examples (the nuances of which had to be patiently spelt out for me) they found quite hilarious, although none were allowed to distract them from the sense of mission with which they described their plans for the future.

These young people, two men and two women, were from villages themselves, albeit villages closer to Colombo and less remote than Tenna. They were all first-generation graduates, and what they were encountering in the uncouth children of Tenna was, I suspect, only a somewhat exaggerated version of the problems they had encountered when they returned home from university. 'Improvement' is as much a cultural as a material process. It is a recognition of this which lies behind the old men's evaluations of the past I started with. They now live with a complex structure of feeling: at once regretful at the passing of much that was familiar in the old ways yet simultaneously ashamed of those parts of the past (hunting, caste, drink, attitudes to marriage) they have now been taught are somehow not really 'Sinhala,' not properly 'Buddhist.' For it is, I believe, the moral authority of the new Buddhist teaching—which is also to say the new emphasis on Sinhala-Buddhist identity, 'children of a single person'—upon which the whole complex of attitudes hinges.

NOTES

[1] The following section is largely taken from Spencer (1984a).

[2] Variants on this account of rural change recur in Obeyesekere's work; see, for example, Obeyesekere (1984b: 159; 1975: 17).

[3] SLNA 45/9 12 June 1864; 45/12 14 June 1865; cf. Leach (1961a: 30).

[4] SLNA 6/551 Malcolm to Lusignan 4 April 1818; Knox (1681 [1911]: 10).

[5] See Spencer (1986: 92–100).

[6] SLNA 45/333 13 February 1911.

[7] SLNA 43/346 24 March, 1934; 45/337 19 September, 1919.

[8] On the village expansion scheme see SLNA 45/343 3 September 1931; 45/346 1 February, 19 August 1934.

[9] For a similar local initiative in establishing a school see Obeyesekere (1967: 12).

[10] For an account of the unexpected consequences of the building of one such model village in the 1980s see Brow (1988). It is significant that the new village had a name ('Samadhigama'—'meditation village') redolent of high Protestant Buddhism and quite unlike the prosaically descriptive place-name it replaced.

[11] 'The record among the Sinhalese of local-level voluntary, quasi-statutory and statutory representative organisations is poor' (Moore 1985: 228). This does not correspond with my own experience of a plethora of local self-help organizations in Sinhala rural areas, of which the Tenna *subhasādhika samitiya* is only one (cf. Obeyesekere 1967: 12). Even so, such organizations tend to be ephemeral—launched in a wave of improving enthusiasm, they tend to quickly fade and die. This is probably because of their uneasy coexistence with the divisive forces of local party politics. There seems to be a tendency for each organization either to become a front for the ruling party or else a base of support for the opposition. Neither situation is conducive to long-term survival.

Chapter Six

The World at Arm's Length

A thread of dislocation again runs through this chapter. This time, though, the dislocation is in the values of everyday life, and while affected by the kinds of changes described in earlier chapters, it can also be linked with certain basic assumptions in the Buddhist view of the moral universe. I start with two of those assumptions—the power of desire and the necessity for detachment—and trace their influence in different area of life. The first point I discuss is the peculiar emphasis on 'shame' (*lajja*) without a corresponding positive code of honour, a combination which has important resonances in daily life. To describe those resonances I have used a metaphor—treating the world at arm's length—which I develop and elaborate in the course of the chapter. On the way the discussion touches on many matters—disputes, violence, suicide, the pain of kinship, inequality, jealousy—without necessarily exploring any of them exhaustively. The movement is from the general to the specific, from the teachings of the Buddha to the minutiae of gossip and trouble in the village.[1]

In this the loss of one unifying idiom of social standing— that of landholding and tenancy described in Chapter Four—is but an aspect of a more generalized shift toward indeterminacy. The challenge for me in writing this has been to convey this indeterminacy as coherently and clearly as I can, without betraying the pervasive spirit of irony which informs so much public sociability. And one corollary of this state of affairs is the fact that public assertions of social position can never be unambiguously confirmed by the response of other villagers; such assertions are always threatened by the possibility of private irony. Put simply, to be somebody—or perhaps to be sure of being somebody— eventually involves the ratification of one's position by someone outside the immediate circle of peers: More often than not, this someone has been the State, and we have here one of a number of factors which have converged to give politics its centrality and form in a village like Tenna. That is the argument which is picked up in the next chapter.

Two Versions of Desire

The Four Noble Truths of canonical Buddhism concern *dukkha* (usually glossed as 'suffering'), the origin of *dukkha*, the cessation of *dukkha*, and the way or path to the cessation of *dukkha*. Here is a definition of the Second Truth (the origin of *dukkha*) in a translation by Sri Lanka's most distinguished contemporary scholar-monk:

> It is this 'thirst' (craving, *tanhā*) which produces re-existence and re-becoming . . . and which is bound up with passionate greed . . . and which finds fresh delight now here and now there . . . namely, (1) thirst for sense-pleasures . . . (2) thirst for existence and becoming . . . and (3) thirst for non-existence (self-annihilation). (Mahavagga in Rahula 1978: 29)

Craving or desire and suffering are two sides of the same coin, two moments in the same process; attachment to the things of this world, and its concomitant dissatisfactions, binds one to the wheel of birth and rebirth. Even the renouncer, in the final stages of the journey, has to transcend the desire to renounce desire. It is *tanhā*, variously translated as 'craving,' 'thirst,' 'desire,' 'attachment,' which provides the motive power in the moral universe.

Towards the end of my first period of fieldwork I spent a few weeks accompanying friends who were working gem-pits around the village. They told me tales of treasure (usually said to have been buried by the old kings, often in or under anthills and protected by local guardian spirits (*bahirayā*)), and of the means of finding it. The stories revealed a number of things. First and foremost they were part of a wider genre—tales of miraculous happenings—that bore witness to a widely-felt need for enchantment.[2] Secondly, in their description of a partly-miraculous landscape they fitted in with the gemming lore I was collecting. The god Mangara, I was told by the *kapu mahatmayā*, used to wander all over Tenna at will, but now people are too many and he has retreated from their uncleanness to the fringes of the plateau (see above p. 146). Older villagers told of hearing his flute from their chena huts in the past, but now he hides from people—one expression of the partial loss of enchantment in the landscape.

But one story, told not at the gem-pit but in the *pansala*, and not by a gemmer but by the village priest, stuck in my mind especially. In the old days of the kings (*rāja kālaya*), when a king or some other powerful person wanted to hide a treasure he would take with him a servant. When the treasure had been secreted in its hiding place, the king would call the servant over and say something like 'Look at that; wouldn't you like that?' The servant would be seized by involuntary desire, and at that very moment the king would kill him. Because of the excess of desire (*āsāva*) at the moment of death, the murdered man would be tied to the place as a *bahirayā*, a guardian spirit who would watch over the treasure in perpetuity.

The story fits well with other ideas about death and desire. People who die still clinging to the world—their hearts perhaps filled with concentrated hatred for an enemy—are liable to linger on as malignant spirits (*preta* or *bhūtayā*). Gombrich, in an interesting discussion, makes the observation that 'although cognitively—and logically—*preta*s can be anyone's relations, the only *preta*s of whom people usually think and with whom they interact are their *own* dead relations' (1971: 163). Even (or perhaps especially) relationships with close kin are liable to suffer from an excess of feeling. Most of the funeral and post-funeral rites at a death are concerned with the transfer of merit (*pin*) to the dead person, and justified by reference to the threat of the dead returning as a *preta*.

It is, moreover, the intensity of *feeling*, whether good or bad, love or hatred, that ties the dead so unhappily to the world. For example, in the case of possession involving a Muslim girl in Tenna (as diagnosed by a succession of Sinhala exorcists), the girl was said to be possessed by her dead grandmother in the form of a *bhūtayā*;[3] in itself, one exorcist told me, this would present few problems. A *bhūtayā* who returned through an excess of love could more easily be persuaded to leave the afflicted object of that love alone. But the *bhūtayā* had received a *varama* ('warrant') from the goddess Pattini; it would be necessary to secure Pattini's blessing before she could be freed. And the immediate circumstances of the patient's possession were a gift of three charmed toffees by a Muslim boy with whom she had 'formed a connection.' So the causal sequence in the aetiology of the possession runs as follows: the grandmother, through excess of love, remains around her family as a *bhūtayā*; the goddess Pattini helps her in her possession of her granddaughter (at other times various demons also use the grandmother's spirit as a vehicle); the *bhūtayā* gains access to her granddaughter through the agency of a slighted lover. The whole is a symphony of affective excess. As Obeyesekere notes, ideas about *pretas* reflect ambivalent feelings to close kin: 'the *preta* loves me, and it is his excessive attachment that makes him hover round me; yet *pretas* in fact can do no good, so all these troubles of mine are due to his action' (1981: 117).

I shall return to this ambivalence of feeling in kinship later in the chapter. For now I am more concerned to establish the importance of desire or attachment as a causal influence in everyday affairs. The first example is the more striking; no mention is made in the priest's tale of any punishment being visited on the king for the murder, only of the entrapment of the servant by the king's trick. One can read it as an example of the almost amoral implications of a profoundly Buddhist moral imperative, with the letter of the karmic law overwhelming its spirit, rather as in one of the Buddha's own satiric discourses on the sophistry of other spiritual teachers. The second example emphasizes still further the malevolent effects of attachment within the closest of personal relationships—kin and lovers. Neither example should be approached without caution; the whole question of *bhūtayā*s and *preta*s was the object of considerable scepticism from some people in the village (not least the priest who told me the first story, who was firmly of the opinion that the afflicted girl in the second tale should be in hospital rather than in the care of exorcists). The next examples, though, reveal a more general, if less explicit, set of assumptions about the importance of attachment and detachment in the world.

Shame without Honour

I first came across the world *lajja* in my dealings with small children. I would be visiting a house, and one of my hosts' small children might peek around the door, or scutter away at my approach, or hide if I pointed a camera at them. The standard explanation would be: 'Don't worry; she is *lajja*.' Not surprisingly, I took the word at first to correspond to 'shy' or 'bashful.' But, during the election campaign, political opponents were quick to explain Cyril's more provocative actions as the result of an absence of *lajja*: 'When he takes drinks he doesn't know fear (*baya*) or *lajja*.' After the fight at the gate of the *pansala*, Uberatna's propensity for violence was explained as a result of the death of his mother some years earlier: 'He has no mother; he does not care what people think; he does not know *lajja*.'

Obeyesekere translates the concept as 'shame,' explicitly comparing it to the Mediterranean world of honour and shame, with the proviso that in Sri Lanka the place of honour is taken by the idea of status or prestige. He discusses the term in its common manifestation as part of the compound *lajja-baya* (shame-fear) which he translates as 'fear of ridicule or social disapproval' (Obeyesekere 1984a: 504). He describes how the idea is drummed into small children, whose every minor misdemeanour is likely to be met with the imprecation '*Lajja nädda, mokada minissu kiyannē?*' (without *lajja* what will people say?) (Obeyesekere 1984a: 505). The result of such insistent socialization is a powerful fear of public ridicule and consequent loss of self-esteem.

In his subsequent discussion, Obeyesekere describes examples of the play on this threat in widely differing contexts. The concept enters his discussion through the example of *ankeliya* (the horn game), a now almost moribund village ritual, fought as a struggle between two teams in which obscene joking and verbal humiliation are powerful components. The idiom of *ankeliya*, he argues has survived the disappearance of the ritual itself; he describes students at Peradeniya University in the late 1970s gathered in groups and shouting abuse (*'aiyo gandayi'* oh, you stink) at other students on their way into their examinations:

The kinds of verbal abuse, pantomiming, and humorous songs of vilification characteristic of *ankeliya* are performed here also, but intensified and divested of the rules that keep the latter within civil bounds. Thus the *model of ankeliya* is pervasive in Sinhala society: from the socialization in the family to interaction within dyads; from public debates in Parliament to the literary debates of intellectuals; from ditties sung in public schools to university dormitories; from public-school cricket games to, let me add, a lawyer cross-examining a hapless witness. (Obeyesekere 1984a: 508)

To this list we can add the exaggerated licence of the electoral carnival described in Chapter Three. Indeed, even more than Obeyesekere's examples, electoral politics represent both the most concentrated and the most pervasive moments of licence and ridicule in contemporary Sinhala life.

But Obeyesekere's examples raise a number of problems. What he documents is the *suspension* of constraint and *lajja* on the part of the taunters and humiliators, not the reaction and response of the taunted and humiliated, still less the quiet workings of *lajja* in normal life. Moreover, his examples suggest a world of almost permanent carnival, a society of clowns and satirists ready to lampoon and shame at every opportunity. Obeyesekere's examples are deliberately drawn from what is known in Sri Lanka as 'middle-class' society,[4] and from the actions of men rather than women. *Lajja* is not, then, regarded as a homogeneous element in society. It becomes more marked as one moves up the social scale (reaching 'its epitome in urban educated people' (Obeyesekere 1984a: 504)), and although it is expected to be emphasized more in female behaviour, its consequences, according to Obeyesekere, are more evident in male activity: 'This is because men have public roles and hence must be more sensitive to the reactions of others' (Obeyesekere 1984a: 505).

One kind of example of *lajja* in operation will indeed be familiar to most casual visitors. A tourist in a post office has failed to accomplish some minor piece of business: the telephone lines to the capital are not working, it is not possible today to find anything in the *poste restante* section, it is not possible to send a telegram because that counter is closed. The tourist starts to get annoyed and raises his or her voice. As this happens, the clerk at the counter looks down and pretends to be working on a pile of papers in front of him. The tourist, accustomed to a raised voice eliciting an equivalent response, grows angrier and starts to shout; the clerk becomes more detached, giggling nervously if really frightened by the European's anger. The whole situation is a classic example of schismogenesis: the tourist responds to the clerk's withdrawal with anger and shouting, calling attention to the situation in order to force a response, but it is precisely the enforced public attention that drives the clerk away from the encounter. What the tourist reads as studied insolence is *lajja*, the fear of ridicule and public humiliation. The classic encounter of this sort is in a post office or bank, where petit-bourgeois concern with standing and dignity is at its highest; a tourist acting in a similar way toward, say, the ticket-boy on a private bus is much more likely to meet shouts and anger in reply.

Two further examples, from Tenna. A young woman, an unmarried mother and again pregnant, was caught red-handed stealing from one of the village shops. After the police had dealt with her she took refuge with a sister who lived at the furthest fringes of the settlement; her immediate family were rarely to be seen around the village in the following weeks. They were, I was told, *hari lajjayi* (very *lajja*). A young man was arrested on a trumped-up charge laid against him by a political opponent; after his release from custody he too was rarely to be seen in the more public spaces at the centre of the village. Rather disingenuously, he insisted to me that this was pure coincidence and nothing to do with *lajja* - *whatever people might be saying.*

So far so shameful. But what of a young bride who enters her own wedding feast, with head bowed, eyes directed modestly at the floor? Her attitude too is said to be one of *lajja*, which is how a girl of good character is expected to behave, especially when she finds herself briefly the centre of attention. She has done nothing, either in our terms or theirs, 'to be ashamed of.' What she is doing is exhibiting a socially-approved modesty and restraint in her behaviour. This, it seems to me, is the common element in my various examples of behaviour described as being caused by *lajja*: restraint, a holding back from the gaze of others, keeping intense encounters at arm's length, whether this be the combined fear and shyness of a small child meeting a huge European or the understandable reticence of an unmarried pregnant woman. *Lajja* touches on many areas we might talk of as 'shaming,' but to gloss it as 'shame' is to ignore its positive valuation as something to be inculcated in all children as a proper ingredient of all good public behaviour (cf. Carrithers 1982: 40).[5]

If 'shame' is an inadequate translation of *lajja*, is there a convenient opposed term corresponding to 'honour,' or in Obeyesekere's revised formula, 'status and prestige' (Obeyesekere 1984a: 504)? There are a number of terms which suggest themselves as possibilities. The urban middle-class, university students, and their families (usually richer villagers with hopes of extra-village employment) can all be heard to speak obsessively of *tattvaya*, which means 'position,' 'circumstances' or 'situation.' Thus, as well as overhearing talk of 'my *tattvaya*,' it is also possible to read in the newspapers of *arthika tattvaya* 'the economic situation,' and so on. But *tattvaya* is usually individualistic in its connotations and does not in itself imply any particular merit; it can be low or high, good or bad.

Nambuva is closer to status or prestige or (justified) pride in one's position. So, for example, on my return in 1984, and after an outbreak of trouble and gossip, a friend apologized to me for the way he and his friends had first received me in the village: 'We did not tell you everything. *gamē nambuva, ratē nambuva nisā* (because of the *nambuva* of the village and our country) we did not want you to know about the bad things here.' 'Cognizance of standing in the world' might be a long-winded gloss on this; 'pride and status' a shorter translation.

But *nambuva* is open to question at a quite profound level. Here is one of the first *vahumpura* settlers comparing Tenna when he first arrived in the 1930s with the position in 1982:

It was very strict regarding caste in those days. When we visited the home of the [*goyigama*] *vidānē* they gave us a mat on the ground to sit on. They gave us water to drink in a coconut shell. I did not drink. Later they began to give us cups and plates, but earlier they wouldn't They were people greatly concerned with *nambuva*. Now there is no *nambuva* here.

So we have on the one hand a young man talking of *nambuva* for his village or nation, and on the other an old man talking of the end of caste *nambuva* as expressed in the minutiae of eating and drinking. It is in part because of the decline of one kind of *nambuva*—that of ascribed status—that assertions of the other are now possible at all.

I return to caste in more detail later in this chapter. Before that I want to deal with the implications of a third term which comes closest to being an exact antonym to *lajja*. This is *ādambara*, which can be easiest glossed as 'excessive or unjustified pride.' For example, one day I was walking down the street in the village with a packet of twenty cigarettes (not a lone *bidi*, or a half-smoked butt behind my ear) and a lighter in my hand. 'Who's this *ādambara* man coming along?' called out a friend, drawing attention to the unintended swagger in my pose and my ostentatiously displayed cigarettes. He was teasing, but that is the point. Accusations of *ādambara* are the stuff of teasing, joking, and horseplay; they are also at the basis of the kinds of deliberate humiliation Obeyesekere describes. Anyone whose concern for his own self-importance becomes at all visible is liable to accusations of *ādambara* and muttered comments behind his back (I use 'his' deliberately; I never heard such accusations directed at women). 'Look at him. He thinks he's some kind of big man (*loku minihā*). All that's big is his head.' *Ādambara* can here be read as a lack of modesty and self-effacement, an over-eager pushing of one's claims in the public eye, an absence of proper *lajja*.

It is one of a number of crude and ineffective moral levelling devices in daily life. These are very obvious on the campuses of Sri Lankan universities. Most students belong to the first generation of their family to leave home for a college education; they are subject to quite serious cultural pressures and strains as they try to balance their domestic identity and origins against the new world of the university, with its wider culture and apparently open social world. The result is an intense emphasis on conformity within the student body itself. The jeering at the examination candidates described by Obeyesekere is but one of a number of ways in which humiliation is used to counter the threat of the slightest tendency to nonconformity. Others include initiatory 'ragging' of new students in frequently grotesque ways, threats, bullying, and attacks on anyone who stands out for whatever reason. A woman told me how her time at Peradeniya University in the late 1960s was one of abject misery and fear as she was mercilessly bullied for being a posh Colombo girl; a young Tamil man, beaten up by fellow students at Peradeniya just before the major communal violence of 1983, said his assailants accompanied their kicks with remarks like, 'That will teach you to get all those good grades'; a male student who forms a romantic attachment with a member of the opposite sex (as most of his fellows would like to) runs the risk of assault, of being thrown into ponds, and of the usual unrestrained teasing. What is being drummed out of the students in all these cases is the real or imaginary sin of *ādambara*.

And then, of course, when the student returns to his or her home community the whole process starts again. In 1983 one of the village's undergraduates returned for the Vesak celebrations at Tenna *pansala* and helped his brother coach a group of young men and women in a performance of *bhakti gī* (devotional songs). The performance was a conscious imitation of urban fashion: a choir of young people dressed in pious white sang popular Buddhist songs in the manner of Sinhala pop stars like Victor Ratnayake.[6] There was no doubt an element of self-advertisement as the two young men, immaculately dressed and with expressions of the purest devotion, led the singing of their choir, squeezed onto the temporary stage at the *pansala*. What doubt there might have been was quickly dispelled when Lionel and a group of his friends gathered on the road outside the *pansala* and started to jeer at the performers, to the mortification of some of the audience—and, I suspect, to the quiet amusement of others. What they were objecting to was not devotion or singing or even the choir itself, but the posing—the *ādambara*—of the two leaders (who were also especially bitter political opponents of Lionel and his friends).

There are moments, then, when it is possible to challenge what may be thought to be unjustified public assertions of status. The Mediterranean language of honour, to paraphrase Julian Pitt-Rivers, concerns both a person's *claims* to position and public acknowledgement of the *right* to position (Pitt-Rivers 1977: 1). The working out of such claims and acknowledgements is a constant process, built into the structure of daily encounters, and manifest in 'the logic of challenge and riposte' (Bourdieu 1977: 15). But the young men at the *pansala* did not respond to the jeers; they ignored them. Some weeks later, it is true, their elder brother refused to attend a funeral because of the presence there of Lionel, and explained this to me as a consequence of Lionel's bad behaviour at the *pansala*. But this was a gesture bordering on the private; the riposte was not manifest in some nuanced interaction, but in a principled avoidance of interaction. And challenges themselves only rarely take the form of public ridicule—festive occasions (public holidays and, of course and above all, the election) with a lot of drink involved were the only occasions where I witnessed outbursts of this sort. But almost no private conversation passed without some acid challenge to the public persona of an absent neighbour or enemy. In place of overt challenge there is in Tenna a kind of institutionalized irony.

The functional complement of *ādambara*—the view from above—is *irisiyāva* (jealousy). If the young men who were so unceremoniously jeered at for their singing had been asked why they should have attracted this abuse, they too would have immediately replied '*irisiyāva*.' It is an inescapable axiom of daily life in Tenna that the slightest good fortune, any improvement in position or prosperity, would inevitably attract the jealousy of those not blessed. (It is the commonest explanation for misfortune invoked by visitors to sorcery shrines; Kapferer 1988: 106–8.) In practical terms this means that people accused of getting ideas above their station—of *ādambara*—can instantly explain away such accusations as so much *irisiyāva*. With such a perfect semantic complement, the only thing left quite unresolved is just what the station or standing of the person involved should rightly be.

Irisiyāva is always imputed to others, indeed assumed of them, never admitted by oneself; it is always someone else's flaw. A statement like, 'I felt quite jealous' is unimaginable. When I was looking for a house to lodge in, I was advised on one occasion not to be too friendly with two particular families because they were not very popular with their fellow villagers. When I was asked why this was, I was told that until quite recently they were quite poor and now they were more prosperous. This was felt to be sufficient explanation. When one of the members of these families was arrested, I went to the police station (along with all manner of well-placed and well-disposed friends of his) to testify to his good character and innocence. When he was released it was his former school principal who claimed to have finally convinced the police of his innocence: 'They asked me if there was any reason why he should be unpopular and I said, people are jealous, of course, because his family have grown prosperous. They said if he'd only told us that we would have set him free straight away. They had asked him if he had any enemies in the village and he had said no.'

Jealousy is another example of an excess of desire, in this case usually desire for a neighbour's material possessions or position. It not only inspires conscious maliciousness, but also provokes the blighting influence of the evil eye (*āsvaha*) and evil mouth (*kaṭavaha*). Like the unwitting servant of the king whose involuntary desire ties him to the world as a malevolent spirit, those afflicted with the evil eye or evil mouth are able to bring misfortune on others simply through their unreflective craving. A couple with a young child of good health and fine looks explained its dowdy and ragged clothes to me as protection against the evil effects of the covetous glances of passing women, and there is a growing national market in protective measures against the evil eye.[7]

Surface and Reality

The fourth of the much recited Five Precepts (*pansil*) is an undertaking to abstain from lying. Despite this, Sinhala peasant mendacity has attracted the attention of earlier visitors. Knox, for example: 'They make no account nor conscience of lying, neither is it any shame or disgrace to them, if they be catched in telling lyes: it is so customary' (Knox 1681 [1911]: 101–2); he later notes that they approve of their own lying but disapprove of the lying of others (Knox 1681 [1911]: 103). Gombrich too:

Truth I would hardly described as a *major* value in fact—affectively—however much lip service is paid to it. The very frequency in villagers' conversation of the sentence '*Boru kiyanta honda nä*' ('Lying is bad'), usually uttered with a light intonation in the context either of mild accusation of a third party or of protestation of one's own sincerity . . . may be offered as evidence for the frequency of lying; while its tone suggests that the offence is not really considered heinous. Lying is bound to be frequent in a culture much concerned with the preservation of status (*tattvaya*) and dignity (*nambuva*)—saving face; the most trivial matter which might in any way appear discreditable to the speaker is concealed almost as a matter of course. (Gombrich 1971: 262–3)

The first part of Gombrich's report is easily corroborated in everyday observation, where '*boru nä* (no lie) is one of the most frequent collocations in every conversation.[8] The second part was repeatedly drawn to my attention by my neighbours, warning me that someone or other should not be trusted, as they were a *māha boru kārayā* (huge liar), and pointing out a frequency of dissembling in daily life which they felt to be excessive.

The point is not that I found there was a greater or lesser incidence of conversational falsehood, measured against some abstract scale of cross-cultural veracity; it is that the people of Tenna themselves assumed a high degree of lying and concealment of awkward truth in their everyday lives, so much so that they felt obliged to warn me about it. This does, of course, pose ethnographic problems. My friend's confession that in order to preserve the dignity of his village and country he had concealed all manner of minor unpleasantnesses from me was not an isolated indication that all was not quite as it seemed. There was also the MP's lamentation (see above p. 75) that no one would ever tell him what he or she really felt.

The uses of the lie in Tenna can be compared with Gilsenan's classic description of lying and honour in a Lebanese village (Gilsenan 1976). In both cases an opposition between the real and the illusory is fundamental to the religious traditions—Buddhism in Tenna, Islam in the Lebanon—to which the villagers subscribe. In both cases lying is important as a device in the negotiation of standing and reputation. But in the Lebanese case both lying *and* truth, illusion *and* revelation, are considered potentially present. Indeed one mark of the holy man—the sheikh—is his ability to see through the illusions of everyday life; conversely, an inability to detect an obvious falsehood was the means by which the villagers were able to discount the claims of a visiting would-be sheikh (Gilsenan 1976: 206–8; Gilsenan 1982: 116–41). In Tenna I heard of no one with such gifts, and the possibility was never acknowledged that there might be people who could cut through the veils of deliberate distortion in everyday interaction. Instead there were moments—*crises révélatrices* (cf. Sahlins 1972: 143)—when people forgot themselves and revealed their 'true' feelings. These were by definition abnormal and untoward—moments of drunkenness, anger, loss of control. Revealed malice was considered the mark of the 'real'—however intermittently displayed—and the confirmation of unremitting speculation on the possibility of concealed malice. The only interpretation of daily ambiguities which could not be argued with was that revealed in outbursts of naked hostility. The logic of the lie could reveal challenges to implicit or explicit claims to position; what could never be displayed *in these terms* was a validation of such claims.

Without the election and its immediate prompting of *overt* expressions of hostility, I have no idea how long it would have taken me to see the other side of daily *politesse*. By the time of my friend's confession in 1984 I knew all kinds of unseemly tales about the pasts of my friends and neighbours; most of these were picked up as the inevitable consequence of being in the right place—if not at the right time, at least for long enough. A widower remarried, and the evening before the wedding I learnt not only of the terrible death of his last wife, as the result of a botched abortion, but also of his affair with a neighbour's wife (this in turn explaining the burning down of this neighbour's house two years earlier—an event which had puzzled me at the time); my informant, seeking a suitable comparison to illustrate the situation, unwittingly let slip details of another affair, between one of the *mudalāli*s and the elder daughter of a highly respectable household. Her family, consumed by *lajja*, had immediately sent the pregnant daughter to stay with another married daughter many miles away; I had been baffled by her disappearance two years before.[9] Time and again, while it was generally agreed that it was not good to tell me of all these bad things, the fact that I had witnessed an incident meant that I got to learn some of the background. A public event—a murder or suicide or death in the area—brought forward quick reminiscences of previous similar events; a day or two later and the excitement would be over, and with it the brief flood of related gossip.

But quite apart from my ethnographic problem, the axiom of concealment had important consequences for the texture of daily life. At the time of the election in 1982, politically active friends would confess their worries to me; if the other side won (I was the SLFP's confidant, so the 'other side' meant the UNP), they would bring in thugs to attack their houses, holders of government posts would be transferred to unpleasant and inaccessible parts of the country, opponents would use the police and the law to harass them. 'Are you sure?' I would ask, 'they seem friendly enough.' 'Of course,' came the reply, 'these people are always nice to your face, but when your back is turned we know they are saying and planning terrible things.' After the election, the only serious damage to SLFP pride was from the public tauntings and celebrations of their opponents. But some of the SLFP supporters did not accept that this proved their earlier fears wrong: Mr Ariyaratna assured me that serious violence had only been averted because one or two of the young SLFP men had made their protective presence felt, thus frightening off their enemies; one of the UNP leaders, on the other hand, told me that there had been no trouble because the President had expressly asked his supporters to behave, and he and his fellows had kept their side in check. Either view was a credible account of what happened; neither was accessible to any kind of check. The SLFP supporters, like Mr Ariyaratna, believed the version that fitted their expectations. Public events do not necessarily alleviate private fears.

This is the point. Wrong-doing and evil intent are assumed to be concealed; good fellowship and amity are expected of all but the most unusual public encounters. As a result, *no* public expression of good intent can offset the fears of someone convinced he or she is surrounded by enmity. One result is a propensity to believe or fear the worst. Some months after the election, a boy I was friendly with told me how upset he was at our priest's imminent departure. I had heard nothing of this and immediately sought further confirmation. 'It's true,' I was told; 'he, and all the other SLFP supporters who teach at the same school, are to be transferred out of the area.' The priest himself confirmed this, adding that he had not mentioned it to the *nāyaka* (a UNP supporter) because it would only have upset him. Two years later no transfer-papers had arrived and they were all still there.

Although it is assumed that many facts may be concealed in advancing claims to *nambuva* or position (for example, new settlers may hide their true caste origins), the assumption is most powerful where mischief is suspected. In 1984 a rumour reached us that the body of civil servants assessing claims to the new land under the Tenna tank, was due to report. This was not the first such rumour, nor would it have been the first such report; several earlier allocations had been abandoned under the protests of the disappointed. The first indications of something about to happen were complaints from SLFP supporters that they had been deliberately excluded from the list; some even said that they had been on the original list and knew for a fact that Cyril, vetting for party loyalty, had crossed their names off.

This view was given some unexpected encouragement when I found myself at a wedding with a few other well-placed neutrals in conversation with Cyril over a bottle of arrack in a neighbour's back room. Cyril, ostensibly *in vino veritas*, suddenly raised the subject of the impending land allocation. 'It's shocking,' he said, repeating the remarks of his political opponents, 'it's extremely unfair. I've been to see the MP to complain about it. You know me, you know how much I do for the village, yet when they give out this land I get nothing. Fine, I don't mind, I don't expect a reward. But then you see who has got land'—and here he mentioned a couple of new settlers on the list (virtually the only completely politically innocent recipients in the event)—'What have they done to deserve it?' I, along with the rest of the audience, nodded sagely and sympathetically, as appropriate, through this increasingly impassioned speech. The list was published the following day. Cyril, it is true, did not receive any land. His seventy-year old father-in-law and both his brothers-in-law and his wife all received full allocations, though; elsewhere the list revealed all the signs of Cyril's meticulous influence, as much of the land went to his friends and kinsmen and political connections.

This example is unusual because we were all equally sceptical of Cyril's protestations of innocence, and events were very quickly to support our scepticism. But no one was at all shocked that Cyril should choose to bluff away his activities so shamelessly. In fact, I suspect the shock would have been far greater if he had admitted to his part in the affair, if he had said something like 'What about the land list? I really put one on them there, didn't I?' Although no one was likely to believe them, Cyril's protestations of altruistic disinterest were precisely what was expected of him.

The result of such expectations is a disorientating experience for an ethnographer. At first, as for the first five months of my stay in Tenna, all around me was gentle, smiling concord. Then, suddenly, a dispute flared, and my notebook bulged with abuse and allegations of covert evil. But even in a conflict as traumatic as the 1982 election in Tenna, the veils of normal tranquillity were swiftly restored. Shortly after the election, Cyril's mother died at her home in Belangala; all of Cyril's enemies in the village, including those who had assured me they would have nothing to do with the man again, went to visit the funeral-house to pay their respects to the bereaved family. Even at the worst point of the dispute itself, after the first shouting had died down, the protagonists did not maintain their argument in public but simply avoided each other, especially avoiding any opportunity for mutual public recognition; they hurried past each other in the street, eyes downcast.

Medicine of the Antisocial

From time to time I would discover that a particular person known to me was unpopular, disliked by many of the villagers.

When I enquired into these cases and asked what it was that had made them unpopular, by far the commonest explanation was that the person in question was very 'strong' or 'harsh' (*sära*) and given to scolding neighbours and acquaintances. The word used for 'scolding' in this context is *dos kiyanavā* 'saying *dos*'.[10] Gombrich translates *dos* (sing. *dosa*) as 'evil influence' (1971: 341); Obeyesekere, in a lengthy discussion of the concept, points out that the word is used both to describe the three humours of Ayurvedic medicine, and more popularly to mean 'fault' (1984a: 40) or 'misfortune.' The 'fault' or flaw revealed by scolds could be said to be the fault or flaw of non-harmonious personal relations. What earns their neighbour's opprobrium is failure to contain their anger (the work of *lajja* in proper circumstances), the making explicit of antagonisms in the everyday world. Again the socially-approved way is the way of detachment, of holding back, of avoiding the intense (*sära* means strong, harsh, fierce, committed and is used to describe the sharp-tongued). There are circumstances, though when the socially-approved is not attained. Women, more than men, are said to be unable to restrain their tongues, spreading malicious gossip (whether true or not is hardly the point), and fanning the flames of argument and quarrel. And so although violence is almost entirely a male activity, it is as often as not blamed on women: they stand at the well all day telling lies and passing on bad things, and when their husbands come in they do not have food ready for them but bad talk, so the men themselves get angry and are likely to fight.

A second context in which trouble is expected, if not exactly sanctioned, is any situation involving the use of alcohol. A generation ago all the men of the old villages were regular drinkers of toddy (*rā* palm wine) and smokers of *ganja* or *kansa* (marijuana). This is the source of some embarrassment nowadays; people used to tease the very devout old *beravā* bachelor known as *upāsāka mahatmayā* because, like his contemporaries, he used to be a habitual drinker of toddy in his youth. On such occasions he would look increasingly discomfited until, in desperation, he would blurt out to me 'But, *mahatmayā*, we didn't know it was wrong then.' A century of Buddhist reformist temperance agitation has put paid to that: no one can now claim ignorance of the un-Buddhist nature of alcohol. (The Fifth Precept invokes the promise to abstain from intoxicating drink.)

Almost all the adult males in Tenna—I knew of a small number of genuine abstainers—drink alcohol some of the time; almost none of them are actually to be seen drinking at any time by a casual observer. At the first wedding I attended, I spent a long and dull afternoon sitting on the verandah of the bride's house listening to speeches from the guests. Every now and then one of my companions would stand up, with exaggerated nonchalance, look around, and wander off into the compound. Minutes would pass and then he (for, again, this ritual was for men only) would return and resume his place. Then someone else would stand up, look around, and wander off. After several hours of these quiet comings and goings the man opposite me stood up, teetered briefly, and crashed to the ground in a drunken stupor. At the bottom of the compound was a stash of hooch, and the visitors would take it in turn to wander down to it, take a few large draughts and then return to the public proceedings. (The room in which Cyril protested his innocence over the land deal was on that occasion the functional equivalent of the coconut clump at the bottom of the compound; it was a tribute to two year's ethnographic experience that I was there rather than at the wedding.) Similarly, during the post-election celebrations there was the bottle hidden under the mattress in Cyril's back room while its owner made a spectacle of himself in the street outside.

Violence was almost always attributed to the effects of drink (and women and politics—there is some scope for layered causality here). When they take drink they do not know *lajja* or *baya*, as Cyril's behaviour was explained to me. It is assumed that people who drink alcohol will no longer be in control of their actions and easily aroused to anger which would be likely to spill out in physical violence, given the opportunity.

This, of course, gives scope for the deliberate manipulation of public expectations (cf. Amunugama and Meyer 1984: 58). On one occasion there was to be a meeting at the *pansala* of the *subhasādhika* committee. Those who turned up straggled in late and chatted amongst themselves while the organizers of the meeting tried to get through their business. Into the midst of this walked Mr Perera the postman (and sometime office-holder on the committee), apparently very drunk. He then proceeded to scold the membership, berating them for turning up late, for leaving all the work to a handful of members, for not contributing their fair share of effort. I was surprised the next day when a number of people, far from deploring the presence of a drunk at the *pansala*, praised Mr Perera's behaviour. They claimed that he had all along wanted to scold the members and the members fully deserved it; but of course one couldn't simply shout at people in normal circumstances, so he had to go away and take a few drinks (though not, I was assured, as many as it seemed) in order to justify his speaking in that way.

Politics also provides a context in which one is expected to speak evil of one's neighbours. Indeed, it is possible to see a great part of village politics as little more than the dressing up of domestic disputes in the trappings of party political competition, exploiting the public expectation of trouble which accompanies party politics in order to settle private scores in the idiom of public affairs. Party politics are established so firmly in rural Sri Lanka, in part because of their elective affinity with those divided or dividing communities which otherwise lack an everyday idiom in which to characterize their own disunity: politics provide just such an idiom.[11] From these roots in the contingency of local argument can be traced at least part of the apparent ideological and sociological incoherence of political party allegiance: X is a member of the UNP because his sworn enemy Y is a member of the SLFP, Y is a member of the SLFP because his father joined it in the hope of getting a job back in the 1960s, and so on. If politics provide a necessary medium for the working out of local disputes and grievances, they do so by appeal to forces and powers outside the local community. As I shall argue in the next chapter, this is a recurring pattern in rural Sri Lanka which helps to explain the otherwise puzzling taste for litigation, petitions, and land disputes in the colonial period.

There are two possible interpretations of the evidence

offered so far which I particularly want to avoid. The first would contrast the 'ideal' order of communal amity with the 'real' world of conflict and discord. In fact the supposedly ideal world is the more tangible of the two, being acted out and thus remade and re-emphasized in almost every public interaction. Meanwhile much of the world of dispute and disorder is intangible, invisible, and, inevitably, in part the creation of a fearful imagination starved of trustworthy signs of true intent. A perfectly sane woman, the wife of a village *mudalāli*, calmly told me that once a meal was cooked she never let it out of her sight—in case someone had a chance to slip poison in it. Less spectacularly, I was forever warned to keep my door locked at all times and not to trust anyone at all (cf. Gombrich 1971: 260).[12]

A second possible interpretation would treat the 'normal' and pacific world of the everyday and the sudden wild bursts of conflict—induced by politics or drink—as functionally related, so that both are moments in one homoeostatic system in which the latter cathartically relieves pressures built up by the former. This ignores two points. First, because violence, for example, is defined as being the product of a *total* loss of social sanction and awareness of others' disapproval, it is often terrifying out of control when it does occur. Murders are very frequently associated with drink and tend to be sudden, brutal affairs, exploding out of some minor disagreement in a matter of seconds. Secondly, an election differs from a ritual like *ankeliya* in a number of ways: the rules are constantly being rewritten, so that no one knows what to expect; the same side may lose again and again, thus building up resentment and discord rather than releasing it; and, again, the public expression of antagonism is still defined as resulting from a loss of control—people may be caught up in the excitement of the rallies and processions and find themselves abusing and jeering at old friends of a different party with whom they had no earlier quarrel. Moreover, politics and drink are not available to all people as safe media through which to channel pent-up resentments, anger, and hostility. Very few women drink, and only a handful actively take part in public politics in Tenna.

The most tragic objection to a functional reading of this

evidence comes from a different kind of medicine of the antisocial. Suicide is common and apparently growing more common in rural Sri Lanka (Kearney and Miller 1985); although there were no suicides in Tenna during my stay, there had been several in the past, and several occurred in neighbouring villages. (For the record, there were two murders, one involving Muslim men at Gonagala and the other involving settlers on the fringe of the settlement; these were the first murders anyone had known of in Tenna itself.) As well as the local suicides I was told about, I had access to newspapers which carry daily reports of coroners' verdicts from all over the island. At the risk of doing violence to a complex subject, it is possible to create an ideal-typical rural suicide. The victim is young, late teens or early twenties, male or female. The suicide usually follows a minor domestic dispute—the father or mother refuses to give the son or daughter the money to go to the cinema, a husband complains to his young wife about his meal. The victim goes out and buys weedkiller, drinks it, then presents the family with the consequences; the poison used in almost all of these cases is well known for its slow and agonizing effects—effects which the mother, father, or husband then has to watch in horror.

It is as characteristic for the suicide to present himself or herself to the person left to be in the wrong in the initial dispute as it is for the relationship between them—child to parent, wife to husband—to be one in which the overt expression of anger is quite simply unthinkable. I was not alone in discerning a strong aggressive element in these cases; the Tenna priest suggested to me that the majority of suicides he knew of had been committed to cause pain to the mind of someone else, usually a parent or spouse. This is perhaps the most striking example both of Obeyesekere's 'ambivalence of kinship' and of the perils of affective excess in personal relations.[13]

Inequality and Standing

Drink is a valuable example because we have some clear evidence of changing attitudes. What was once a relatively open activity has grown shamefaced and concealed. It is not necessarily that drinking has decreased to any appreciable extent; it is simply that its significance, the whiff of spiritual brimstone that now accompanies it, is different. And perhaps most important, the old villagers have learnt that what went without saying in the past is not necessarily approved of in the present. It is one of a number of areas where assumptions about everyday behaviour have had to be accommodated to the imperatives of new styles of Buddhism, disseminated through the *pansala*, the school, and more recently the radio, newspapers, and the speeches of politicians. Social inequality is another such area, as too is marriage and the social control of sexuality, to which I shall return later.

The recent history of studies of caste in Sri Lanka is not encouraging. Early clarity has been steadily replaced by confusion and obscurity. Yalman's emphasis on purity and pollution has been deftly destroyed by Gombrich's observation that the concept of pollution (*killa*), associated with menstruation, birth, and death, is never associated with caste (1971: 183; cf. Yalman 1960, 1967). McGilvray, working on the Tamil-speaking east coast, not only failed to find ideas of purity and pollution associated with caste but eliminated any possibility of a role for the 'coded bodily substance' of recent American studies of Indian caste (McGilvray 1982). In the place of these ideas there has been a revival of support for Hocart's (1950) model of caste as a division of liturgical labour based on the idea of service to the king; Dumont was quick to point this out for Sri Lanka, even as he denied its appropriateness for the Indian mainland (Dumont 1972: 262–3). The best support for the contemporary relevance of Hocart's model (e.g. Kendrick 1984), though, is based on evidence from temple villages where the religious institution (often the deity itself) has taken the place of—but retained the focal role of—the monarch. The persistence of caste elsewhere in Sri Lanka, without kings and royal service, or brahmans, or purity and impurity, or untouchables, remains something of a mystery (cf. Stirrat 1982; Ryan 1953).

A number of general points do emerge nevertheless. Caste is habitually explained by reference to the acts of kings in the past. In Sinhala parts of the island the highest caste is also the biggest caste; the *goyigama* constitute an absolute majority of the population in Tenna now, just as they did in Udawela and Medawela in the past. There are only limited areas of formal inter-caste transaction; many villages were formerly occupied by a single caste, and caste specialists were only called upon in major *rites de passage*. Given the size of the *goyigama*, competition for status within this group cannot be settled in caste terms, and without the formal support of the State (which was implicitly maintained by the British through most of the colonial period), there is a large and growing area of potential status-indeterminacy (cf. Rogers 1987a: 150).

There is every reason to believe that in the past inequality and its expression were at the heart of every social encounter. The Sinhala language is blessed with a large number of alternative second-person pronouns, graded to reflect fine differences in the standing of speaker and spoken-to. With these went a choice of lexical subsets, again varying with the relative positions of the partners to a conversation. Christian missionaries in the nineteenth century attempted to counter what they saw as native prejudice in this area; a translation of the Bible into Sinhala appeared, resolutely using the second-person pronoun throughout. The pronoun chosen—*tō*—was usually restricted to address from someone of greatly superior status to someone of greatly lower status. When this translation was introduced into the Anglican churches in the 1840s 'the most prominent Sinhala Christians in Colombo rose in a body and retired from the church' (Malalgoda 1976: 200).

Inequality was not only expressed in language; it was written into one's appearance, the style of one's house, the physical stance adopted by one person in conversation with another. An Old Tenna *goyigama* man recalls his youth:

In those days the low-caste people were shunned. Those *beravā* people, their women were not allowed to wear jackets, or enter the houses of high-caste people. When their women came they only wore a cloth around their waists with nothing to cover the body. If any of them came near a house they were chased away. The headmen did not allow it. When they came to the village on the *gansabhāva* road they wore no jacket on the body. From Gantota to here [the speaker's current house about half a mile from the centre of Tenna], as it was in the jungle, they wore jackets until the village came into view, about half a mile from the village. The customary rules were very strict . . . Looking back, those were bad customs.

A *beravā* man:

In the past it was very severe (*sāra*). Terrible. Could not enter a house, could
not go to a house wearing a new shirt like this. Now it's not like that. When
you go to a house everyone will be treated alike.

The *vahumpura* man quoted earlier (see above p. 144).

One day the Gantota dispenser came to the *vidānē*'s house at Udawela. The
vidānē's wife said to the dispenser, 'Mahatmayā, I prepared this tea for you
[*umbaṭa*], drink it and go [*bīla palayan*].' That's exactly how they used to
speak.

Umba is a standard literary second-person pronoun, widely
considered to be demeaning in conversational use; the *palayan*
form of the imperative is undoubtedly offensive in all contexts
today, being the form used to give instructions to servants.
My notebooks are full of assertions that caste is a thing of
the past. The three men just quoted: 'Now, little by little, it's
been given up . . . In those days the people were like beasts.'
'All the castes of men live together without any difference
. . . Now all live together like children of one person.' 'Now
there is no *nambuva*.' The principal of the village school
assured me that since the children go to school together, sit
together, and play together, by the time they grow up they will
have forgotten all about caste.
Various reasons are put forward to account for this state of
affairs. The *goyigama* man quoted above described in careful
detail how the etiquette of eating and seating had changed
over the years, a coconut shell giving way to an old cup, and
this in turn being replaced by a new cup for giving tea to a
member of a different caste; he was not more specific about
why these changes should have come about, merely seeing
them as parts of a more general civilizing process as he and his
fellows were gradually led out of the ignorance and squalor of
their early lives. The *beravā* man was more explicit: it was the
preaching of the first incumbent at the new *pansala* which
reformed the high-caste villagers. Certainly it is a matter of
general agreement now that caste is a rather un-Buddhist
institution. One very distinguished local monk went so far as
explain to me that caste was not Sinhala at all, but a recent
importation by the last Nayakkar dynasty of Kandy, who had

brought it with them from India; its persistence in the area, he assured me, was all an unfortunate misapprehension.

The *vahumpura* man provided some more robust detail on the demise of caste. His uncle was a famous *ayurvedic* healer, and came to Tenna from time to time to administer cures. In due course he got to hear of how the Old Tenna people addressed his kinsfolk; one day he got drunk and stormed from house to house in the old village berating the occupants for their disrespect and threatening not to treat them in future if they refused to change their ways: 'Afterwards he told me, "Look here, boy, after this they won't treat you like that, giving you water in coconut shells and speaking to you like that." ' No doubt the influx of newcomers, some of murky caste and family, others—like the *vahumpura* healer or his relative, Kiriyansa, the founder of the *pansala*—with a formal caste position out of step with their wealth or standing in the community, has done much to reinforce the preacher's message that caste is not a necessary or desirable part of society.

But all the pious expressions of equality and fraternity which I recorded do not in themselves amount to the death of caste. Certainly it is not, and possibly never was, the fundamental ordering principle of local social life. But it is the source of much interest; nobody much wants to talk about their own caste position perhaps, but there is considerable enthusiasm for discussing the caste of others.[14] Caste is perpetuated in marriage: all of the Old Tenna marriages were intra-*goyigama* (although there was an occasional suggestion that outsiders of distant low country origin like Cyril might be members of the *karāva* fishing caste); almost all *beravā* marriages were within the caste (there was one *vahumpura* man married to a *beravā* woman), and all the central members of the cluster of *vahumpura* families were married to *vahumpura* spouses. I knew of at least a dozen cross-caste marriages among more recent settlers, all but one hypergamous. These aroused no particular outrage or disapproval among the Old Tenna villagers; as long as they were not required to recognize kinship with the low-caste immigrants, it was of no particular consequence who married them. There was no particular feeling, then, of collective identity as *goyigama* which needed to be protected. Rather, *goyigama* identity was but one indication of standing—with kin ties, place of birth and residence, and source of income—amongst the old villagers.

On many occasions I witnessed *goyigama* men sitting with *beravā* or *vahumpura* men, eating or drinking together. What I saw far more rarely was a lower-caste man sitting on a stool or a mat while a higher-caste man sat on a chair, or a lower-caste man drinking or eating from a different serving vessel, or a high-caste man refusing food or drink from a low-caste kitchen. It was not the case that all were prepared to eat, drink, or talk in conditions of neat equality—far from it. But it was the case that, by a kind of tacit consent, moments of confrontation were on the whole avoided. If a *vahumpura* man had good reason to suppose that a particular *goyigama* man would give him his tea in a coconut shell, then he would avoid visiting him and thus bringing the matter into the open. When the postmistress daughter of Kirisanta, the *vahumpura* ex-*vidāne*, married in 1983, the family were very careful in their issuing of invitations to accompany the bridal party to the groom's house. Apart from a few close relations, the party was made up of people of some standing but either of indeterminate caste identity (myself, Mr Perera the postman) or known to be liberal in their attitude (Cyril); potential ill-feeling and embarrassment were avoided by not inviting any Old Tenna people who might raise objections to feasting and celebrating with *vahumpura* people, however respected these people might be as individuals.[15]

Caste, rather like drink or enmity, is always present but almost never seen. It lies just beneath the surface of daily life, threatening to intrude or upset at any moment: in 1982 a casual joke from a *goyigama* youth, asking a *vahumpura* boy to get him a piece of jaggery—an allusion to the *vahumpura* duty of carrying the box of cakes at a wedding—was sufficient to provoke a brawl in the street. But caste was always 'shamefaced' (to use Dumont's expression); only the *beravā*— the *gurunännsēlā* as they were known—were happy to be known and referred to by their caste identity, and they were as unhappy as anyone else if this should turn into what they thought of as humiliating or degrading treatment. Perhaps the most significant evidence I collected was not the absence of caste-regulated interaction, but the fact that no one I interviewed, young or old, high caste or low, was prepared to defend or justify caste in any way. They were not necessarily going to defy it—especially when it came to marrying—but nor were they ready to draw public attention to it.

The repertoire of public deference is still visible and can be seen on many occasions: children greeting their parents formally (at a wedding or a homecoming after a long journey); villagers meeting a big gem-dealer; poor villagers calling on richer patrons at the New Year celebrations; indigent men approaching one of the village *mudalālis* for a loan or some other promised payment. Holders of government jobs or other people of equivalent status (anthropologists for example) are addressed as *mahatmayā* or *sir* (if male), *nōnā* or *miss* (if female). But the full glory of public deference is reserved for relations with the Buddhist clergy, the *hāmuduruvaru*, the 'lords' (see above p. 55). The 'de-secularization' of the term *hāmuduruvō* itself, the process by which it has become restricted in the present to the Buddhist clergy, is symptomatic of the way in which the *sangha* in post-Independence Sri Lanka has become a social pivot, just as Buddhist (or Sinhala Buddhist) identity has become a cultural pivot (cf. Marriot and Inden 1974: 989).

The world of wealth and poverty (and that of power and powerlessness) is described in terms of 'big people' (*loku minissu*) and 'little people' (*poḍi minissu*). For example, when describing the poorest squatters, Tenna political leaders would invariably use the standard phrase *poḍi ahinsa duppat minissu*, 'small *harmless* poor people'. This imputation of harmlessness is the complement of the village-eye view of the big gem-dealers as glamorous and good, mentioned earlier. I never heard much overt grumbling or resentment from the poorest sections of Tenna society directed against the richest; rather, self-interested acts like the advancing of money or seed for cultivation by a richer neighbour were described to me by the cultivator, who would have to pay them back at interest, as favours testifying to that neighbour's good character. Occasionally political leaders of both sides would claim to be speaking on behalf of the *poḍi* people and against their rich fellow villagers, but I never heard this view propounded by the poorest themselves. My position in the centre of the village and my friendliness with richer villagers must explain some of this, but not, I suspect, all.

What was missing in Tenna in 1982—but which might have been present amongst sections of rural youth in the turbulent 1970s, and may again be reappearing in the late 1980s—was a coherent criticism of the order of material things in the village comprehensive enough to relate the wealth at the top to the poverty at the bottom. As so much of this wealth came from trade or links with the state, rather than from the more brutal appropriation of manual labour or crops, this failure is not so surprising. The little people really did seem to be harmless—which I took to mean unthreatening as moral agents. Material inequality did pose a threat to the more prosperous in contexts where jealousy (*irisiyāva*) was perceived to work, that is, within a small band of people of almost, but not quite, equivalent material position.

Material change was certainly not an unproblematic feature of Tenna life. One evening I was talking with a group of men at one of the village shops, and one of my companions raised the hypothetical case of a poor man with rich relatives who, because of *lajja*, would not approach his relatives for financial help. Was this man, he asked, stupid (*moḍa*) or not? The question was passed around the group before all turned to me for some kind of authoritative answer. This was extremely embarrassing, because the man who had raised the question had borrowed fifty rupees from me earlier in the day, explaining that although he had rich relation (three siblings in government employment, while he scuffled a living as a sharecropper) he would not approach them because of *lajja*. I never fully sorted out the subtleties of this conversation. But my early suspicions that all concerned would realise the man was talking of his own case were quickly dispelled; all four men taking part in the conversation had at least one close relative a great deal richer than himself: a sibling or a wife's sibling in a government job, or running a store, or, at the least, the recipient of a few acres of government paddy land on the new colonies. Far from being just the product of one man's obsession, the conversation touched on a very general condition.

Sinhala kinship terminology is the subject of an extensive

anthropological literature, of which Yalman's work (1962, 1967, 1969) is both the best known and the most misleading.[16] The most significant aspect of the terminology for the present discussion is the rather simple observation that it does not divide the world into separate categories of kin and affines. To this we can add the practical point that kinship tends to be reckoned laterally—by virtue of a potentially infinite number of links in the present—rather than vertically by reference to genealogical recall (Brow 1978: 68–70). Every marriage, then, has the important implication that for a wide range of kin of each partner it will either reinforce existing kin-links or else introduce a whole new set of fellow kin. At the same time, it is generally agreed that relations with one's kin should be amicable, co-operative, and altruistic. Marriage, as a moment when it is possible to choose just whom one should or could be amicable and co-operative with, is thus of some strategic consequence.

What that consequence is will of course depend on the circumstances of the partners to the marriage. Tenńa marriage patterns are broadly in line with Tambiah's (1965) ingenious model of Sinhala kinship. New settlers stand to gain most from marrying locally, establishing a network of kin-ties in their new surroundings. The result in their case is a high incidence of local in-marriage, which, because of the nature of the settlement, is in kinship terms out-marriage into new groups of kin. Inherited property is only an issue for a tiny proportion of people in the village, and this in itself had little bearing on marriage strategies: usually there was too little to warrant any endogamous strategy to preserve it. The local evidence I collected which best fits the property-based aspects of Tambiah's model concerned *radala* marriages in the late nineteenth and early twentieth centuries, in which the same names cropped up again and again as marriage after marriage took place within the same very limited group of local elite families.

Old Tenna marriages have changed a great deal in the past fifty years. As elsewhere in the island, the average age of marriage has increased; most Old Tenna men now marry in their late twenties or early thirties, women in their early or mid twenties. Their fathers usually married in their early twenties, their mothers as young as fourteen or fifteen. Marriages in the past were rarely marked with any special ceremony, the agreement of the family on both sides being secured by an intermediary. Many of these marriages were, and still are, unregistered.[17] This pattern persists, not among the Old Tenna households which are themselves the elite of the village now, but among the poorest of settlers. Young men with aspirations to salaried employment and respectability delay marriage for many years; when they marry they are likely to marry a partner from outside Tenna and to mark the occasion with an expensive celebration (*magul gedara*). Covert love affairs, which can so easily lead to pregnancy or forced marriage, pose a constant threat to the orderly arrangement of kinship. They are not in themselves a new phenomenon, but the later age of marriage provides a great deal more time in which they can develop and flourish. For every Old Tenna marriage contracted in the last ten years, I eventually learnt of at least one 'love case' involving one of the partners before the arrangement of their marriage. In the past, when most marriages involved two local parties, and caste was the biggest limiting factor, many of these would have simply become *de facto* marriages. Some still do, but only at the cost of rupture and dissension within the immediate family of one partner or both. For example, Mr Ariyaratna's eldest brother-in-law had two married children by the time I left Tenna, but both, a son and a daughter, had married clandestinely. At the second of these, the young man's mother was said to be very angry and unwilling to allow him into her house. The objection was not, I was told, to the new daughter-in-law, a *goyigama* girl from a neighbouring household with which they were on ostensibly friendly terms; it was to her mother, said to be a scold. The son's headstrong action had foisted an unwanted, unwelcome, but inescapable (because so close at hand) set of new kin on his family.

A tendency to extra-village marriage amongst the richer families in the village, it is generally agreed, reflects their interest in creating alliances with similarly-placed families in other villages (Tambiah 1965: 169). But when I looked at recent Tenna marriages, I could not help noticing that the new alliances were being formed with families further away than seemed practical for the regular exchange of visits and support. There had been, for example, five or six marriages into families who all lived near the same big village ten miles beyond Belangala on the Ratnapura road. A visit to one's kin was the best part of a day's work and not to be undertaken lightly. It was true that the new kin-links were exploited for all kinds of small favours, but it seemed that neither end of the alliance could stand to gain a great deal politically or economically from such distant kin.

A good friend of mine who was preparing for his daughter's wedding explained the criteria involved in arranging such a marriage. He agreed that there could be certain advantages in having the other family close at hand, ready to help out in emergencies, but on the whole it was better to marry at some distance from your home. If there was trouble between husband and wife, for example, the wife might rush straight to her family if they were close at hand, and the trouble would no longer be confined to the couple themselves but would start to involve everyone else. Or, he said, you know what people are like here; if you made a lot of money suddenly, everyone got to hear about it at once in the village; your new kin would expect to share in your good fortune straight away. Better, he concluded, that you should marry some distance away, so that while you could still profit from your new kin they would not be so close as to prove a nuisance. Behind this lay the tacit admission that circumstances now made it harder to maintain the norms of good fellowship expected of close kin. The best way to deal with this was to arrange for any new kin to be far enough away for the relationship not to be stretched too hard or too frequently.[18] The appearance of amity could again be best preserved by placing the relationships involved at arm's length; the ambitious attempted to restrict their local kinship obligations in a frequently futile effort to evade the pervasive contradictions between sociability and economic position.

So the poor marry much younger, with little or no ceremony, and their unions often break up. The better-off delay marriage more and more and mark it with new and more ornate ceremonies—ceremonies which emphasize the virginity of the bride (the post-nuptial inspection of the sheets, the bride's exchange of a white for a red dress after her wedding night). The pre-marital control of female sexuality is an element in claims to social position (while it is tacitly assumed that the young men may take their pleasure at the houses of well-known poor, often lower-caste, women). And after marriage it is assumed that sexuality is ultimately uncontrollable out of the public eye. This was not, as I have suggested, a state of affairs of which people necessarily approved, and my own knowledge is limited by people's reticence on the subject. Obeyesekere is reported as finding, twenty years ago in a remote village, that 'nearly all the adult males there had committed adultery when opportunity arose' (Gombrich 1971: 260). I suspect that this was a little less true in Tenna—adultery, like sorcery and poisoning and other kinds of mischief, being most commonly found in the suspicious minds of the respectable. But I do not have the evidence to prove this either way.

The evidence in this chapter is partial because it is so dependent on my particular experience and my particular position in Tenna. It is biased toward the centre of the village, and toward that part of the village most concerned with its own dignity and position. It is also a view derived from conversations with men and observations of the predominant-ly male world of public behaviour. This is also true of the description of public events in Chapter Three. Occasional fragments of evidence suggest that the assumptions and judgements reported here are also shared by at least some of the women; but, rather than claiming to present an impossibly complete picture of the community, I think it better for now to admit the partiality of my description and call for more study of women, especially of rural women, in Sri Lanka.

The general picture I have presented is of an assumed discrepancy between an often poisonous world of personal relations and a public world where, as far as possible, the poisonous and the unpleasant are concealed from sight. The value placed on detachment and restraint and the perils associated with desire, as I have suggested, are both at the heart of Buddhist teaching. Other values discussed here— *irisiyāva, lajja, nambuva, ādambara*—are more specifically Sinhala. Some of the manifestations of those values are even more specifi-cally a product of the particular history and circumstances of Tenna, while others are more general but located in some parts of Sinhala society—the world of men, or of those aspiring to 'middle-class' respectability—more than others. But one aspect of the historical experience of Tenna is common to most other Sinhala communities: the effect of Protestant Buddhist teaching on the values of everyday life, on drink and violence and enmity, and on caste and marriage and sexuality. It is acceptance of this teaching which makes the old men so ashamed of their disreputable and rather inadequately Buddhist past, and it is this teaching which has further increased the known discrepancy between the way things are (as well as the way they were) and the way it is felt they ought to be.

There are two difficulties in assessing the degree of change in this area. The first is that we have few reliable records of the moral texture of everyday life in the past. Outsiders' versions are almost invariably coloured by the wider assumptions about rural society discussed in Chapter Five, while the memories of the old are also affected by their current circumstances. These memories, though, are almost unanimous in their support of my view that caste, for example, has become increasingly 'euphemized' in everyday life (cf. Bourdieu 1977: 191). Similarly, we know that marriage involved less ceremony and less waiting in the past. But national trends suggest that the pattern of overt rural violence has been stable; what may have increased is the practice of covert attack on one's enemies.

The second difficulty concerns the distribution of different values within the village. Obeyesekere, for example, connects the practice of sorcery (rather than immediate overt aggression) with the growth of 'ethical rationalization' and the life-circumstances of a stratum he identifies as the 'lower middle class': 'gainfully employed, economically well off, hardworking, and perhaps thrifty—the good middle class of the village or small town' (Obeyesekere 1975: 14). In general terms this would seem to describe the most active members of the *pansala* committee, the ritual innovators, the people whose marriages are most carefully organized and celebrated, and whose affines are kept at the most respectful distance; people, in short, like Mr Ariyaratna and the most successful of the

Tenna farmers. But we have to be careful because there are at least some people among the richer villagers in Tenna who spend more time partying than attending ceremonies at the *pansala*, and whose ethical conduct is impulsive rather than rational; Lionel, Cyril, Uberatna, and their cronies are the best examples of this trend, and it is not surprising to note that *their* material fortunes are based less on thrift and systematic work than on the vagaries of gemming, trade, and politics. Finally, there are intermediate cases, traders like Appuhami *mudalāli*, whose everyday conduct inclines to the restrained—he is one of the very few villagers who on religious grounds neither drinks nor eats meat—but whose religious inclinations encompass both the Protestant Buddhism on offer at the *pansala* and a very great deal of highly irrational 'magical' Buddhism, much of it of his own devising. And then there are the poor and the settlers, who also vary at least as much among themselves in their values and actions. As Weber reminds us, 'In religious matters "consistency" has been the exception and not the rule' (Weber 1948: 291).

But this variation in the ethical orientation of the rich villagers is particularly important for another reason. Sinhala society is at least as much concerned with standing and status as most other societies. I suggested in Chapter Four that in the past a central medium for the expression and validation of claims to position was landholding and agricultural activity, in particular paddy cultivation, which was at once a subsistence activity and a set of embodied statements about social identity and social difference. But most economic change has taken place in the socially residual area formerly dominated by chena agriculture, but now occupied by a diversity of activities—cash-cropping and gemming most notably—which involve limited and particular social ties, and from which it is only possible to make equally limited and particular social inferences.

People in Tenna made statements about their identity and standing in many different ways. One, which was growing especially popular as a result of the consumer boom of the post-1977 years, was through consumption: houses, bicycles, cars, sewing-machines, clothes. To a European of my age and class—still caught up in the blue-denim anti-materialism of a misspent 1960s youth—there was an ingenuous charm in the way people responded to my camera, my tape recorder, and my motorcycle. My supposed anti-materialism, I realise, was anything but that in reality. It was rather a particular sophistication which insisted that consumption should appear as little like consumption as possible—jeans should be old and torn, clothes should be 'practical' not showy, the hand-made was always preferred to the machine-made, the 'natural' to the 'synthetic.' In short, it was an aesthetic of prosperity. The villagers, in contrast, displayed the innocence of the poor (Stirrat 1989; cf. Gell 1986).

But it was that innocence—after all, many of the things which were being bought and displayed had only been known in Tenna in the previous four or five years—that reduced the possibilities of consumption providing the kind of nuanced language of inclusion and exclusion in which most European people (and most anthropologists) are used to expressing themselves. Employment provided another claim to status—if nothing else, a job as clerk or schoolteacher guaranteed the honorific recognition as *mahatmayā* or *nōnā* (lady) in everyday speech. It was also relatively stable, the threat of punishment transfers notwithstanding. Politics and political connections provided a somewhat larger number of people with the chance to assert themselves (and to become the target of vilification). Those excluded from political power because of electoral misfortune, or employment, or even the new language of things, could still use the *pansala* as a point of social reference; their route to standing was conspicuous piety and the emulation of a model of 'respectability' represented by people like Mr Ariyaratna.

The problem was not an absence of routes to public assertion. If anything, there were too many ways—often mutually exclusive—of claiming a position in the world, so that one had the feeling of people constantly talking past each other. One of Cyril's notable characteristics, for example, was a considerable capacity for self-indulgence which, while quite acceptable (even chic) in the urban middle-class circles I knew, made a wholly negative impression on someone like Mr Ariyaratna, whose own emphatic piety and respectability were the subject of jokes and scorn in Cyril's circle. Claim and counter-claim were being expressed in incommensurable languages; all they had in common was a shared unease that somehow the proper message was not being received.

This is where the significance of Obeyesekere's substitution of 'status and prestige' for 'honour' is most telling (Obeyesekere 1984a: 504). The sense of honour described in Mediterranean anthropology is both a way of making statements about social position and a way of validating them. Every action is subject to interpretation by the group, and the group is itself defined by this ability to agree on the criteria of interpretation (Bourdieu 1977: 15). To accept a challenge to one's honour is to acknowledge the right of the challenger to inhabit the same moral universe. So it is that shared assumptions that individuals or families are inherently antagonistic can bind people together precisely because the assumptions—and the ways in which they are expressed and challenged—are shared, as in John Campbell's classic description of a Greek shepherd community:

In competitive institutions, although feelings of hostility may remain unabated, opposition becomes a form of mutual dependence; the more men are opposed in this way, the more they have need of one another. The values of prestige recommend the intense consideration of own interests and honour, accentuating always the exclusiveness and separation of one family from another. Yet they also impose the condition that prestige depends on the attentions and opinions of others. They separate; and, at the same time, they create a necessary and close interdependence in the common membership of a community in honour. (Campbell 1964: 320).

The 'community in honour' is bounded and autonomous. Campbell's transhumant shepherds deny that the settled villagers among whom they move possess true honour, just as the villagers despise the shepherds as uncivilized (Campbell 1964: 213); in the Andalusian *pueblo* the sanction of ridicule is denied to two classes of people, the 'shameless' and the upper class, each in its own way beyond the boundary of the 'community in honour' (Pitt-Rivers 1977: 27).[19]

Without public challenge and without common criteria for challenge, the struggle for self-assertion in Tenna cannot create a similar unity out of mutual antagonism. The counter-moves which challenge assertions of position are in normal circumstances hidden from sight. When they do come into view, in the carnival of electoral politics or in moments of drunken abandon, it is under circumstances which are by definition abnormal. As Obeyesekere points out, there is a rich vein of satire in areas of Sinhala popular culture, but the fact that this is often concealed means that nobody knows quite who is challenging their right to the position they claim, nor on what terms; but everyone who tries to claim a position of any worth in the village is quite sure that someone somewhere is making some challenge.

Recent history and economic change have combined to reduce still further what common experiential ground there was for a local idiom of social position based in work and landholding, just as Buddhist revivalist teaching has undermined much of the authority of caste as a principle of social differentiation. But even caste and landholding ultimately referred questions of status and position upward and out of the village—to the king or to the colonial courts, or through petitions to the colonial administrators. The pervasive irony and indeterminacy of everyday life I suggest, are the product of a long history in which status and position have never been settled at local level but have always required the ratification of higher powers. That is one of the factors which have made politics so central and absorbing in villages like Tenna, and it is one of the reasons we have to remember that politics is at once a kind of moral evaluation and a kind of material relationship.

Avurudda

The Sinhala New Year (*avurudda*) celebrations in mid April recapitulate in a couple of days my own ethnographic journey from the detached *politesse* of public formality to the anarchy of desire and feeling believed to lurk beneath the surface. For weeks in advance people clean up their houses and compounds, buy, if they can, new clothes, and make other preparations. The New Year is at once the affirmation of the proper order of social things and an expression of its negation. It is the occasion on which married children visit their parents, clients their patrons, tenants their landlords. The junior partners in such visits offer worship and deference, the senior partners hospitality and acceptance of their visitor's worship; and all exchange gifts. But it is also a feast and a celebration, an occasion for drinking, gambling, and excess. It is notoriously a time when the murder rate in the country rises dramatically.

My notes of the events on the two occasions when I was present in Tenna for *avurudda* are inadequate, but for rather different reasons. On the first occasion I had only been resident for a couple of days, and amidst so much that was strange I noticed nothing that was especially strange about the New Year. The following year I threw myself into the occasion, dressing up to pay formal visits on close friends. I had managed to traverse three quarters of the day unscathed when I walked in on the secretary and treasurer of the *pansala* committee, who were just beginning their second bottle of arrack; I could hardly refuse an invitation from two such stalwart pillars of the Buddhist community, and much of the rest of the day remains a blur in my memory.

My experience is not untypical. The day had started out with groups of people, laden with gifts, dressed uncomfortably in new best clothes, setting out on their visits, calling on kin and close friends, where they would be greeted with tea and oil cakes. Younger kin would go on their knees and worship their elders, while the men would quietly slip off to a back room to share a drink. As the day and the round of visits wore on, the morning's clean clothes grew rumpled and dishevelled, the men grew livelier with the drink, and each new group of visitors brought stories: X's house had burnt down, the police had come to the sixteenth mile-post and arrested Y after a fight, a man had killed his brother-in-law in an argument at Gantota. By the evening, the strains of the reunited families started to tell, drink loosened restraint and old grievances were aired, while gambling in many houses provoked new grievances. Arguments and fights, a common accompaniment to any bout of sustained drinking, broke out—in some cases lethally. In Tenna in 1983 the damage was confined to three arrests, three houses burnt down (a result of the popular custom of igniting celebratory firecrackers too close to thatched roofs), and a large but unquantifiable increase in ill-feeling. Elsewhere in the immediate area there were at least two murders (in both cases victim and murderer were brothers-in-law) and a number of fights and brawls.

The contrasts of the celebrations were similar to the contrasts which I detailed in Chapter Three, and which I hope I have gone some way to explaining in this chapter. The restraint and formality of the morning crumbled inexorably into the drinking and gambling of the evening. Hierarchy, equality, and amity were all acted out in exemplary fashion, only to be challenged later by the intrusion of the unruly forces of hostility, frustration, and aggression. So too with my experience of the village. If the first months could be summed up in the image of children marching down the village street chanting their celebration of 'our village,' the later months were dominated by another procession—the victors' charivari crowing outside the homes of the electorally vanquished. The two images meet, in characteristically confused fashion, in that moment of scuffling and invective outside the temple gate with which I started this book.

A story I was told by a neighbour provides a perfect metaphor with which to close. It is one of a large body of local tales about poison: how to make poison by baking a monitor lizard over a fire, how to apply different poisons so that they go undetected. Sudden deaths in the area, whatever the medical circumstances, usually provoke some suggestion of poisoning, the classic recourse of the secret murderer close to his or her victim: husband, wife, brother, sister, or brother-in-law or sister-in-law. My neighbour explained to me that a very popular way of administering poison was to dip the tip of a betel leaf into a colourless, odourless poison, before offering it to the victim. The offering of betel (*bulat*) is a central element of the formal etiquette of amity: one invites a guest to a wedding by offering a sheaf of betel leaves between the pressed palms of the gesture of worship; at a wedding the bride and groom together offer betel leaves to all their guests and kinsfolk; on any formal visit, at a funeral or *dānē* or at the New Year, the host offers betel to the guests. The poisoned betel leaf—the exemplary gesture of friendship with its hidden deadly message—can stand as a metaphor for the strained and anxious world in which I lived.

NOTES

[1] Commenting on Knox's assessment of the moral climate in the seventeenth century, Gombrich remarks: 'The difficulty is, of course, that neither Knox nor I have been similarly exposed to other peasant societies for comparison' (1971: 259). Neither have I, and there is a danger throughout this chapter that I describe as culturally specific, of distinctively Buddhist, some trait or assumption which is to be found in all small-scale communities. My main concern, though is not to describe the axioms of everyday life as expressions of some embracing Sinhala culture, but merely to describe the texture of daily life in Tenna as I found it. In fact my observations are largely in harmony with Gombrich's (1971: 244–68), and even Southwold's assessment of village morality (shared by no Sinhala villager I have met) can, with a little imagination, be fitted into the pattern described here (Southwold 1983: 54–9).

[2] The need is more pronounced as one moves out of the village and up in the social scale: urban middle-class acquaintances were especially avid enthusiasts for my stories of rural spirit-possession.

[3] The term *bhūtayā* was used to describe the possessing spirit throughout this case, although most people were happy to gloss it as *preta* and I was never able to establish any satisfactory semantic distinction between the two terms.

[4] Sri Lankan folk sociology postulates a two-tier stratification of society into 'villagers' and 'middle class'; the latter category embraces messengers and clerks in minor government positions, MPs and ministers, and the very wealthiest elite elements. I use the term in its Sri Lankan sense, and imply no further analytic precision.

[5] It is clear that the term 'shame' has been used to gloss similar areas of restraint, shyness, and holding back in Mediterranean ethnography, and that in some cases these may be positively-valued attributes: e.g. Pitt-Rivers (1977: 20); Herzfeld (1980: 344).

[6] *Bhakti gī* performances are a recent fashion, spread in part through the recently introduced national television network. On Victor Ratnayake and his following see Seneviratne and Wickremaratne (1981).

[7] Most of the demand for such protection is urban. I particularly treasure the memory of a conversation between a visiting academic of pronounced rationalist views and a leading Sinhala Marxist intellectual. Tired of what he thought to be sensationalist talk of black magic and demons and possession, the visitor quietly asked the other if people really believed all this stuff, or was it not just a case of anthropological exaggeration; 'Come on,' he asked, 'what proportion of people really believe in demons?' 'Ninety per cent,' was the immediate reply, 'especially people like doctors in private practice, who are always using *vas kavi* (sorcery) to stop their competitors stealing their patients.' In Tenna I suspect that scepticism runs somewhat higher than it does among urban sophisticates.

[8] A bizarre legacy of colonial rule is April Fool's Day, which, under the name *boru kiyana davasa* (lie-telling day), is observed in every village. In 1983 a domestic dispute led to the deliberate burning of one house in the village on 1 April. Its owner, a carpenter, was working some miles away, and for some time refused to be 'tricked' into going to see his destroyed dwelling!

[9] It was in fact at the end of this long recitation of sexual irregularities (told to me on my return in 1984) that the friend in question made the apology for concealing bad things from me quoted above.

[10] I am grateful to Robert Simpson, then of the University of Durham, for first drawing my attention to the significance of the idea of *dos* in this context.

[11] The most daring interpretation on these lines is Paul Alexander's (1981) description of the 1971 Insurrection; where he was working, on the south coast, the Insurrection, he claims, was predominantly an expression of intra-elite rivalry with little real revolutionary intent.

[12] In July 1983 the Sinhala areas of Sri Lanka were gripped by a collective panic following an increase in separatist guerilla activity in the Northern Province: amongst the rumours that reached me were tales of Tigers (Tamil guerrillas) reaching Colombo by hanging under trains from the north; of Tiger attacks in the centre of Colombo and elsewhere (see Spencer 1984b; n.d.b); Kannangara (1984) provides an account of similar rumours in the 1915 riots. How much of this propensity to believe rumour in a time of crisis can be attributed to the effect of everyday insecurities is unclear.

[13] While the evidence suggests that murder rates, while high, remained at a fairly constant level in Sinhala Sri Lanka between the late nineteenth century and the 1950s (Rogers 1987a: 122–56), suicide (Kearney and Miller 1985), and perhaps sorcery too (Obeyesekere 1975; Selvadurai 1976; Kapferer 1988), appear to have grown in recent decades. Like the question of gender, the management of aggression deserves a study in its own right; the comments presented here should be compared with Wood's report (1961) and Obeyesekere's (1975) subsequent criticisms of it. Most of this chapter was written before I had a chance to consult Rogers' admirably clear and lucid summary of the pattern of violent crime in colonial Sri Lanka (Rogers 1987a; cf. Rogers 1987b). Amunugama and Meyer (1984) provide a useful summary of both the Buddhist background and the actual incidence of violence in social practice. The basic pattern that emerges from all these studies is that crimes of violence tend to be unpremeditated; Obeyesekere points out that premeditated aggression is channelled into sorcery (*vas kavi*). Whatever the mechanisms involved, the end result is the same: covert enmity and overt amity. Gombrich, too, has some interesting observations on passivity and masochism (1971: 265–6; cf. Malalgoda 1972: 167–8). I have attempted to summarize this evidence and develop the line of argument found in this chapter in Spencer (n.d.b.).

[14] This is probably truest outside the rural areas altogether. The urban middle classes are much given to discussions of caste, especially as a catch-all explanation for the otherwise baffling twists and turns of rural politics. Doubtless this accounts for much of Jiggins's (1979) caste-based interpretation of post-Independence politics (on which see Moore 1981a).

[15] Much depends on the fact that in Tenna enough people are prepared to ignore caste etiquette in particular circumstances. I know of one case (in a village fifty miles away) where a similar set of influences has led to a near-total rupture between castes; rather than run the risk of humiliation, lower-caste people simply avoid all interaction with those of higher caste. A critical variable in this case may be the politicization of caste identity (the MP for the area, closer to Colombo, is himself low caste and depends on a considerable caste vote). Closer to Tenna, visitors from other villages around Belangala were sometimes surprised to discover how lax was the separation of caste; the distinguishing factor between Tenna and their home villages seems to have been the sheer quantity of settler immigration in Tenna—an over-rigorous stance on caste dignity would be as unworkable there as in a crowded urban street.

[16] See also Leach (1961a), Obeyesekere (1967), Tambiah (1958, 1965), Brow (1978), Robinson (1968), Moore (1981b), Stirrat (1977).

[17] This is the source of some embarrassment now. From time to time local officials in different parts of the country hold registration campaigns, thus making respectable some very venerable partnerships; the Tenna *grāma-sēvaka* told me of his plans to hold such a campaign before too long.

[18] The distances involved in selecting a marriage partner are oddly symmetrical with the distances travelled to sorcery shrines; in both cases distance is used to restrict other people's knowledge of one's actions (Obeyesekere 1975: 5–6).

[19] It is true that, as mentioned earlier, fear of the malign consequences of jealousy (*irisiyāva*) is largely concentrated on a thin stratum of near-equals, and this also accords with the general imputation of harmlessness to the really poor. If this would seem to suggest the emergence of something analogous to a 'community in honour,' it must be remembered that it can only ever remain an implicit community, lacking as it does any positive medium for its own expression.

Chapter Seven

Politics as a Consuming Passion

This chapter concerns politics—*dēsapālanaya* in Sinhala—as material relationship and moral form. In discussions of the national question in Sri Lanka it has often been pointed out that the Sinhala language is unable to discriminate between 'people,' 'race,' and 'nation,' all of which are usually subsumed under the term *jātiya* and its derivatives (e.g. Roberts 1979a: 60). What has less frequently been observed is that when people speak of 'the State,' as often as not they still speak of kingship: one of the two commonest terms for 'government' or 'the State' is *rājaya*, a term whose etymological connotations are, I assume, self-evident.[1] The point is not that people think of the President or Prime Minister as kings—there are quite adequate and popular neologisms for both positions—but that there is an area of continuity between the pre-colonial and the post-colonial in the language used to invoke government, its works, and its possibilities. It is reasonable then to see if we can discern parallel continuities in the way people perceive and respond to the State.

In this chapter I shall look at the relationship between peasant and State from two different perspectives. I want first to detail the role of the colonial and post-colonial State as a provider of resources, and as a key instrument in local social mobility; and then to look at the State as a provider—perhaps guarantor is a better term—of social standing in a less material but equally important sense, filling the space in the sociology of reputation identified in the last chapter. We can only understand the importance of political division if we take into account both of these factors.

Politics as a public activity has grown in importance in rural Sri Lanka over the past half-century (since the introduction of universal adult suffrage in 1931). In particu-

lar, between the populist victory of S. W. R. D. Bandaranaike's SLFP in 1956 and the Presidential election and subsequent referendum in 1982, village party politics became, I
believe, a 'central cultural performance,' a cultural arena
within which all sorts of contradictory social and cultural
impulses might be represented and worked through. Such a
phenomenon needs to be interpreted broadly and historically.
The material interests involved are national rather than
local in their scope, while ideas about the State and its role
in local society are complex developments of a set of ideas
about the polity inherited from the pre-colonial State but
mediated, and to an extent overturned, by two hundred years
of colonial and post-colonial history. Throughout this chapter
I shall be providing what I consider to be the peasant's eye
view of the State (*rājaya*) and politics (*dēsapālanaya*), rather
than the metropolitan political scientist's view from the top,
and I shall be concentrating on politics as an expressive
public activity rather than the politics of electoral swings and
statistical culculation. This, then, is a partial view of
the political process which ignores many questions better
dealt with in national analysis by those properly qualified for
the task.

   I start with evidence which shows little, if any, relation
between social class, if defined in terms of the control of local
resources, and political affiliation. This is because politics, far
from reflecting some prior reality like class position, in many
cases constitutes it. From the early nineteenth century onward
the relationship to the State has been the most effective
guarantor of personal position, as well as the critical
instrument of social mobility, for a growing segment of the
rural population of Sri Lanka; throughout this period State
resources, broadly defined, have been the chief medium of
economic and social advancement.

   Although my evidence stems from one small corner of
southern Sri Lanka, there is every reason, as I shall indicate,
that we are in the presence of an historical structure of the
long run which can be traced through from the pre-colonial to
the post-colonial polity. The long-term pattern in peasant–
State relations is a moral as well as a material structure; the
State has been treated not only as a source of material

resources but also as an arbiter of social standing among a crucial—and growing—section of the rural population. Political party identification can be seen as the successor to the nineteenth-century penchant for litigation and petitions to the colonial authorities; alternative political parties also represent alternative criteria for personal position within the community. But if the State is seen as an arbiter of personal position, politics is frequently seen as a medium of collective moral disorder, and it is in this essentially *cultural* contradiction that we can discern some of the more obvious patterns of local politics.

Political Affiliation

Let me start with the relation between political affiliation and local relations of production. Here, as elsewhere, I will rely for my general observations on Mick Moore's important recent monograph on peasant politics in Sri Lanka (Moore 1985). My point of departure is in fact an apparent contradiction in Moore's argument: on the one hand he claims Sri Lankan political parties show a remarkably coherent right-left division (Moore 1985: 203) with correspondingly clear socio-economic differences in their electoral bases (Moore 1985: 221–3); local politics, on the other hand, are strikingly free of ideological division and are dominated by the question of the division and distribution of state resources which he calls 'welfarism':

A stable pattern of inter-party competition over publicly distributed resources encourages voters to define themselves in terms of their roles as actual or potential consumers of these resources. Politics is about who will be employed by the Ceylon Transport Board as bus conductors (Moore 1985: 224).

If party affiliation is largely based on socio-economic position, why is it that local political discourse so rarely exploits the apparently obvious antagonism of rich and poor?

Moore's first point is the most obviously contentious, as he himself recognizes. The conclusion that the two main Sri Lankan political parties—the left-of-centre SLFP and the right-of-centre UNP—draw their support from socioeconomically distinct sections of the population is, says Moore, 'implied' but 'not often strongly stated, and coexists with a certain degree of doubt and ambiguity' in the literature (Moore 1985: 221); he describes the equivocations of earlier political scientists as 'unnecessarily cautious' (Moore 1985: 223). The following is a fairly representative example of this political scientific caution, taken from a recent general survey of Sri Lankan politics:

While it is generally argued that the SLFP appeals most strongly to the poor and the UNP to the rich within the villages, both have to appeal to those with some small investment in property or position, as they may well be the numerical majority in rural constituencies, and will normally make up the great bulk of actual workers for both parties. There is thus no substantial, predictable vote based on class, as in industrialised nations. (Jupp 1978: 208).

A more recent anthropological summary of recent agrarian change, based on a great deal of as yet unpublished ethnography from the late 1970s and early 1980s, gives a slightly sharper version of this:

Ideological differences between supporters of the two main parties are not strongly pronounced. Nor do class differences appear as the only, or in many cases even as the most decisive, basis of party political affiliation. . . Party political cleavages in the villages, then, remain no less vertical than horizontal, and increasing class differentiation has, for the most part, not been effectively translated into a local, class-based politics. (Brow 1986: 6–7; cf. Brow 1988: 315).

Moore's argument is subject to a number of qualifications, not least that he is talking of voting patterns (on which he has a small amount of suggestive evidence) rather than public political allegiance which is Brow's and Jupp's obvious concern. I have no reliable data on voting and shall instead concentrate on public political allegiance.

Party political identification is extraordinarily strong in all sections of Sri Lankan society (outside the secessionist north and east of course). People and whole families are habitually referred to by their party identification: 'he is an SLFPer,' 'they are an old UNP family,' and so on. The most public expression of such identifications comes from attendance at party rallies, which can attract a crowd of several hundred in a village like Tenna and up to 10,000 in a small town like Belangala, and also provide the opportunity for individuals to signify a change of allegiance. From attendance at rallies and a careful sifting of local political gossip I gained a fairly good idea of the most salient political allegiances in Tenna. What I could not do—and I certainly tried hard enough—was provide any coherent socio-economic explanation for the resulting pattern of allegiances. If the leadership of the UNP and SLFP tended to be drawn from the richer villagers (although both parties had very poor settlers in prominent positions too), the foot-soldiers on each side involved as many of the poorest recent settlers as the richer landholding residents.

An explanation in socio-economic terms naturally presupposes that a pattern of socio-economic difference can itself be relatively easily adduced in a place like Tenna. This of course—and not uncoincidentally—is not the case. Both of my mysteries, party political identification (why did each party have its particular supporters) and socio-economic position (what made rich villagers rich), were clarified when I started to trace out the life-histories of the village political leadership.

The dominant figure in the village UNP was Cyril, whose brother was the local MP's chief local aide. Cyril had moved from Belangala to Tenna in the mid 1970s, renting and running one of the two small shops in the centre of the village. A couple of years after his arrival he married the daughter of one of his neighbours, a member of the handful of richer *goyigama* families in the settlement. After the UNP victory in 1977, despite his limited farming experience, he was appointed Cultivation Officer for the surrounding area. Uberatna, his wife's younger brother—one of his closest friends and staunchest political allies—was rewarded with a post as a schoolteacher. Her two elder sisters also hold government jobs—one in a bank in Ratnapura and the other as a schoolteacher in Colombo. Almost all of Cyril's numerous siblings have government jobs of one sort or another. The third key figure with Cyril and Uberatna in the Tenna UNP leadership was Lionel, a cousin of Cyril's wife. Again his family were from the more prosperous section of the village population; his father had left the village to work his lands at a new government colony ten miles away, his eldest brother was a successful farmer, and his two youngest brothers made a living from a mixture of trade, gemming, and some farming. Lionel, alone of the village leadership, had not taken a government job after the 1977 victory; but his main sources of income—gem-dealing and timber-dealing—were both on the fringe of legality and clearly dependent on his political protection for their success. All three of these men had obvious 'family' allegiances to the UNP, but they also had equally long histories of private quarrels with individual leaders in the opposite camp: Cyril with a rival trader who had tried to oust him from business when he first established his shop in the 1970s, and Uberatna with almost all of the village SLFP leaders because of his famously short temper and record of brawling; Lionel's family had been involved in a bitter land dispute with a group of kinsmen who were especially prominent in local SLFP activities.

The other office-holder in the village UNP was Perera, a very poor Sinhala Christian settler in the village, popular for his willingness to help his neighbours in times of need but the butt of frequent jokes for his heavy drinking. After 1977, when the new government provided the village with a sub-post office, he was appointed village postman. The post office itself was located in the house of Kirisanta, the oldest and most respected of the *vahumpura* settlers and a long-time UNP supporter; his daughter became the village's first postmistress.

The most prominent anti-UNP leader in the village was Mr Ariyaratna. He came from a village about fifteen miles away, where his family were rich *goyigama* farmers and strong supporters of the prominent left-wing politician Philip Gunawardene. After a period at college in the provincial capital he was appointed as a teacher at the village school in the early 1960s; like Cyril, he had soon married into one of the richer village families and established himself as the most prominent lay Buddhist leader in the community. He had used the financial base provided by his teacher's salary to buy land in the area, as well as making the first village profits from gemming with his brother-in-law in the mid 1960s. His eldest brother looked after the family lands in his home village; other siblings were employed in government posts elsewhere in the district.

Most of the other richer villagers at the centre of Tenna were—or had been—strong SLFP supporters. And as I made my census enquiries into their family circumstances I would hear of the brother who had a job as a clerk in a government office, the sister who was a schoolteacher, the father now working on colony land provided by the government. Although many of the younger men had achieved a degree of prosperity from gem-dealing, and in recent years from trading in vegetables and running small shops, they still tended to invest the profits either in immediate consumption—a new house or motorcycle—or else, significantly, in the education of a younger sibling whose time at university should later ensure some chance of official employment.

None of this is especially dramatic—to the politically connected go the spoils of victory—nor is it especially novel. But what I want these examples to show is not only that the better-off villagers have benefited from political patronage, although they clearly have; I also want to show that in virtually every case it is the spoils of politics that have done most to make them better off in the first place. If we look at the richest farmer in the village, we discover that his father accumulated much of his land while serving as *vel vidānē* in the 1930s and 1940s; the man himself now has three siblings in government employment outside the village. His brother-in-law—the landless but prosperous farmer mentioned earlier (see above p. 131)—may seem quite free of State support in his prosperity; but his farming success is based on ingenious manipulation of tenancy reform laws introduced by the SLFP government of the 1950s—without political support it is very doubtful that he could have established his many highly profitable tenancy relations. The only source of profit to rival the State as a means of achieving relative wealth within the community is petty trading, which again involves the control of resources flowing in and out of the community, not the control of the community's productive resources themselves.[2]

Local Elites and the State

There is a pattern here which can be traced back at least as far as the beginnings of British rule in the area in 1815. In the early years of their rule the British were forced to depend heavily on the stratum of Kandyan nobles who had engineered their arrival, and the area around Belangala, including Tenna, was dominated politically by one particular family of the *radala* subcaste from 1815 right through to the post-Independence era. In part they were the beneficiaries of British administrative sociology, which required a class of landed worthies to act as intermediaries for them in the rural areas. As British ideas about this supposed class of 'old county families' (as one Government Agent described them) developed, so British policies, wittingly and unwittingly, ensured that they were indeed 'landed.' A royal grant of the lands of a particular village near Belangala (reward for their support during the rebellion of 1818) was used fifty years later in a largely successful claim for thousands of acres of new tea-land on the mountains behind that village; rents from this land seem to have been the main source of income for this family in later years. But the additions to their property were new resources (tea estates, newly irrigated paddy tracts), developed as a result of colonial economic policy, not old resources like village paddy lands on which the local peasantry were dependent. Descendants of these families still owned the largest single block of paddy land in Tenna in 1982.[3] The politically and economically dominant group in this area through the colonial period was not some sort of 'dominant peasantry' dependent on local peasant production, but rather what official accounts described as the 'headman class,' for whom property acted as a qualification for office but *not* as the main source of power and wealth (cf. Meyer 1982).

Similar patterns are quite generally reported in the literature (e.g., Obeyesekere 1967: 211–47; Leach 1961a: 29). Alexander, writing of a low country area in the late 1960s and early 1970s, describes how a *pelantiya* (status group) which had accrued wealth through land ownership in the nineteenth century used that as a base from which to establish itself as the sole intermediary between government and the local population:

Direct appropriation of surplus value through the control of land, the initial economic foundation of the *pelantiya*, while not insignificant, had become less important by 1970. Because of their marriage, kin and school ties with the urban ruling class, the *pelantiya* had almost complete control of goods and services provided by the central government . . . While direct appropriation through landlord/tenant or landlord/wage labour relationships remained important for the social reproduction of the *pelantiya*, it was control of the local levels of the political structure and consequent control of the goods and services in a highly centralized economy, which was the source of *pelantiya* power. (Alexander 1981: 120)

The basic process described by Alexander covers all the cases of which we have evidence: a small local economic advantage provides a springboard for positions within the local administration which in turn provide the means for far greater economic advantage in the long run.

Even so, these examples would seem to involve only a small stratum either outside, or on the very top of, village society. *Their* material interest in local politics may be clear enough, but what of the rest of the population? Nothing mentioned so far would seem to explain their fascination with parties and politics. Not everyone can expect to become a bus-conductor after the election.

But apart from direct employment as schoolteachers and clerks, state resources have flooded into a village like Tenna in a number of ways (see Chapter Five). From the 1940s to the late 1970s every household received a free rice ration from the government as well as subsidised wheat flour: in the period of operation of the scheme the state provided 'between one-third and two-thirds' of annual consumption of these two basic staples (Moore 1985: 99). The current government abolished the scheme in the late 1970s but replaced it with a food-stamp scheme which, although allowed to decline in real value and restricted in reach by a series of *ad hoc* measures, still in 1982 reached all but a handful of households in the village (only twenty-three out of 173 were excluded on grounds of income).[4] Cheap flour and bread were still available. Every year of my stay there were relief works (usually to alleviate the effects of drought) in which most households participated and for which they received a mixture of food-stamps and 'dry rations' (lentils, tinned fish). Government contracts for road and irrigation work provided casual wage-labour for poorer villagers. And the number of permanent government employees resident in the village had grown from one in 1963 to twenty-three by 1982 (a number which has since increased). It is hard in such an economically diverse settlement to quantify the effects of state intervention in the local economy, but, put broadly, if there was no household which was wholly free of direct or indirect state subsidy there were many which depended on state resources for their very survival.

Village political discourse reflected these basic facts of everyday life. Political meetings in the village during the election provided the opportunity for village and district political leaders to address the faithful. While the MP or a senior opposition figure would expend at least part of their oratory on the needs of 'development' or the threat to the country of debt, virtually all the village leaders' talk would be of the water supply we got for you, the school we built here, or, conversely, of how the existing administration had heedlessly neglected this community and only favoured its own supporters. The consistent aim of political discourse at this level was to personalize the blessings of the State, to make 'us' the channel and 'you' the recipient.

The Roots of Welfarism

From about 1850 onward the colonial State started to take an active role in improving the conditions of the Sinhala peasantry, particularly through occasional relief works and sporadic investment in major irrigation schemes like that at Gantota (see Roberts 1973). After the turn of the century, emerging nationalist criticism encouraged the administration to take upon itself even more of the mantle of protector and defender of the peasantry; key elements in contemporary 'welfarist' policies—on Crown land, for example, the creation of the Land Commission in 1928—were established in the years immediately before the beginning of mass electoral politics in 1931 (Samaraweera 1981). What has happened since 1931 is that the scale of State support for the non-plantation rural population has increased steadily. Although the general principles involved were already well established, electoral politics has had the effect of freezing the terms of discourse. As one politician quoted by Moore put it in Parliament in the 1970s: 'The function of government was to provide welfare facilities to backward areas and not to impose taxes upon the poor' (K. Jeyakody in Moore 1985: 112).

What of taxes upon the poor? Until 1893 the main burden of taxation on the peasantry was the Grain Tax, levied at one-tenth or one-fourteenth of the crop, with many lands exempted altogether; this compares with an equivalent rate of one-half of the crop in British India (Roberts 1973: 134). The tax was replaced with a compulsory commutation system in the 1880s. The effect of commutation in some areas where widespread evictions and distress were reported added the final touch to a movement for abolition which had been gathering force in parts of the administration for years; the taxes were abolished altogether in 1893. The main sources of revenue were customs duties, 'primarily import duties on rice and other commodities consumed by the plantation economy' (Peebles 1982: 227). From then until the 1940s the main burden in Tenna was the annual requirement for labour on the roads administered by the revived Village Council. What contribution the contemporary village population make to the State's finances comes almost entirely from sales and other indirect taxes. In the late nineteenth and early twentieth centuries the low level of taxation in the rural sector was possible because of the existence of strong, alternative sources of income in the plantation sector. Since Independence, those alternative sources have been used not only to support the existing administrative structure, but also to provide direct subsidies (like the rice ration or the food stamp scheme) to the population.

At least since Independence, and arguably for most of the preceding century, the State has effected a major transfer of resources from the plantation sector—especially tea, but also rubber and coconuts—to what Moore describes as the 'smallholder sector': 'export crop producers have been the milch cows of the economy' (Moore 1985: 101), surpluses being drained off by the state through export levies, indirect taxes on plantation crops, and a complex but effective system of exchange control. Since the nationalization of the tea estates in the 1970s the productivity and contribution of this sector has declined; but the post-1977 government has more than compensated for this through the exploitation of new sources of revenue, most notably the huge increase in development loans and grants from Western agencies.

The point of closest connection between peasant and State in the long run has been the State's claims on land. In 1840 the colonial State enacted legislation which codified the existing assumption that the State, as the inheritor of the old kings' privileges, was the outright owner of all land on the island for which title could not be demonstrated. It was this land which was sold off so profitably for the expanding plantations in the nineteenth century, and it was this legislative assumption which partly justified the colonial State's repeated attempts to forbid or control swidden agriculture. Nationalist historiography has repeatedly stressed the State's position as appropriator of peasant land. Since the 1930s, though, (and strongly influenced by just such historiography), the State has been a huge net distributor of land. In Tenna old residents received LDO lands under a village expansion scheme before Independence, then their share of the partitioned highlands under the Land Settlement scheme in the 1950s and 1960s; newcomers have settled on licenses on the remaining areas of Crown land, and others have moved on to land granted on colonization schemes elsewhere.

The control over swidden is a good example of the way in which the State, rather than the market, became the mediator between people and the means of their own reproduction (see Chapter Four above). The colonial government's policy on chena did not 'work'—since chena continued much as before—but it had unexpected effects. It made the peasants potentially vulnerable to legal restriction on what was their main economic activity. So the effect of the policy was to bolster the power of, and provide additional income for, local agents of the colonial State who controlled the flow of information between village and administration.

This is the paradigm for the State's nominal control of local resources, then as now. Legally, that control is strong; practically—administratively—the State's ability to exercise it is relatively weak. There is thus a gap between the State's potential impact on the villager's means of physical reproduction and its actual practical effect. This gap was filled in the past by the 'headman class'—the *radala* holders of local office throughout the colonial period and their local subordinates, the village headmen (*āracci*) and irrigation headmen (*vel vidāne*)—who were able to channel selective local information to the higher administrators; at the same time they could exploit the power this gave them over the ordinary village cultivators, who needed their help and support in order to cultivate their chena plots, to carry on hunting with their unlicensed guns, and to farm their paddy plots free from expensive legal battles over ownership. Their place is now taken by local politicians.

At present almost all of the village's houses are built on Crown land, leased by a licence system on nominal rents. In the last fifteen years population growth has brought an end to chena in the immediate area. But the same lands that were used for chena in the past are now used for permanent dry-land cash-cropping, usually of vegetables like beans which are marketed in Colombo by traders who also advance seed, fertilizer, and pesticide for the cash-croppers who then resell the crop to them at an agreed price. Land is not the scarce resource in this process; it is control of capital which gives the traders profit. But obviously, a change in government land policy, or simply the arrival of a determined official with some reason for malice, could deprive the villagers of almost all the land on which they make their most important cash income. The main alternative to cash-cropping in the recent past—gemming in small teams in shallow pits along the stream beds—is in theory licensed and controlled by the State, like chena in the past. In practice, virtually all gemming in the area is illegal, which renders gemmers similarly vulnerable to the actions of zealous agents of the State. So too with timber felling in what remains of the hillside forests. The bulk of the population has to confront the State in order to gain access to the means of its own reproduction. The gap between the State's legal pretensions and its real power privileges those with secure access to the State—the politically connected (who as often as not *are* its local agents in any case).

The Moral Appeal of the Opposition

All of the evidence discussed so far reveals that the State has been a growing element in rural Sri Lankan political economy since at least the beginning of the British era. But I have also alluded to evidence of other avenues to economic advancement: the accumulation of land in the nineteenth century in Alexander's account; the role played by the Sabaragamuva *radala* as agents, speculators, and absentee landlords in the expansion of plantation agriculture; trade as a source of wealth. What is interesting about these phenomena, though, is the way in which they have been used as the means to a greater end, and this greater end is the 'official' recognition of position and standing. In this, the part played by the State in the long historical run seems to have remained the same as that ascribed by Peebles to the early nineteenth-century 'native' officials, the *mudaliyars*; 'The mudaliyar's relationship to the sovereign appears to have been the converse of the feudal baron's: acquiring legitimacy from the connection rather than bestowing it' (Peebles 1973: 29). Legitimacy seems to be another of the good things thought to emanate from the centre.

A striking feature of the colonial records for this area is the eagerness with which would-be intermediaries presented themselves to the new rulers in 1815—and the vitriolic comments they passed on each other (see e.g. Pieris 1950: 139, 226). It was the divide between king and 'nobles' (*radala*), as well as the various divisions amongst the *radala* themselves, that allowed the British into the Kandyan area in 1815. The most successful local beneficiary of British rule in the early period was a minor Kandyan official promoted to the position of *disava* in 1817, who was eventually made *adikar* ('chief minister' under the Kandyan king) in 1835 as a reward for spectacularly accusing a large number of his fellow *radala* of sedition (Pieris 1950: 576 n.49). His descendants continued to dominate the area politically until the 1970s.

Throughout the colonial period the petition was the most common mode of expression of such covert accusations. Petitions to the Government Agent (the most accessible British civil servant) accused minor local officials of all manner of sins (Wickremaratne 1970). When the position of *āracci* (headman) for the area which included Tenna fell vacant in 1941, the Government Agent received a letter containing the following information on the various candidates: 'This is an uneducated person who is very unpopular in the village'; 'About three years ago this man took an action against his wife and another for misconduct and divorce. The correspondent in this case proved that this was a made-up story to get rid of his lawful wife, and that he had been keeping sixteen other wives and got rid of all cunningly'; 'This man has no education whatever, and is hardly doing his present Vel Vidaneship (irrigation headman)'; 'A criminal action had been instituted against this man by one Bandara of the same village for molesting him seriously' (SLNA 45/1064; cf. Meyer 1982: 229–30). The author of the letter, needless to say, was himself a candidate for the job.

Nineteenth-century petitions seem to have frequently foundered on a basic difference in assumptions about the proper place and purpose of the State:

Petitions mirrored a certain divergence of attitudes with regard to the obligations of the rulers towards the ruled. For example, that a great many petitions drew attention to the lawlessness prevailing in certain districts was not *per se* particularly significant. There were, however, a closely allied group of petitions reflecting a widespread belief that the government's duty to protect its subjects necessarily involved its intervention in private disputes which—as the government agents were never tired of reminding the petitioners—should have been referred to the courts of law. (Wickremaratne 1970: 224)

But even the recourse to colonial courts seemed to many British officials to be based on the wilful and inappropriate intrusion of private animosities into areas of public law. So much so that at one point in the nineteenth century the use of colonial law in minor disputes came to be seen as a serious administrative problem. As one Governor put it, 'In their attempts to adapt our system to their wants they . . . have abused the process of criminal procedures, as the cheaper and more efficacious mode of enforcing their civil rights and of avenging their petty quarrels' (Sir Hercules Robinson in Samaraweera 1978b: 193). According to another British observer, the apparently low proportion of convictions to complaints indicated 'a great disposition among natives to bring forward false, and frivolous charges, engendered by ill-feeling, arising from imaginary or real wrongs' (Capper in Samaraweera 1978b: 194). A judge complained that 'We have fostered the spirit of gambling in the Courts for mere Victory, a form of excitement which has pauperized tens of thousands of them individually' (Berwick in Samaraweera 1978b: 194). The official response to this deluge of legal complaint was the attempted restoration of the *gansabhāva*, the supposed pre-colonial village council.

Recourse to the courts was certainly very popular in nineteenth-century Ceylon. John Rogers estimates that in the 1860s between seven and eight per cent of the population were accused *each year* of some criminal offence, but less than ten per cent of those accused were convicted (Rogers 1987a: 60, 62). Rogers argues against those who have suggested that British justice was an alien imposition on the peasant population and suggests, convincingly, I think, that the peasants simply adapted the colonial institution to their own purposes. In particular, he points to a parallel between the use of sorcery and demon rites and the use of the colonial courts: both represented an external and amoral source of power; while manipulable, this outside power was nevertheless capricious at times; in both cases ritual intermediaries were necessary, and these intermediaries addressed the power in an incomprehensible language (Rogers 1987a: 68–77). Rogers's argument tells us *how* people may have used the colonial legal system, but in itself it does not tell us why they used it in such numbers.

It is worth reflecting on the language in which civil servants expressed their bafflement at the alleged 'litigious nature' of the Sinhala people; they talked of the 'spirit of gambling,' of 'a form of excitement.' As Edmund Leach put it in his description of Pul Eliya in the 1950s: 'Litigation might be described as a favourite village sport' (Leach 1961a: 41). This corresponds exactly with more recent descriptions of party politics: 'Mass sports or entertainments are unknown in the villages and politics remains a consuming passion' (Jupp 1978: 162). From the first, elections in this area were conducted with robust enthusiasm. The Village Council elections in 1933 were marred, according to the Government Agent, by the activities of 'a small clique of low-country people, traders and contractors': 'When they found they had no following, [they] adopted terrorist methods, employing rowdies, using threats, and even attacking the cars used by their opponents.' This group apparently accused the headmen of working against them, a complaint which the Government Agent was quick to dismiss even though he had to concede that the victorious candidates were themselves mostly 'of the headman class.' The first State Council election in 1931 had been uncontested, but a by-election two years later was bitter enough for the Government Agent to describe subsequent criminal proceedings against some of those involved as a 'riot case.'[5] The two subsequent elections, in 1936 and 1943, were if anything even more bitterly contested (Jiggins 1979: 96–111). Since 1956 the acrimony and excitement has increased with each election, spreading out of the towns and engulfing villages like Tenna.

What these examples have in common is the use of the State as an arbiter in local disagreement (as well, perhaps, as a source of local entertainment). Litigation, appointments to office, petitions, elections—all, it could be argued, embody real material interests; indeed that is the very point I developed at length in the first part of this chapter. But they are more than that; they all involve claims or challenges to individual position, standing, or status—*tattvaya* as it is usually put. Through all these different manifestations the common pursuit is the State's recognition of the legitimacy of one's position in the local community. In most cases it is even more than this—the position that is being contested (headman, *raṭē mahatmayā*, member of the State Council, MP) is itself part of the State apparatus. The legitimacy of your social position does not flow upward from the acclamation and accord of your neighbours; it still trickles downward from the State. The State is greater than the sum of its parts and, in true **Durkheimian** spirit, it bestows on those in its favour that sparkle of difference which Durkheim called the sacred.

I think this is also the key to the mystery of party affiliation. It is true that party membership can, in certain circumstances—for a minority of members after an election victory—provide material reward; but it is equally true that most party members most of the time have little or no prospect of such reward. There are insufficient rewards of the right kind to go round, and there is always a chance that your party will find itself in opposition. On the other hand the material disincentives of party affiliation are far more tangible. For government employees there is the prospect of the punishment transfer to some inaccessible and undesirable corner of the island; for most people in a village like this there is the threat of official harassment over all those economically necessary but legally dubious activities—from gemming to collecting firewood—on which everyday life depends; in the last resort there is even the possibility of removal from the Crown land on which your house and garden lie.[6] Plenty of people do avoid public politics altogether (traders are a common example, usually preferring a quiet deal in a back room to the dangers of public politicking). So why, given all these reasons, do so many persist in such an apparently dangerous game?

The answer seems to be that politics—like those other earlier uses of the State—has become the crucial arena within which local differences of all sorts are worked through. 'Worked through' not 'resolved,' because to stay in opposition is to deny the legitimacy of your opponents' current, doubtless temporary, ascendancy. This is what Scott, describing an analogous situation in Malaysia, calls 'the moral appeal of the opposition' (Scott 1985: 133). This is also one point at which differences of political ideology can fuse with local differences: a rich farmer can afford to stay in the SLFP, publicly justifying the decision in terms of, say, the UNP's refusal to help the 'little people,' while also enjoying the opportunity thus afforded to abuse his long-detested neighbours in the UNP. To change sides in a situation like this—as many old

SLFP supporters started to do in late 1982—requires a display of at least nominal deference to your erstwhile enemies in the local leadership of the other party. In fact, very few of those who remained in the SLFP justified their decision to me in terms of some insoluble difficulty in the other party's policies; indeed, quite a few were prepared to concede grudging approval of some of the post-1977 changes. The main obstacle between themselves and departure from the sinking ship which was the SLFP by late 1982, was, I surmised, that too much pride would have had to be swallowed. In all this, different parties represent different moral communities, neither of which accepts the legitimacy of the other's estimation of different individuals' social worth.

Political alignments then, are embedded in the particularities of local disagreement, and there is thus a high degree of contingency in party political affiliation in any particular locality. Politics, like petitions and court cases in the past, has become a medium through which villagers can act out all sorts of ostensibly 'non-political' disagreements. All manner of rifts and disputes may become expressed as political differences; class could, in some cases, certainly be a factor, but so too could caste, religious community, family disagreements, minor economic rivalries, and bad blood of all kinds.

So, at this most general level, we are confronted with an enduring pattern. In theory, anyone can make a living. And it is still just about possible to do this untroubled by the attentions of the State; the countryside where I worked is long used to groups of masterless men and women drifting through to work a season or two of chena before moving on. But if you want to be *somebody*, to be a lord, or a freeholder, or an official—to be anyone of standing—then it is necessary to establish relations up and out of the local community, to a higher source of social worth. This can be seen in the prevalent 'top-down' explanation of caste as a product of kingship, and it can be seen in the use of landholding (the key medium of pre-colonial power) as an idiom of standing. It can also be seen in more general observations on Sri Lankan society: Moore points out that 'relationships in civil society and in the state organisation are not easily separable' (Moore 1985: 173); Kapferer talks of the hierarchical 'encompassment' of persons by the state (Kapferer 1988; cf. Nissan 1984: 176).[7]

But this pattern has been affected by other major developments, of which politics itself is one. The pre-colonial State was primarily a ritual organization, as described by Hocart (1950, 1970). The colonial State was at its upper levels a bureaucratic apparatus, although it was dependent on non-bureaucratic semi-hereditary officials at the lower levels. Since Independence, politicians have moved in to assume the 'personalistic' ties between the lowest levels of the administration and the population, at first uneasily co-existing with the official bureaucratic structure of the State, but more recently quite eclipsing it. In many cases this has been made easier by the fact that the politicians are the same people as the old *raṭē mahatmayā*s; the local *radala* were closely related to S.W.R.D. Bandaranaike, and from 1960 to 1977 the MPs were the son and daughter-in-law of the last *raṭē mahatmayā*. As one old man described the 'populist' election of 1956 to me: 'We were used to these people (i.e. the local *radala* families) coming and asking for their share of the harvest; when they came and asked for our votes, we gave those too' (cf. Brow 1978: 46).

But if the appeal to the State is as old as I have suggested, politicians—whatever their pretensions—are not divine kings, and it would be foolish to ignore the considerable changes that have taken place in the texture of hierarchical relationships as a result of mass politics. Political leadership in a local community is as likely to attract opprobrium as adulation— the spoils of politics, especially State employment, are more attractive than any purely political position. Unlike petitions and litigation, politics is, above all, an idiom of *public* vituperation in a local arena, which makes it all the harder for those politically bested to recover whatever dignity they had before. In Tenna this can be seen in the way the UNP have systematically attacked the local *radala*. Cyril, for example, celebrated the 1977 victory over the SLFP by giving an old *radala* honorific name, 'Banda,' to his dog. The effect of a half-century of political competition is to make people aware that there are alternatives, that nobody can occupy a position of importance unchallenged. At the same time the power of politicians means that the holders of most bureaucratic posts are particularly vulnerable to public humiliation by local party bosses. As the pursuit of individual *tattvaya* (standing, position) grows ever more obsessive, so the principle route to its attainment, politics, *by its very nature*, undermines all claims to dignity and honour (*nambuva*).

Similarly the island has seen two hundred years of capitalist expansion. Access to the State has not been the sole route to fame and fortune. In fact the relationship between the colonial and post-colonial State and capitalist penetration has taken two characteristic patterns. Money made elsewhere has been invested in claims to official position; and official positions have been a crucial way of making money. There have been exceptions to this closed circle of wealth and power: minority groups like the Muslims, who until recently ignored (or were ignored by) the State, and in many areas confined themselves to their own trading domain, or the Indian and Ceylon Tamils, an account of whose different, changing, and often tragic relationship to the colonial and post-colonial State would obviously require another book.[8]

The scale of State impact on local circumstances has also varied over time and space. I have suggested that the position of the State as the provider of good things can be traced back at least as far as the 1850s, although this is a theme which is strongly figured in the ideology of pre-colonial kingship. Until the 1930s though, outside areas of major development (like the Gantota irrigation works in the 1890s) the State was a fairly minor figure in everyday material circumstances, and the beneficiaries of State employment, the *radala* and their headmen, constituted a relatively thin stratum on the top of rural society. But with mass politics, 'welfarist' policies have greatly enlarged the State's role in the peasant economy, while the proportion of the population which might reasonably expect some more specific benefit (a job, an allocation of new land) has steadily grown. This is still true despite the supposedly liberal economic policies pursued since 1977; recent research suggests that the State's role in the distribution of resources has continued to grow in the last decade.

In contemporary Sri Lanka, State-peasant relations can be described in material terms: the State distributes, the peasant consumes. The resulting material interests explain why politics are so important—because almost everyone is heavily dependent on the State. The frequent electoral reversals between 1956 and 1977 (in which the incumbent government was defeated in each successive election) can be most easily explained in these terms: each incoming government was forced to promise to deliver more but was able to deliver less; only the UNP government between 1977 and 1982, through its cultivation of external sources of aid, was able to deliver something of what it had promised. This was certainly the view I heard most often expressed to explain their victory in the first vote of 1982. But there is no reason to suppose that this government can continue indefinitely receiving favoured treatment from the international agencies which have so far propped it up. Without the prolonged security crisis in the north and east the recurrent contradiction between material promises and the ability to deliver would have almost certainly become more evident by now.

But village politics are more than that. Alasdair MacIntyre has pointed out that a science of comparative politics presupposes the identification of cross-culturally comparable political institutions and practices. But institutions and practices are themselves 'always partially, even if to differing degrees, constituted by what certain people think and feel about them' (MacIntyre 1971: 263). So the State has been many things in the recent history of Tenna; a capricious source of trouble, a growing source of wealth, an unpredictable ally in the pursuit of local disputes. These are the experiences upon which politics have become based. But these experiences have been interpreted over time through a mesh of differing and sometimes incompatible ideas about government: the language of kingship is still an important element in much ritual,[9] but it now coexists with the bureaucratic idiom of the modern State, as well as the populist appeals of the local politician. If talking in these terms makes 'politics' look less like a unitary area of life, this may be because the institutions and practices labelled 'political' (by the villagers of Tenna as well as by observers like me) are themselves fluid and changing, as people's ideas and understandings change.

As an idiom, politics combines, in a particularly beguiling manner, all the themes I have discussed; in politics it is as easy to invoke images of the good society while advancing your own chances of material reward as it is to use the language of unimpeachable moral worth in order to subvert the everyday norms of neighbourly fellowship. All who participate in it seek to project their ideal of what society ought to be like; all who observe it see evidence of what society is like. Politics, as well as being an idiom of abuse, and a channel for resources, is also a discursive space; a context in which different people can articulate their vision of their society. In the next chapter I turn to this final aspect of politics and the State—the vision of nationalism.

NOTES

[1] The other term used is *ānduva*.

[2] There has been a steady growth in interest in trade (*bisnis* in village Sinhala) amongst younger men in the village. There is evidence that, at different times and paces in different areas, trade has moved out of the hands of 'outsiders' and into those of 'insiders' in many Sinhala rural communities over the past thirty or so years (Brow 1978: 129–30 n.15; cf. Yalman 1967: 53). It is possible that in the 1980s the often reported glamour of government employment is being slowly eclipsed by the attractions of merchant capital as a medium of social advancement.

[3] A more detailed account of the career of these families in the colonial period, and full references, can be found in Spencer (1986: Ch. 3).

[4] The supposed cut-off for the scheme was a monthly income of more than 300 rupees; in practice the local official charged with its administration included all the households in the village, except those with a full-time wage-earner, the most successful half-dozen village traders, and the two most prosperous farmers. The government's main effort to check the scheme had taken the simple form of refusing all new applications for some years. In 1982 households received stamps worth 15 rupees a month for all those over the age of twelve, 20 rupees for those between eight and twelve, and 25 rupees for those under eight.

[5] SLNA 45/345 17 May 1933, 14 October 1933, 16 October 1933; SLNA 45/346 1 February 1934.

[6] These were all threats felt by SLFP supporters and reported to me in 1982.

[7] Ironically, Moore's point is brought out in a rather odd comparison with India, and Kapferer's in an even odder comparison with Australia. Neither cites Hocart on caste (Hocart 1950).

[8] Colonial official sociology, by defining groups as appropriate or inappropriate intermediaries, did much to substantialize caste and ethnic

groups and determine their different attitudes to alternative routes to advancement. To paraphrase a low-caste informant of Meyer's, 'They wouldn't give us jobs so we became planters' (Meyer 1982: 230). Similar patterns are unevenly distributed in the modern era; although one might expect caste to be further substantialized in areas with a known caste vote, elsewhere (probably most of the country) employment patronage has been much more homogeneously distributed in the population than it was in the colonial period. The significant exception to this is of course northern Tamil youth, who have been excluded from political patronage since the 1960s (their area represented by regional parties condemned to opposition); the effects are obvious enough.

[9] Kapferer's persistent failure to distinguish between 'kingship' and 'the (modern) State' is one source of confusion in his analysis of Sinhala nationalism (Kapferer 1988); it is, of course, a confusion he shares with most nationalists.

Chapter Eight

Experience, Interpretation, and the Nation

About suffering they were never wrong,
The Old Masters: how well they understood
Its human position; how it takes place
While someone else is eating or opening a window or just
    walking dully along

W. H. Auden 'Musée des Beaux Arts'

The July Troubles

And so it was that I found myself one morning in late July 1983 sitting with a group of men who were taking a break from work in the paddy-fields at Udawela. This was the second or third day of a nationwide curfew imposed after the outbreak of serious anti-Tamil rioting in Colombo. 'Aren't you worried about the curfew?' I asked the field-owner. 'No, that only really applies along the road where the police might travel,' was the reply, 'this is jungle'. The paddy needed attention and the troubles were far from Tenna. Try as I might, though, I found it hard to concentrate on the details of harvesting procedures and soon returned to my room to listen to the radio for any further news from the cities.

On 23 July 1983 thirteen Sinhala soldiers were killed in an ambush by Tamil separatists in the Jaffna peninsula. When the bodies were brought back to Colombo for a collective funeral the next day, a large crowd gathered which moved on from the cemetery to attack Tamil shops and properties in the immediate neighbourhood. The following day much of Colombo burned while the government remained oddly silent.

The violence spread out to other towns in the south of the country. Much of it was the work of relatively small, well-organized groups of men, methodically identifying Tamil properties from electoral lists and systematically setting fire to them. But this routinized destruction was punctuated by moments of panic and frenzy in which innocent Tamils were set upon, beaten, killed, in some cases burnt alive. Within a week the violence abated, leaving whole suburbs of Colombo razed, an unknown number—probably several thousand—dead, many more homeless in refugee camps, and the country's political process deeply traumatized.[1]

I had in fact been staying with friends near Kataragama (where the annual festival was just ending) when the first news of the trouble reached us on 25 July. I returned to Tenna by back roads the next morning and stayed there for the rest of the week. At the end of that week I managed to scrounge enough petrol—there was almost no public transport and no petrol to be obtained during the days of trouble—to rejoin my friends for a few more days. I did not visit any of the areas worst affected by the violence for another two or three weeks. I was not, then, an eye-witness and can claim no special authority in assessing those events.

Obviously, though, they posed a problem—emotionally as well as intellectually—for me. But this was as nothing to the problems of the victims, or those of people all over the country in villages like Tenna who are still living with the political consequences of those days. Writing shortly afterwards I put it like this: 'Like many others, I found myself desperately trying to make sense of that familiar paradox—the perpetration of evil by apparently nice, decent people' (Spencer 1948b: 187). But the people I knew had perpetrated no evil; nothing had happened in Tenna, the farmers went back to the paddy-fields, the priest stayed in the *pansala* listening to the radio, the handful of Tamil families were left unscathed. All were, though, intensely worried by what was going on elsewhere and I took part in some of their conversations as we all tried to make sense of a mélange of rumour and heavily censored—often plain false—news from the radio.

My mistake in my first hasty response was to accept the polarization of the times—the division of the world into

Sinhala and Tamil, absolute good and absolute bad.[2] For example, one evening during the week of troubles at Appu-hami *mudalāli*'s house, a friend of his tried to spell out the situation for me: this is a good, Buddhist country given to us by the Buddha, but these Jaffna Tamils are always doing bad work, killing people, spoiling it. 'But who are killing people now?' I interrupted. 'Ah, but the things they have done in the past,' replied Appuhami's wife. 'Once they dropped a Sinhala baby in tar and set fire to it.'[3] It was widely accepted that the Tamils 'had started it,' and while the attacks on innocent Tamils were regretted by many of my friends, it was still somehow 'their fault' for letting the separatists operate for so long (cf. Nissan 1984).

The fragments of news and information that reached Tenna were being filtered through a mesh of received ideas about Tamils: that they were inherently violent, potential attackers of individual Sinhala, and potential destroyers of the Sinhala-dominated polity. These stereotypes are themselves derived from many overlapping sources: school textbooks in which Tamils are portrayed as outsiders, the descendants of anti-Buddhist invaders who destroyed the old dry zone kingdoms (Siriwardena 1984); newspaper accounts of the Tigers' attacks on the security forces; politicians' ruthless exploitation of popular fears, and so on. In addition a host of rumours sprang up, in which specific acts of violence were explained as responses to imagined attacks by the Tigers on Colombo and other southern towns. Indeed it seems clear that many of the worst atrocities were seen by their perpetrators as defensive reactions to Tiger attacks; so strong was the fear of the Tigers—largely whipped up by a sustained campaign in the Sinhala press in the previous few months—that any attempt at self-defence by individual Tamils, even the act of running from the mob, was read as evidence that the person involved was 'really' a Tiger intent on destruction (Spencer 1984b; cf. Spencer n.d.b.).

Gradually the government regained a semblance of control. On the night of 28 July President Jayewardene made a national broadcast; he announced the outlawing of separatist parties in order 'to appease the natural desire and request of the Sinhala people to prevent the country being divided' (quoted in Nissan 1984: 178). The next night the Prime Minister made a broadcast blaming 'anti-government' forces for the trouble. The following day three left-wing parties were proscribed and another senior minister made a national broadcast, this time giving further details of a subversive conspiracy, somehow linking the Tigers to anti-UNP forces in the south, designed to foment violence and bring the government down. What the various ministers were doing in these speeches, which were listened to with rapt attention by almost everyone I knew in Tenna, was gradually assembling an interpretation of the trauma which shifted the responsibility for the violence from the Sinhala population, and specifically from those cadres of the UNP who were already being blamed for the organized destruction in Colombo.[4]

Interpretation and Ritual

Gradually things returned to something like normality. I was never sure how much of the government's version of events was accepted by people in Tenna. Some strongly anti-UNP villagers were sceptical of the alleged conspiracy behind the riots, although the possibility of active UNP involvement was only whispered rather than discussed aloud. I went back to the paddy-fields and the gem-pits. My fieldwork was in any case coming to an end. I was due to leave Tenna in late September and return to England.

During these weeks there was a gradual shift in village political alignments. This was made publicly manifest at a wedding in early September. Although it was held at the house of one of Cyril's strongest political opponents, both Cyril and Mr Ariyaratna were invited and both made particularly telling speeches. First Cyril, who stressed his kinship connections with their host before asserting that 'we are all kin (*okoma näyo*) in this village'; it was true, he admitted, they had been divided in the past because of politics; but despite all criticism, all that he had ever wanted to do was improve the village and unite the village. Mr Ariyaratna's speech followed almost immediately: he was happy because he had taught both the bride and groom at

different times; the bride's father was his friend, a good
Buddhist and a strong supporter of the Tenna *pansala*, just as
the groom's father was himself a strong supporter of the
pansala in their village, and one of the groom's brothers had
been ordained into the *sangha*; our host, he emphasized, was a
good man, a Sinhala man, a Buddhist, with only Sinhala
Buddhist blood, which was how it should be in our country,
which was a Sinhala Buddhist country.

The next major public occasion appeared to seal the
rapprochement indicated by the presence of these two enemies
at the wedding. It was decided to organize a special ceremony
at the *pansala* to mark my departure from the village, and both
Mr Ariyaratna and Cyril were heavily involved in the
planning and organization. Various friends and local worthies
were invited, I had a special protective *pirit* recited over me by
a phalanx of monks, gifts were exchanged, a child recited a
poem, and speeches were made, the most memorable of which
came from Mr Ariyaratna. He reminded the company of how
I had lived the same life as a Sinhala person, eating the same
food, enjoying the same comforts; now I was to go back to
Oxford and write about Tenna, and my writing would be
published and would be read all over the world, and I would
say that Sinhala Buddhist people are the best people in the
world, and that Sinhala Buddhist culture (*sanskṛtiya*) was the
best culture in the world.

Like his earlier speech at the wedding, Mr Ariyaratna's
speech seemed to be a kind of oblique commentary on the
recent national disturbances, an attempt to reassure his
audience of their own worth and to re-establish a position for
them in the world. As he warmed to his theme of the virtues
and longevity of Sinhala culture I found myself growing
increasingly uneasy. If Sinhala culture was so important and
self-evident, why was it necessary to take this occasion to
remind everyone of the fact? Perhaps—and I do not recommend this as a comforting thought to happen on the final day
of fieldwork—the problem was precisely that Sinhala culture
was not at all self-evident, central, or secure. Speeches like
this, in which cultural continuity was such an insistent theme,
could only be read as symptoms of some implicitly recognized

discontinuity. The problem they addressed was the problem Mr Ariyaratna recognized when nobody organized the *perahara* among the poorest settlers (see above p. 67), the problem that all of the invented rituals at the *pansala* could be seen to address: people here are not united.

The way in which I have to chosen to describe this problem in earlier chapters is the loss of shared experience. In Tenna, a gap has grown between people's received understandings of the world and the events and circumstances with which they live. This is the gap filled by the rituals and symbols of the nation:

But do you know what a nation means? says John Wyse.
Yes, says Bloom.
What is it? says John Wyse.
A nation? says Bloom. A nation is the same people living in the same place.
By God, then, says Ned, laughing, if that's so I'm a nation for I'm living in the same place for the past five years. So of course everyone had a laugh at Bloom and says he, trying to muck out of it: Or also living in different places. (Joyce 1971: 329–30)[5]

Sociologically and culturally, the people of Tenna, like those of Bloom's nation, live in different places: their childhoods were different, their educations were different, potentially they live in different worlds. These differences cut through the village along a number of axes: differences of geographical origin; differences of generation; differences of education, employment, and experience.

There are two obvious ways to patch together the gap between experience and common understanding. One is to offer public interpretations of disparate, worrying events so that they become tied to more familiar common understandings; another is to create common areas of experience in which everyone can participate. And then these areas of created experience can provide the common understandings to which subsequent public interpretations can lead. Public ritual creates a basic ground of common experience; public discourse, like Mr Ariyaratna's speech on my departure, can then offer an interpretation which links otherwise new and worrying events to the safe core of common experience. The wedding is made into an occasion for healing national

wounds. The leave-taking ceremony finally creates a place for
the outsider who has witnessed the splits and antagonisms
behind the surface of village life: he will record and celebrate
our unity and goodness. The symbols around which both
rituals and interpretations coalesce are the central symbols of
Sinhala Buddhist nationalism.

Mr Ariyaratna, like the President and his ministers in the
post-riot broadcasts, was offering a set of interpretations. In
both cases the end-product was the same: a bundle of
intertwined assertions about the worth and place of Buddhism, the Sinhala people, and Sinhala culture. In both cases
the raw material for interpretation consisted of events or
circumstances which might be thought to challenge such
assertions—the bitter realities of village politics, the terrifying
spasm of communal violence. The style of interpretation in
both cases reproduces the style of interpretation of the
chronicle. The purpose, for chronicler and nationalist, is to
demonstrate underlying continuity, eternal verities, in the
face of change and disruption. Each chapter of the Mahavamsa ends with a formulaic homily. Each speech delivered in
Tenna by Mr Ariyaratna or Cyril or one of the handful of
other skilled speakers in the village led back to the necessary
unity of the village, the importance of Buddhism, the identity
of the nation as a community of Sinhala Buddhists, and a few
other favoured themes.

Incessant public emphasis on community presupposes the
idea of absent community. Repeated assertions of historical
continuity—the 2,000 years of Buddhist culture beloved of
Sinhala politicians and the Sinhala press—are, I would
suggest, indicators of the fear of discontinuity. Nationalism,
says Eric Hobsbawm, combines two phenomena—a 'civic
religion' intended to bind the citizen to the modern State, and
a 'mode of confronting social changes' (Hobsbawm 1972:
404). Its appearance is broadly coeval with the spread of
market relationships, although it first takes root 'in areas (and
perhaps strata) for whom "modernisation" was sufficiently
present to present problems . . . but not sufficiently advanced
to offer solutions' (Hobsbawm 1972: 399). The solutions
advanced by nationalists involve remaking the present in the
image of a common past—possibly real, usually imagined.

Nationalism moves forward, in Nairn's terms, by a 'certain sort of regression' (Nairn 1981: 348); nationalists confront the new, often create the new, in terms which evoke the old and hallowed. Nationalism is a peculiar form of the modern political imagination concerned, above all, with the problem of change and the 'secular transformation of fatality into continuity, contingency into meaning' (Anderson 1983: 19).[6]

In Tenna, Hobsbawm's two phenomena are simply two aspects of one process, two ways of delivering the same message—a message about who we are and what our relationship to each other is. The message is endlessly reiterated in village oratory, and endlessly enacted in village ritual. At this level we are dealing with a kind of endogenous nationalism, created and recreated at the local level by local agents for whom it provides perhaps the only clear image of the good social life in a world of dizzying change. If we step back a little, though, we can situate it more accurately on the boundary of change and in the cultural gap between local knowledge and the wider world.

The circumstances of change I have described for Tenna are sufficiently large to need little further emphasis. In fifty years the population has increased more than ten times, and much of this increase came in a wave of immigration from more crowded districts elsewhere in the island. There has been a transformation in health as a result of the near total eradication of malaria; death in childhood, still the norm fifty years ago, is a rare occurrence now. Children of Tenna now go to university in the cities; fifty years ago there was no school. Contact with the *sangha* and the formal institutions of Buddhism was limited by distance, and religious values were preserved and transmitted in idiosyncratic local oral traditions; now the *pansala* serves as a focus for village activity, and the teachings of the Buddha are available in pamphlets, books, and preaching (both at the *pansala* and over the State radio service). Newspapers arrive every day and are read avidly. The economy was based in the past on paddy and chena and was very largely oriented to subsistence. Now there is a great diversity of work, including important cash-based activities like gemming and cash-cropping. Traders in the past, were almost by definition outsiders—itinerant Muslims who would barter salt and cloth for chena crops. Now sons of Tenna are running vegetables to the Colombo markets while others engage in elaborate and ruthless wheeler-dealing in the gem trade.

The bulk of these changes can be traced back to the crucial decade between 1935 and 1945. In that period the road to town was constructed, the *pansala* founded, the school started, and malaria reduced by the first spraying. In other words 'material' change (population, transport) and 'cultural' change (school and temple) are coeval. The agents of change were the State, which built the road and provided health care, and local people who operated on the boundary between the old order and the inrushing new. The founder of the *pansala* was a *vahumpura* immigrant who worked for the *raṭē mahatmayā*, as well as trading along the new road, and working the old village paddy and chena. The school was started by overseers on the commercial chena operation which swept across the village during the Second World War. More recent cultural innovators have been people like Cyril and Mr Ariyaratna, both of whom have married into the village from outside, and both of whom are, in their rather different ways, familiar with the different cultural nuances of town and village, schoolroom and paddy-field.

The village is being gradually reimagined in the image of the nation. The rituals at the *pansala* were explicitly intended to bring people together. This is done by emphasizing what is common—Buddhism as represented by the bo tree and the *sangha*—and finding new ways of enacting that commonness, for example, the division and reaggregation of the community in the arrangements to mark *vas*. The Christians in the village—now mostly Sinhala in terms of the national divide (Stirrat 1984)—tended to participate uneasily on the fringes of these activities. The Muslims remained excluded. And, all the while, the process of reimagination involves false trails and contest—stories and interpretations which fail to find a sympathetic audience, refusal or rejection of some new version of the present or the past. I have described elsewhere some of the ways in which local interpretations are resisted and contested (Spencer n.d.a). The Muslims who stand apart from the *pansala* rituals can remind us of all the groups who are excluded by the national style of political imagination. The most tragically visible of these, of course, are the Tamils of the north and east.

The village in which I lived was absorbed in a long process of remaking itself in a new image. This can be seen in the response when I asked the smallest children at the village school to make a picture of 'our village.' All of the pictures represented the village through three borrowed symbols: tank, paddy-field, and stupa. These are the three national symbols of rural order, and it mattered little that one of these had only recently been rebuilt, the second provided work for only a fraction of these children's parents, and the third did not yet exist. The children had been provided with a visual mnemonic for 'our village' which, more than anything, made 'our village' an integral part of the nation as an imagined community of villages (cf. Moore 1985; Tennekoon 1988).

Politics and the Nation

In the course of this book I have tried to reverse the terms in which we customarily understand rural politicization in Sri Lanka. Nationalism, often treated as a survival of older, 'primordial' ties, is, I have argued, both a symptom and a cause of much recent change. Party politics, on the other hand, which are often thought of as a recent and disruptive arrival in the countryside, are partly an old and familiar phenomenon dressed in modern form. At its most fundamental that phenomenon is the inability to settle differences of standing and position within a purely local idiom of social worth. At least since the period of British rule, the question who you are and what you are worth has been habitually referred upward to various agents of the State for settlement. In the nineteenth century these agents—the judges confronted with obsessively litigious peasants, the Government Agents reading endless petitions of complaint—were largely baffled by the role they had inadvertently assumed. The emergence of party politics since the introduction of universal suffrage in 1931 has provided a different institutional form for many of the same processes. At the same time, the growing role of the

State as a distributor of resources in this period, means that
the allocation of worth has as often as not taken a material as
well as a moral form.

One tempting way to view this—implicit in much village
talk of politics—is to treat politics and nationalism as
complementary but different things. Nationalism is a necessary idiom of unity and amity; politics an equally necessary if
regrettable idiom of division and abuse. For example, one day
I came upon Appuhami *mudalāli* reading a pamphlet called
Kavuda Koṭiya? (Who is the Tiger?). On the cover of the
pamphlet was a cartoon of the TULF leader Amirthalingam
starting back from a mirror, out of which, in place of his
reflection, sprang a ferocious tiger, the symbol of the
separatist fighters. The pamphlet was one of a number
distributed at the time of the 1981 communal unrest by a
notoriously anti-Tamil cabinet minister.[7] 'What's this?' I
asked. 'I didn't know you were interested in politics?' 'This
isn't politics (*dēsapālanaya*),' was Appuhami's reply, 'this is
about the national question (*jātika prasnaya*).'

Implicit in this was the view that nationalism was somehow
'above' politics. Politics, in village discourse, provided an
explanation for all sorts of personal animosities. Differences
and arguments which seemed to me to have their roots
elsewhere were frequently represented as political differences.
In January 1983 one rich Old Tenna farmer organized a large
kirimaḍuva to bring Mangara's blessings down on his old and
sick mother, who had recently suffered a stroke. As is the way
of these things, the farmer stayed up all night drinking while
the ritual proceeded. By the next morning he was in a state of
advanced emotional disarray. At this point he remembered
his simmering disagreement with another farmer whose
buffaloes, he claimed, had eaten his paddy crop. He
announced that he was going to kill his adversary and set off
to find him. Fortunately for all concerned, mutual friends were
easily able to forewarn the buffalo-owner while the other man
was still crashing drunkenly along the jungle paths to his
house. Afterwards, though, everyone explained the event to
me as the result of the first man having recently transferred
from the SLFP, of which the buffalo-owner was still a
stalwart, to the UNP. It was much more convenient for

everyone concerned to treat this as the cause—rather than merely another symptom—of the rift.

But Appuhami's distinction was, for all that, disingenuous. After all the author of the pamphlet was himself a leading politician of less than spotless reputation. And any attempt to apportion responsibility for the continuing national crisis in Sri Lanka must start with the politicians and the dynamics of the political process. In 1931, electoral politics were thrust upon a small, heavily Anglicized and politically docile elite who were accustomed to a favoured status as intermediaries between the colonial rulers and the colonial ruled. To ensure the continuation of that status in the future a new relationship had to be created with the ruled. As Nairn rather cynically puts it in his assessment of nationalism as a global phe-nomenon, 'The new middle-class intelligentsia of nationalism had to invite the masses into history; and the invitation-card had to be written in a language they understood' (Nairn 1981: 340). In fact, in Sri Lanka this invitation took place in two stages. The 'middle-class intelligentsia of nationalism' wrote the invitation all right—this took the form of cultural revival and religious assertion in the second half of the nineteenth century—but they never delivered it. This was left to a slightly different group, the more culturally remote elite figures— figures like the Oxford-educated Anglican-turned-Buddhist S. W. R. D. Bandaranaike— who emerged as Sri Lanka's new political class in the 1930s.[8]

The structure of the political system (neither Kandyan politician nor Jaffna politician needed to worry about offending the other's constituents) and the circumstances of the new politics (power was given without asking and no show of unified opposition was needed to wrest it from the colonial rulers) both encouraged the use of sectional appeals in the writing of the invitation. Even so, the first generation of political leaders was wary of unnecessary communal division. It was Bandaranaike's populist election triumph of 1956 which set the terms for the future uses of national rhetoric in political appeal. Bandaranaike's appeal was boosted by popular enthusiasm for the celebrations of the Buddha *jayanti* (the 2,500th anniversary of his death) that year, and by the active participation of many Buddhist monks in his campaign. The key issue of the campaign was language—the replacement of the colonial language with Sinhala as the language of government. Within two years the ousted UNP was itself using the combined appeal of religion and language in its opposition to the first and most promising attempt to settle the Tamil problem, the Bandaranaike–Chelvanayagam pact. Another year and Bandaranaike was dead at the hands of a Buddhist monk, apparently acting on the orders of one of the country's most senior and powerful Buddhist leaders.[9]

Since 1956 some public agreement with the tenets of Sinhala Buddhist nationalism has been the precondition for almost all participation in national political power. Individual Muslims, Christians, and Tamils have been members of successive cabinets, but none of them have been able to use this position to challenge the central vision of nationalist ideology which remains a *sine qua non* for all national political discourse. The main challengers, of course, have been the representatives of the Sri Lanka Tamil population; their reward has been their exclusion, first from a share of power, and since 1983 from parliament. Meanwhile, every major opposition party since 1956 has used the charge of abandoning Buddhism and betraying the interests of the Sinhala people as one of the simplest and most effective ways of challenging the authority of the government. Such tactics have been sufficient to destroy every settlement and deal with the slightest prospect of appeasing the disaffected Tamil minority. Since the 1987 peace agreement with India, a number of left-wing politicians have publicly aligned themselves with the terms of the agreement and the need for communal harmony; they (and leading figures in the UNP) have been subject to a campaign of intimidation—which has included the assassination of popular leaders like Vijaya Kumaranatunga, Mrs Bandaranaike's film-star son-in-law—apparently by the resurgent and increasingly chauvinist JVP.

But there are a number of reasons why we should be wary of simply endorsing Nairn's view of nationalism as primarily a product of the attempt of 'peripheral' elites to enlist the political support of 'the masses.' The first is that the originators of nationalism are different from the subsequent users of nationalism. The ideas which someone like Bandaranaike employed were already in circulation before his birth; his achievement was to make them the stuff of public political discourse. They were born in circumstances of large-scale social change in the nineteenth century, and similar ideas are being remade and renewed in places like Tenna which are now going through similar changes. In other words, the concerns of those who first put together the ideas were not necessarily—still are not necessarily—the cold-blooded man-ipulation of popular passions.

They were rather the concerns of people attempting to make sense of a particular set of historical circumstances—people like the turn-of-the-century leader Anagarika Dharma-pala, born to a rich Buddhist family, but educated at a Christian school. The problems from which his propagandiz-ing sprang, according to Obeyesekere, were first of all personal problems:

His lack of roots in the traditional social structure—the absences of village, caste or regional identities—impelled him to seek his identity in Buddhism. Moreover, insofar as he lacked local identities like caste he could appeal to all sectors of the educated Sinhalese. His religious conflicts led him to be an inveterate and implacable foe of the Christian missions, and he brought into Buddhism the zeal, enthusiasm and bigotry that characterised the missionary dialectic. (Obeyesekere 1979: 302)

The source of Dharmapala's new synthesis of Buddhist identity and Christian proselytizing was his own sense of sociological weightlessness. The appeal of his teaching was to other people similarly placed, at once part and not part of the world of their own childhood, people, to paraphrase Hobs-bawm, for whom modernity constituted a problem without offering a solution.

The fact that nationalism appears to emanate from points in the social and historical order for which there are no simple or convenient labels must be one powerful source of its continuing appeal. The patrician politicians of the 1930s who sought to inherit the colonial mantle were far too distant from their would-be subjects in terms of class, culture, and style of life to come up with a set of political images with this kind of appeal. The appeal of nationalism is above all a vertical appeal which cuts across differences of class. This fact explains why nationalism is so often used by those who would seek to attract the support of people whose class interests are very different from their own. It does not explain why it is nationalism that has that appeal.

If we need to differentiate the origins of nationalism from the first political uses of its imagery, we now need to take account of a further process. The generation of politicians in power in Sri Lanka during my work in Tenna, with a few exceptions like Jayewardene himself, were people who had grown up politically since the first electoral triumph of Bandaranaike's populism in the 1950s. If nationalism has an appeal which can cut vertically across divisions of class and culture, then it can command the passions of those at the top as much as it can command the passions of those at the bottom. The political and class interests of Sri Lanka's rulers in the late 1970s and early 1980s would have been best served by a speedy settlement of the Tamil problem. That such a settlement was not achieved must in part be attributed to the rulers' own reluctance to depart from the imperatives of what they saw as national destiny. The force of nationalism can imprison rulers and ruled alike (cf. Kapferer 1988).

But this is to give nationalism a transcendent power and, in the current context, to deny the possibility of ever breaking free of the destructive course of recent Sri Lankan politics. The first flaw in such an argument is obvious enough. If nationalism is born of particular historical and social circumstances, and gathers its strength from those circumstances, then a change in one should bring on a change in the other. It is possible to imagine, given time and a degree of peace, that Sinhala nationalism could sink quietly into the political background. The analogy would be with English identity as a political force; it is certainly present in British political culture—witness the success of the Falklands campaign—yet it remains in large part implicit rather than explicit, only summoned up when overtly (or apparently) challenged. To specify exactly what those 'changed circumstances' might be would—require another, bigger book—a comparative enquiry into the political economy of intolerance. The comparative question is irrelevant for now because Sinhala nationalism has never passed without challenge from at least one corner of the State—the north and east—and such challenges have presented ample opportunity for the constant assertion and reassertion of nationalist ideology.[10]

We can glimpse a second chink in the armour of nationalist inevitability if we return to Appuhami's attempt to differentiate nationalism from politics. To characterize this as 'disingenuous' because nationalism is steeped in the political was ungenerous. It would be better to call it idealistic. Ideally, for someone like Appuhami, nationalism and the national question would indeed be above politics and the seamy dispute of the political. One can see this ideal distinction on every political platform. There on the one side are the politicians and their followers and hangers-on. There on the other side are the *sangha*. But, in nearly all cases nowadays, the *sangha* witnesses the political rally without participating; its presence signifies a symbolic ratification of the legitimacy of the proceedings in nationalist terms. The *sangha* commands the deference of politicians because, as guardian of the nation's destiny, it is above politics. Its many political interventions in recent years have been prefaced with references to this 'time of national danger.' They are not, it is made plain, speaking politics, they are speaking on behalf of the nation; they represent unity not division. But if a monk does address a political meeting he is liable to face a great deal of criticism; that kind of *public* political activity is widely felt to be inappropriate. The only monk I ever saw address a political rally in the Belangala area devoted much of his speech to a defence of his right to speak in such a context.

But of course the *sangha* is involved in politics. References to 'SLFP monks' and 'UNP monks' are as common as references to 'SLFP families' and 'UNP families.' Mostly, though, they are involved in backroom politics rather than the institutionalized acrimony of public politics. When Cyril started arguing with the monk at the Tenna SLFP rally (see above p. 85) there was a great deal of pained embarrassment all round at the resulting cultural dissonance. When Bandaranaike was killed by a monk, there was a wave of hostility to the clergy all over the country, or so I was told by older members of the *sangha* who still remembered being forced to stand on buses as passengers refused to offer them a seat, all the while aware of muttered comments like 'Where has he hidden his gun?' The respect and deference ordinarily visible in all dealings with the clergy is in fact conditional on their staying in their allotted place. If they become too publicly associated with politics they are in danger of losing that place.

It is possible that the power of nationalist discourse is similarly vulnerable to the cynicism which attaches itself to all things political. I argued earlier that while politics is a way of attaining standing and position, it also, by its very nature, undermines all claims to standing. As an idiom of public challenge, it means that the attainment of position is inevitably accompanied by the threat of public humiliation. So too nationalism may become sullied by its long association with the political. The post-1977 UNP government has invested very heavily (and, I suspect, successfully in many cases) in various forms of state ritual—ever grander opening ceremonies, rallies, and so on. But some critics of these ceremonies assert that they are political 'manipulations' of religion (Tennekoon 1988: 306). The very fact that politicians are more and more overtly exploiting the symbolic treasure trove of Buddhist nationalism may, in time, cheapen the force of the symbols. But even criticisms like the ones quoted by Tennekoon gain their force from the presupposition that there is some right, non-manipulatory use of such ritual elements. As Tennekoon points out, the image of culture represented in such rituals is not in itself challenged in these criticisms (Tennekoon 1988: 306).

Perhaps the most important point is that Sinhala Buddhist nationalism is a young creature. The individual elements in its constitution are, in some cases, very old indeed but the package itself is much younger. It has been politically dominant in the country for thirty years. More than forty years ago it had barely touched people in a place like Tenna. During my stay it formed, with politics, the dominant idiom in which people could represent their society and their place in it. But it remains an idiom not a canon. The ways in which people were using the idiom in Tenna were often new and always changing. I doubt very much if Sri Lanka has yet exhausted the possible ways of imagining itself as a community. There are other stories yet untold. And in that fact there lies some hope.

Nationalism, Culture, and Ideology

What then of my disturbing reflections at the *pansala* on the penultimate day of my fieldwork? If I could interpret Mr Ariyaratna's talk of the longevity of Sinhala culture as somehow evidence of its novelty, was I right to suspect that the talk of 'culture' rendered the self-evidence of that ever-slippery concept equally problematic? To start thinking in those terms is to enter an anthropological hall of mirrors, as both the vocabulary of analysis and the terms to be analysed, bounce back from unexpected directions and with unexpected shifts and distortions. In the end, and after much further reflection and heartache, I think the effect of Mr Ariyaratna's reflections was salutary—salutary, because above all they served as a reminder that anthropologist and villager share a common world; they are both trying to make sense of common problems, and to some extent they share the intellectual tools with which they are trying to make sense of them. Those tools are ideas like 'culture,' 'community,' 'history,' and 'tradition.'

The word 'culture' in its anthropological sense can be traced back to that same moment, around the turn of the nineteenth century, to which the modern phenomenon of nationalism is conventionally traced. Herder, for example, is credited with the first use of culture in something like its plural anthropological sense (Williams 1983: 89); and Herder is also claimed as a key figure in the emergence of nationalism in late eighteenth-century Germany (Kedourie 1966: 54–5 and *passim*; cf. Wolf 1983: 387). Moreover, both descriptive and prescriptive uses of 'culture'—high culture and everyday culture—share this provenance. And, according to Williams, rather than dismissing 'loose' or 'incorrect' uses of the term we should instead treat the very diversity of usage as a key to the term's significance: 'The complex of senses indicates a complex argument about the relations between general human development and a particular way of life, and between both and the works and practices of art and intelligence.' (Williams 1983: 91). That was what Mr Ariyaratna's speech signalled to me—not the absence of 'culture,' but the presence of argument. And that, it now seems, is as good a definition as we have of the moment of the nation.

So Gellner, for example, attributes the emergence of nationalism to the necessary cultural transformations attendant upon industrialization and economic growth. Premodern polities were indifferent to cultural differences, whether these were horizontal divisions between ruler and ruled, vertical divisions between different localized units of the ruled, or, as was usually the case, a combination of the two. Modern States depend on their redistributive powers—'universal Danegeld' in Gellner's terms (Gellner 1983: 22)—for their legitimacy, and this requires constant economic and cognitive growth. For this a particular sort of workforce is required: culturally homogeneous and thus potentially adaptable to many different working situations. So the State assumes responsibility for the transmission of culture—through compulsory State-regulated education.

The ideal of nationalism, a unitary bounded territorial State enclosing a culturally homogeneous citizenry, is according to Gellner the product of nationalism, not its prerequisite:

Nationalism is *not* the awakening of an old, latent, dormant force, though that is how it does indeed present itself. It is in reality the consequence of a new form of social organization, based on deeply internalized education-dependent high cultures, each protected by its own state. It uses some of the pre-existent cultures, generally transforming them in the process, but it cannot possibly use them all. There are too many of them. (Gellner 1983: 48)

There are weaknesses in this agrument, most obviously the weakness of all functional arguments which explain a phenomenon by its effects, but as a general description of nationalism it seems to me convincing. Nationalism involves a process of cultural transformation in which local differences come up against an ideal of national similarity.[11] It is a moment of dislocation, then, when a set of familiar and essentially local shared understandings are ranged uneasily alongside a new set of outside assumptions—brought in by way of the schoolroom, the newspaper, and, in Tenna, the *pansala*. Moreover, in Tenna it is also a moment when the force of economic change had already exploded some of the areas of shared activity in which local understandings were based. In this process, fathers and sons, mothers and daughters, neighbours and friends may find themselves talking at cross-purposes, unable to understand the world in which the other is living. Nationalist movements characteristically manifest themselves as 'a species of civil strife between the generations; nationalist movements are children's crusades' (Kedourie 1966: 101). They are, crucially, moments of argument and dispute.

There are various ways in which we might analyse such moments of argument and dispute. The cause can be variously attributed—in approximate order of discursive toughness—to 'uneven development' in the 'world system' (Nairn 1981), the coming of 'print capitalism' (Anderson 1983), the transition to 'industrial society' (Gellner 1983), or, most generally, 'social and intellectual change' (Kedourie 1966). Perhaps 'modernity' (rather than modernization, which implies a unitary process and a known goal) is the safest and most general description of both cause and effect. It is a term which has the advantage of applying equally to the world of the anthropologist and the world of the villager.

The effects of modernity have also been described in various ways. Geertz (1971) talks of the 'struggle for the real' in modern Islamic societies. Gilsenan explains it like this:

For everyone the nature and meaning of society have become a central problem . . . The very bases of political legitimacy and claims to authority are questions of constant relevance and sharply contesting points of view. Social and cultural institutions once part of the taken-for-granted everyday world are equally open to fiercely divergent interpretation. Many of the suppositions and presuppositions that make up culture have come into conscious and often very critical and self-conscious reflection. (Gilsenan 1982: 14)

It is this process of induced—sometimes violently induced- - reflection on areas that in the past could be taken for granted that, in different ways, all these writers are trying to pin down. Bourdieu has characterized this process as a shift from *doxa* to 'opinion,' from 'that which goes without saying because it comes without saying' (Bourdieu 1977: 167). As James Brow, whose description of competing discourses in a northern dry zone village parallels much of my own description of Tenna, puts it: 'Today . . . the social prescriptions of Sinhalese

Buddhist nationalism come in a barrage of saying that is almost incessant' (Brow 1988: 312).

Another way to talk about this area involves the use of that much-abused term 'ideology.' Nationalism is an ideology in that specific and still useful sense of a limited set of ideas about the world which serve as both a model of how the world is and an ideal of how it should be. As Geertz points out, the problem of nationalist intellectuals is in a sense an epistemological one (Geertz 1973: 239); nationalism is one symptom of a 'sort of social changing of the mind' (Geertz 1973: 319).[12] Behind this we can glimpse the decay of an implicit consensus within which the definition of persons and politics were both contained. Both of those are now being avidly defined and re-defined *ad infinitum*. They now come with a plenitude of saying.

Two recent essays on nationalism close with the same borrowed image (Nairn 1981: 359–63; Anderson 1983: 147). It comes from Walter Benjamin's 'Theses on the Philosophy of History,' written in early 1940, the year of Benjamin's refugee suicide on the Spanish border:

A Klee painting named 'Angelus Novus' shows an angel looking as though he is about to move away from something he is fixedly contemplating. His eyes are staring, his mouth is open, his wings are spread. This is how one pictures the angel of history. His face is turned toward the past. Where we perceive a chain of events, he sees one single catastrophe which keeps piling wreckage upon wreckage and hurls it in front of his feet. The angel would like to stay, awaken the dead, and make whole what has been smashed. But a storm is blowing from Paradise; it has got caught in his wings with such violence that the angel can no longer close them. This storm irresistibly propels him into the future to which his back is turned, while the pile of debris before him grows skyward. This storm is what we call progress. (Benjamin 1973: 259–60).

We all aspire to make whole what has been smashed. I certainly saw the storm blowing in Tenna, and in Sri Lanka, and I sometimes hear its presence around me in England too.[13] But what I also saw in Tenna was people battling against the storm, struggling to make something of the debris, building and rebuilding recognizable shapes and structures from the wreckage.

To explain the passion which accompanies that process there is no need, I believe, to invoke sophisticated arguments about 'hierarchy' and 'ontology' (Kapferer 1988). We merely need to see what it is that has been smashed and what it is that is being pieced back together. Lying among the wreckage we can see the comfortable familiarities of place and family, and place and family are the two governing figures in the language of the nation (Hobsbawm 1972: 392). In their self-descriptions, all human societies seem, in different ways, to favour a limited set of metaphors involving begetting and belonging, kin and kind. When, as in Tenna, it becomes less and less possible to maintain the expected amity of kinship and neighbourliness, except by evasion—placing all affectual claims at arm's length—the metaphors do not waste and die as might be expected. Instead they are spread wider. 'Now everyone lives like children of one person' as the old man told me.

As such, these metaphors tap the reservoir of inchoate and contradictory affect—love and hate, desire and disgust—which lurks in our experience of family. Nairn uses a suggestive Freudian parallel in discussing the 'uncontrollability' of the forces released by nationalism:

> The powers of the Id are far greater than was realized before Freud exposed them to theoretical view. In the same way, the energies contained in customary social structures were far greater than was understood, before the advent of nationalist mobilization stirred them up and released them from the old mould. (Nairn 1981: 349)

'The energies contained in customary social structures' may sound suggestive but bland. If so think of the scene in which a young man or woman enters the family home and says 'Father (or mother, or husband, or wife) I have swallowed poison,' as the horrified family have to watch the slow, agonizing—and, as I have suggested, apparently recriminatory—death of their child. This is what Obeyesekere means by the 'ambivalence' of kinship (Obeyesekere 1981: 117), and it is something that happens every day in one village or another in Sri Lanka. We should not be surprised at the depth of feeling sublimated deep within the language of belonging. Nationalism as a genre confronts the threat of meaninglessness and incoherence with a limited but emotionally explosive set of metaphors.

My language has grown more florid and extravagant as this chapter has progressed. To end on such an apocalyptic note would be a betrayal of the dominant tone of my own life in Tenna, a life shared with a group of good and hospitable, if often puzzled and worried, people. I will instead close with a more representative memory. It is of a group of men cutting *kurakkan* on a chena plot in early 1983. The chena has in fact been cleared on land belonging to a big gem-merchant whose rice mill can be seen through the long grass nearby; it has been cultivated by a *beravā* family, who act as his agents and clients in the village. One old man is leading the cutters (including a rather self-conscious anthropologist who has put his notebook to one side to join in) through what he remembers of the old *kurakkan*-cutting songs (*kavi*). This is the only plot of *kurakkan* on chena in Tenna this season; next year there may be none at all. Standing to one side of the group is a young man, a son of the cultivator of the plot, holding a tape recorder with which he is recording what is left of the songs.

NOTES

[1] A very great deal has been written on the July 1983 violence. See especially Meyer (1984), Obeyesekere (1984b), Nissan (1984), Committee for Rational Development (1984), Goonetileke (1984), Tambiah (1986). I provide a slightly fuller account of the view from Tenna in Spencer (1984b).

[2] In 1983 I wrote '[the violence] would have been impossible had there been any measured show of opposition from the Sinhalese population' (Spencer 1984b: 188). One recent commentator has recently repeated precisely this mistake: 'Most Sinhalese did not participate in the killing of July 1983. Nontheless, many watched, without acting, while Tamils burned' (Kapferer 1988:83). Looking back I have to confess that I have no idea what 'measured show of opposition' I could have had in mind; only someone who has never been near a murderous mob could argue that a failure to challenge them can be read as a sign of complicity.

[3] The baby story has been circulating for at least thirty years (cf. Vittachie 1958) and I have also heard it attributed to Sinhala attacks on a Tamil baby. It appears to be a fantasy.

[4] A fuller account of these speeches can be found in Nissan (1984). On the possible role of the UNP in the violence see Tambiah (1986: 32–3); on the background to such involvement see Obeyesekere (1984b).

[5] I am grateful to Mark Whitaker for this quote.

[6] I develop this argument and provide further evidence of local nationalist interpretations in Spencer (n.d.a.). I also make it clear there that I believe the similarity between the Mahavamsa and modern nationalist discourse is

as much a similarity of style as a similarity of content. The Mahavamsa is not itself a nationalist text (Gunawardana 1984; cf. Bechert 1973), it is above all 'about' the proper relationship of king and *sangha*, not people and State. As well as providing key symbols for nationalist *bricolage*, the Mahavamsa shares with contemporary nationalist discourse a common stance toward history and change. Both see history as following a necessary preordained pattern; both, like medieval European chroniclers, display events as 'models of the course of the world' (Benjamin 1973: 96).

[7] The minister in question was Cyril Mathew, who was sacked some months after the 1983 riots and whose name has been frequently associated with the organized gangs at work in the riots (e.g. by the magazine *India Today*; Tambiah 1986: 32–3). For examples of his characteristic style see the extracts from his speeches and writings reprinted in the journal *Race and Class* (Mathew 1984).

[8] For the nineteenth-century sources of national revival see Malalgoda (1976), Roberts (1979b); for the use of sectional rhetoric in the politics of the 1930s see Russell (1982), Meyer (1982).

[9] James Manor's forthcoming biography of Bandaranaike promises to provide much needed detail on the political career of this pivotal figure. On the politics of the 1950s see Wriggins (1960).

[10] There are examples of minorities who have retained their cultural distinctiveness while accommodating themselves to the political imperatives of Sinhala Buddhist nationalism—Christians (Stirrat 1984), Muslims (De Silva 1986), and Indian Tamils. Such 'accommodation' has usually taken the form of turning a blind eye, biting the tongue when provoked, and grumbling a great deal among themselves. De Silva (1986) holds the Muslims up as an example of how to 'manage' ethnic tensions. Kapferer on the other hand seems to argue that the 'ontology' of Buddhist nationalism is inherently intolerant and dangerous if provoked; his solution to the problem is for the government to remove 'ethnic identity and hierarchy as dominant state-sanctified principles of political and social order' (Kapferer 1988: 114).

As for the comparative dimension in the study of nationalism, it seems essential to me that such a study should take account of two crucial variables. The first is the relative 'youth' or 'maturity' (in some cases 'senescence') of any particular nationalism, which, as the example of Tenna makes clear, must include the uneven development of national consciousness within a particular national territory at a specifc historical moment. The second is the 'political ecology' of any particular nationalism—the extent to which it is subject to explicit challenge, either internal or external, verbal or physical. Most material on nationalism concentrates on the stridencies of national awakening. What we lack are convincing studies of the chimerical forms of mature 'background' nationalisms.

[11] The other side of Gellner's description is less convincing in Tenna, or in Sri Lanka more generally. The culture that is being forged in Sinhala

nationalism is transparently inadequate as the ground for a shift into an industrial economy. The language base is simply too small for translation of technical texts to be feasible on a useful scale. Competence in English, despite the 1956 reforms, is a key diacritic in broader class relations in the country, and remains essential for all who aspire to any kind of technical or professional employment. By the early 1980s there were thousands of small, private English classes to be found in both rural and urban areas. It is only an apparent paradox that key local articulators of nationalist ideology, like Mr Ariyaratna, were also the most skilled in the use of English. What the cultural transformation of nationalism seemed to be doing was creating a new homogeneity of experience in certain rather special areas of life: the most obvious loci of common experience were the schoolroom and the *pansala*. In other words there were different spheres of culture emerging: something like a high culture (school, *pansala*), 'English' culture (towns, universities, professionals), and the myriad fragments of different everyday cultures. One could also add areas like trade which used an idiom known as 'pavement *bāsāva*' (pavement language, street talk); this delightful tongue combines English and Sinhala elements in often startling ways ('*hari* [very] fashion' as someone said when I finally succumbed to the clamour to move into slick polyester trousers and out of scruffy blue denim). This again confirms Williams's advice to concentrate on the *different* connotations of 'culture,' and the tensions between them.

[12] Of course, if nationalism is a product of perceived discontinuity, while politics is but a new version of an old cultural game, then we can being to make some sense of the oft-reported absence of ideological difference as a major theme in the discourse of Sinhala rural politics (Brow 1988: 315; cf. Moore 1985: 224). As Geertz says, 'In truly traditional political systems the participants act as . . . men of untaught feelings . . . The role of ideology, in any explicit sense, is marginal' (Geertz 1973: 218). I would hesitate to label Tenna's politics (or anything else) 'truly traditional', but there is some sense in arguing that the understanding of the role of the State has changed less than, say, the understanding of the meaning of 'community' or 'kinship.'

[13] It is worth juxtaposing Benjamin's bleak reflection with a very different use of a similar metaphor. The user is Benjamin's friend Brecht, speaking through his Galileo, in exile two years earlier: 'What is written in the old books is no longer good enough. For where faith has been enthroned for a thousand years doubt now sits. Everyone says: right, that's what it says in the books, but let's have a look for ourselves. That most solemn truths are being familiarly nudged; what was never doubted before is doubted now. That has created a draught which is blowing up the gold-embroidered skirts of the prelates and princes, revealing the fat and skinny legs underneath, legs like our own. The heavens, it turns out, are empty. Cheerful laughter is our response.' *Life of Galileo* I (Brecht 1980: 7).

Epilogue

It is almost five years since I left Tenna for the second time in 1984. Those five years have not been happy years in Sri Lanka. The events of 1982 and 1983—the Presidential election, the referendum to prolong the life of parliament, the anti-Tamil riots, even the Sinhala-Tamil divide itself—can now be seen as symptoms of a longer process of deepening political crisis on the island. It would be foolish to pretend that the experience of one anthropologist in one village could possibly provide the key to understanding this long crisis in the Sri Lankan polity. Moreover, the rise in political violence in the Sinhala south of the country since 1987 precludes, on ethical as well as practical grounds, any detailed discussion of the effect of the crisis on local politics. Instead, I merely want to sketch in the bare outlines of post-1984 political developments, and trace one or two obvious connections between my account of local politics and subsequent trends in national politics.

This book has focused on two problems in Sri Lankan ethnography, both of which are at the heart of the crisis: the central place of party politics in Sinhala village life; and the tenacious hold of Sinhala Buddhist nationalism. The government of the new President, Ranasinghe Premadasa, has faced two serious political threats to its control. From 1987 the north and east of the island were under the *de facto* control of the Indian Peace-Keeping Force (IPKF), a situation which the Colombo government has attempted to resolve through a bizarre mixture of diplomacy (including recent talks with the Tigers in Colombo) and belligerent public rhetoric. Meanwhile in the south, the JVP returned to something like its 1971 strength, although its tactics were now more controlled and more effective; strikes, shutdowns, and selective assassinations instead of the uncoordinated frontal assault on State power of the 1971 Insurrection. The response to this was counter-terror from the security forces, disappearances, torture, and death-squads in southern villages. The two crises were inter-dependent: the JVP demanded the removal of the Indian 'occupiers,' and drew on the popular appeal of Sinhala nationalism to challenge the legitimacy of the Colombo regime.[1]

After the 1971 Insurrection the JVP was proscribed and a number of its leaders jailed. They were released after the UNP election victory in 1977, and for a few years in the late 1970s and early 1980s the party attempted to establish itself in electoral politics. The referendum in 1982, which artificially preserved the parliamentary balance of 1977, ended that hope, and in 1983 the JVP moved underground again after it was rather implausibly accused of involvement in the July riots.[2] In late 1986 and early 1987 rumours started to circulate of a return to the violent tactics of the early 1970s: an anti-JVP student leader was kidnapped and brutally murdered in Colombo, and there were a number of thefts of weapons from the security forces in the south. The signing of the peace agreement between Rajiv Gandhi and J. R. Jayewardene in July 1987, and the subsequent arrival of the troops of the IPKF, gave the JVP its biggest boost. It had by now shed those leaders who favoured a policy of secular, non-ethnic socialism, and had instead reaffirmed its old anti-Indian Sinhala nationalist position. From July 1987, local UNP officials were attacked, as well as representatives of those parties of the left who had supported the peace accord. The level of violence escalated through the election campaign which brought Premadasa to the Presidency in late 1988, and continued through the parliamentary elections of early 1989. Despite occasional lulls, the assassinations, strikes, and disappearances have continued through the first half of 1989.

Even this skeletal outline raises questions which cannot be resolved here. What, if any, continuity is there between the JVP of the early 1970s and the JVP of the late 1980s? Is this a continuity of ideology, a continuity of personnel, or both? The most common and convincing explanation of the 1971 Insurrection attributed it to the growing contradiction between the aspirations of a large and growing sector of well-educated but under-employed youth and the dwindling ability of the State to meet those aspirations. Is this essentially demographic explanation still adequate almost twenty years later?

The evidence in this book is too partial and limited to answer questions on this scale. But it is possible to see how each of the components of local politics I describe in Tenna can be discerned beneath the surface of recent events.[3] Since Independence rural politics in Sinhala Sri Lanka have been based on two central ideological features. One is the role of the State as a distributor of material resources, which, after Moore (1985), I have called the politics of welfarism. The other is the symbolism of Sinhala Buddhist hegemony. One additional feature I have identified is the embeddedness of politics in everyday life, and the tendency for people to pursue what might be thought private grievances in the idiom of public party politics. All three of these features can be seen to have played their part in the background to the current crisis.

The decision to circumvent the need for parliamentary elections by the referendum of 1982 is an obvious point of departure for any analysis of the subsequent crisis. The UNP's decision, and its subsequent tactics, deprived it of whatever legitimacy it may have enjoyed from its electoral victory in 1977. Opposition parties felt themselves cheated out of a chance to regain power; local supporters of the opposition found themselves cheated out of any share in the flood of resources which the UNP government had distributed to its followers in earlier years. But even UNP supporters were unlikely to be satisfied with the decline in available patronage during the mid 1980s as the security crisis took its toll on the economy. The effect of the referendum was to add an extra dimension of bitterness and injustice to the recurrent Sri Lankan political dilemma of too many expecting too much from a State with too little to distribute.

But the deteriorating security situation in the north and east after the 1983 riots at least provided the government with a distraction and some sort of excuse for its failure to live up to welfarist expectations. The Indian intervention in 1987 deprived them of that alibi. The 1987 agreement was seen as a betrayal of the central tenets of Sinhala Buddhist nationalism. The UNP leadership was not merely an inadequate source of patronage for its own supporters, or an unjust monopolist of State power for the opposition; it now became, for many, a group of traitors. Moreover, parliamentary opposition had been steadily devalued by a combination of constitutional tampering, as exemplified by the 1982 referendum, and simple incompetence on the part of the main opposition party, the SLFP. Instead opposition to the Indian presence coalesced around the revived JVP and its often violent tactics of extra-parliamentary protest, and in so doing, added a frightening new dimension to the already vicious idiom of local politics. The government is faced simultaneously with a collapse of welfarist policies, a loss of nationalist legitimacy, and the smouldering resentment in hundreds of towns and villages of too many years of a kind of power which, as the rest of this book shows, intrudes again and again in people's everyday circumstances.

If one word were to describe Sri Lankan politics in 1989 it is 'impossibilism.' President Premadasa demanded the withdrawal of Indian troops, knowing he has no means to enforce his demand, and promised a war on poverty, knowing that the economy could not even sustain the State's current commitments let alone take on any new expenditure. The JVP also demanded Indian withdrawal, but in the unlikely event of it capturing power, there was no reason to think it could enforce this demand. The Indian forces remained in place, partly to protect one set of Indian protégés (the new Provincial Councils) from the attacks of an earlier set (the Tigers, who had now become the main enemy of the IPKF); the stability Delhi is said to want off its southern shore was as remote as ever.[4]

But circumstances change quickly at times of crisis. I still have difficulty recognizing the Sri Lanka I know in the Sri Lanka described in this epilogue, but I still hope to see a peaceful Sri Lanka again. That will not be brought about by the prognostications of anthropologists and political scientists, still less by the erratic interventions of foreign governments. It can only come through the efforts of Sri Lankan people themselves.

NOTES

[1] These are merely the most critical of a series of critical problems; the condition of the economy would in other circumstances be thought sufficiently serious to threaten the stability of the government.

[2] The JVP's subsequent identification with virulent Sinhala chauvinism may make the government's case in 1983 look more convincing than it did at the time, but it is worth remembering that no convincing evidence has ever been produced to support the claim that the JVP, along with other leftist groups, was responsible for organizing that violence.

[3] At the risk of tiresome repetition, I should again stress that this epilogue is in no way based on events in Tenna after my departure, but is merely an attempt to extrapolate from my experience in the early 1980s to accounts of rural politics in the late 1980s.

[4] This is not the place to analyse the tragic consequences of short-sighted Indian interference in Sri Lankan affairs. It is worth noting, though, how positive moves like the 1987 accord have been cancelled by the lingering effects of earlier negative moves like the cynical support of the Tigers in the early 1980s.

Glossary

Terms which occur only once in the text are glossed where they appear and are not listed here. I have, with only a few exceptions, followed the orthography in Carter's Dictionary (1965). Occasionally in the text I have quoted examples from speech in which a few common suffixes have been used; the most important of these are: *-k, -ek* (indefinite e.g. *gama* 'the village,' *gamak* 'a village'); *-ṭa* (dative e.g. *gamaṭa* 'to the village'); *-gē, -ē* (genitive e.g. *gamē* 'of the village'); *-yi* (copula e.g. *lajja* 'shame,' *lajjayi* '(is, has) shame').

Roman entries are Anglo-Indian or Anglo-Sinhala.

ādambara	proud, swaggering
AGA	Assistant Government Agent
akkā	elder sister
Amarapura Nikāya	one of the three primary divisions ('fraternities') of the *sangha* in contemporary Sri Lanka
amunam, pl. *amunu*	unit of sowing extent = 4 *päla*
andē	sharecropping
anicut	dam across river to feed canal
ankeliya	the horn game, a ritual for the goddess Pattini
āracci	village headman
Äsäla	lunar month corresponding to August
äsäla perahara	annual *perahara* in Kandy
asweddumize, -ation	(Sinhala *asvädun karanavā*) clearing and terracing of land for paddy cultivation

aṭasil	the Eight Precepts, taken by the most pious lay people
aṭavaka poya	quarter-moon day
attam	reciprocal labour relationship
avurudda	Sinhala New Year (April)
bahirayā	chthonic spirit of place
bana	formal preaching; hence *bana sālāva* preaching-hall
bǟnā	son-in-law, nephew
baṇḍāra	lord; hence *baṇḍāra iḍam* lord's land (i.e *nindagam*)
bāsāva	language
baya	fear
beravā	drummer caste
bhakti gī	performance of devotional songs
bhikkhu	Buddhist priest
bhūtayā	ghost, spirit
bidi	kind of cheap cigarette, leaf from which this is made
bintenna	flat lowland plains
bisnis	business, trade
bōdhi	bo-tree, under which Buddha attained enlightenment; hence *bōdhipuja* act of worship of bo-tree
bōnci	beans
boru	lies; hence *boru kārayā* liar; *boru kiyana davasa* lie-telling day, 1 April
budupuja	act of worship to the Buddha
chena	(Sinhala *hēn*) swidden cultivation
CTB	Ceylon Transport Board
dāgäba	stupa
dānē, danaya	formal offering of food to the *sangha*
dāyakayā	lay donor to the *sangha*
dēsapālanaya	politics
dēvālē	shrine to a deity

deyyō	deity
dharma	the teachings of the Buddha; also the following of these, the nature of the world as revealed in these, etc.
dos(a)	flaw, blemish, malevolent influence
duka, dukkha	sorrow, suffering
Ealam	putative Tamil national State in north and east Sri Lanka
GA	Government Agent
gama, pl. *gam*	village
gamarāla, māha gamarāla	village headman, chief
gansabhāva	village council, revived by colonial administration in nineteenth century
goviyā	farmer, cultivator
goyigama	cultivator caste, usually thought to be largest and highest Sinhala caste
grāmasēvaka, abbrev. GS	village servant, successor to village headman
gurunnänsē, pl. *-lā*	revered teacher, used to address members of *beravā* caste
hāmuduruvō, pl. *-varū*	lord, now restricted to Buddhist clergy
hari	very
havula	partnership, connection
hēn	chena, swidden
honda	good
iḍam	land; hence *iḍam kacceriya* land tribunal
iḍōra kālaya	dry season
irisiyāva	jealousy
jāti(ya)	kind, variety, caste, 'race', 'ethnic group'
jātika prasnaya	national question
jaya	victory, celebration; hence *jayavēva* may he or she receive victory, hooray

JVP (Janata Vimukti Peramuna)	People's Liberation Front, radical party associated with 1971 Insurrection
kachcheri	(Sinhala *kacceriya*) secretariat, local government office; also, in *iḍam kacceriya*, land tribunal
kapa karu dāyakayā	lay donor with responsibility for priest's welfare during *vas*
kapu mahatmayā (kapurāla)	ritual intermediary with deity
karāva	large low-country (fishing) caste
kaṭhina piṇkama	ritual to mark the end of *vas*
kāvaḍi	decorated arch, and associated style of dancing, in honour of the god of Kataragama (Skanda, Murugan)
kavi	verses
kirimaḍuva	ritual to the deity Mangara
kōralē	division of a province, official (subordinate of *raṭē mahatmayā* in colonial period) with jurisdiction over it
kuli vāḍa	wage labour
kurakkan	kind of millet grown on chena
lajja	shame, shyness, restraint
lajja-baya	fear-shame, fear of humiliation
lakh	100,000
LDO	Land Development Ordinance
loku	big; hence *loku minissu* (sing. *minihā*) big people, i.e. wealthy, powerful
macan	mate, cross-cousin
māha	large, great
mahatmayā	honorific; 'sir', 'mister'
Mahaväli	largest river in Sri Lanka; Accelerated Mahaväli Project large combined irrigation and hydro-electric project

mal puja	offering of flowers
mamoty	pick-like digging tool
Mangara (*deyyō*)	deity in whose territory Tenna is thought to lie
māsa poya	new moon
massinā	cross-cousin
minissu, sing. *minihā*	people
mudalāli	merchant, trader
nambuva	dignity, honour, status
nāyaka	chief, leader
Nayakkar	name of the last dynasty of Kandyan kings, of south Indian origin
nāyō	kin
nikāya	division ('fraternity') of the *sangha*
nindagam, sing. *-a*	aristocratic landholdings = *bandāra idam*
nōnā	lady, madam
pāla	(a) temporary hut for watching crops; (b) sowing measure = quarter *amunam*
panata	sharecropping under the terms of the 1958 Paddy Lands Act; hence *panata ayiti* 'panata owner,' one with a sharecropping arrangement under the act who sublets the land to tenant on the old *andē* system
pansala	temple, residence of Buddhist priest
pansil	the Five Precepts taken by all Buddhist lay people
patala	gem-pit
pavula	wife, wife and children, kin
pelantiya	kin-based status group
perahara	ritual procession
pilimagē	statue-house, image-house
pin	merit
pinkama, pl. *-kam*	major Buddhist ritual (lit. merit-making)

pirit	chanting of protective verses, Buddhist ritual of protection
piṭisara	rural
poḍi	small; hence *poḍiaya, poḍi minissu* small people
Poson	lunar month corresponding to June
poya	quarter-days of lunar month
preta	ghost, spirit
puja(va)	act of worship or offering
radala	aristocratic stratum of *goyigama* caste
rāja(yā)	State, government, king
rāja kālaya	the time of the kings, i.e. the pre-colonial period
rālahāmi	honorific address to village headman
Ramanna Nikāya	smallest of the three primary divisions of the *sangha*
rate mahatmayā	Sinhala colonial official, immediately answerable to GA or AGA
roḍiya	lowest beggar caste
sabda pujāva	offering of sound, i.e. drumming
sādhu, sādhu, sā	devotional cry
samitiya	committee
sangha	the order of Buddhist monks
sanghika	food offered to, and formally accepted by, the *sangha*
sanskṛtiya	culture
sāra	strong, harsh
sāsanāraksa samitiya	Buddhist defence committee
sil, sing. *-a*	vows, precepts; hence *sīla viyapāraya* campaign to encourage the observation of the precepts; see *aṭasil, pansil*
sīmā	boundary, esp. around the *sangha* for certain rites; hence *sīmāgē* boundary house
sirit(a)	custom

Siyam Nikāya	the largest of the three primary divisions of the *sangha*, restricted to *goyigama* ordinands
SLFP	Sri Lanka Freedom Party, in power 1956–9, 1960–5, 1970–7
subhasādhika samitiya	good works society
tattvaya	position, situation, standing
tavumbada	urban
Theravada	the school of the elders, the style of Buddhism found in Sri Lanka, Burma, and Thailand
TULF	Tamil United Liberation Front, main opposition party 1977–83, barred from parliament in 1983
uḍa raṭa	up-country, i.e. Kandyan area
UNP	United National Party, in government 1947–56, 1965–70, 1977–
upāsakā, fem. *upāsikā*	lay Buddhist
vāḍa	work
vahumpura	(jaggery-maker) caste
valavva	dwelling-place of *radala* officials
variga	kind, caste, subcaste
vas	(a) (*vas vāsima*) rainy season retreat of the *sangha*; (b) poison; hence *vas kavi* poison-verses, i.e. sorcery
vāsagama	family name, honorific part of family name
vāva	tank, reservoir
Vedda	(Sinhala *vädda*) supposed primitive aboriginal inhabitants of Sri Lanka
vel vidānē	irrigation headman
Vesak	lunar month corresponding to May, celebration of Buddha's birth, enlightenment, and death on full-moon day of this month
vidānē	minor local official

vihāra	place of worship of the Buddha
Vijaya	North Indian prince said to have first colonized the island
visvāsa	belief, faith; hence *visvāsa karanavā* to believe, trust
viyadam	expenses, costs; hence *viyadam kārayā* provider of expenses
yakā, pl. -*ō*	demon
yāya	expanse of paddy-fields

Bibliography

DOCUMENTARY SOURCES

The main documentary sources employed have been those of the Department of National Archives, Colombo. Apart from a few early letters from Lot 6 (Letters from Ratnapura Kachcheri to the Colonial Secretary SLNA 6/), the bulk of the material has been drawn from Lot 45 (Ratnapura Kachcheri Papers SLNA 45/), especially the AGA's and GA's diaries; a few extracts from these have been recently published (Abeyaratne n.d.). A few records were traced to the offices of the Land Settlement Department and a near-complete copy of land transactions was made in the Land Registry in Ratnapura.

OFFICIAL PUBLICATIONS

Administration Report 1877
————— 1885
————— 1887
Census Report 1871
————— 1881
————— 1891
————— 1901
————— 1911
————— 1921
————— 1931
Department of Census and Statistics. 1982. *Statistical Pocket Book of the Democratic Socialist Republic of Sri Lanka.*
Resources of the Walawe Ganga Basin. 1960. *A Report on a Reconnaissance Survey of the Resources of the Walawe Ganga Basin, Ceylon.* Colombo: Ceylon Government Press.
Sessional Paper XVIII. 1951. *Report of the Kandyan Peasantry Commission.*

OTHER PUBLISHED SOURCES

Abeyaratne, M. ed. n.d. *Ratnapura: An Account of the District from Diaries of Government Agents Supplemented from other Records.* Colombo: Department of Government Printing.

Alexander, P. 1981. 'Shared Fantasies and Elite Politics: the Sri Lankan "Insurrection" of 1971.' *Mankind* 12, no. 2: 113–32.

Amunugama, S. and E. Meyer. 1984. 'Remarques sur la violence dans l'idéologie bouddhique et la pratique sociale à Sri Lanka (Ceylan).' *Études Rurales* 95–6: 47–62.

Anderson, B. 1983. *Imagined Communities.* London: New Left Books.

Bechert, H. 1973. 'Sangha, State, Society, "Nation": Persistence of Traditions in "Post-Traditional" Buddhist Societies.' *Dædalus* 102, no. 1: 85–95.

Benjamin, W. 1973. *Illuminations.* London: Fontana.

Bourdieu, P. 1977. *Outline of a Theory of Practice.* Trans. R. Nice. Cambridge: Cambridge University Press.

Brecht, B. 1980. *The Life of Galileo.* Trans. J. Willet. London: Methuen.

Brow, J. 1978. *Vedda Villages of Anuradhapura.* Seattle: University of Washington Press.

———— 1981. 'Class Formation and Ideological Practice: a Case from Sri Lanka.' *Journal of Asian Studies* 40, no. 4: 703–18.

———— 1986. 'Agrarian Change in Sri Lanka's Villages: Local Initiatives and Government Policies.' Paper presented to Annual Meeting of Association for Asian Studies, March, Chicago.

———— 1988. 'In Pursuit of Hegemony: Representations of Authority and Justice in a Sri Lankan Village.' *American Ethnologist* 15, no. 2: 311–27.

Campbell, J. K. 1964. *Honour, Family, and Patronage.* Oxford: Oxford University Press.

Carrithers, M. B. 1982. 'Hell Fire and Urinal Stones: an Essay on Buddhist Purity and Authority.' In *Contributions to South Asian Studies II*, edited by G. Krishna. Delhi: Oxford University Press.

———— 1983. *The Forest Monks of Sri Lanka.* Delhi: Oxford University Press.

Carter, C. 1965. *A Sinhalese-English Dictionary.* Colombo: Gunasena.

Clifford, J. 1986. 'On Ethnographic Allegory.' In *Writing Culture*, edited by J. Clifford and G. E. Marcus. Berkeley and Los Angeles: University of California Press.

Committee for Rational Development. 1984. *Sri Lanka the Ethnic Conflict.* New Delhi: Navrang.

De Silva, A. 1847. 'On the Corruptions of Buddhism and the Different Tenets, Opinions and Principles of the Amarapoora and Siamese Sects.' Appendix XII. In J. Ribeyro, *History of Ceylon.* Trans. by G. Lee. Colombo: Ceylon Government Press.

De Silva, K. M. ed. 1965. *Letters on Ceylon 1846–50. The Administration of Viscount Torrington and the 'Rebellion' of 1848.* Kandy and Colombo: K. V. G. De Silva.

————— ed. 1973. *University of Ceylon History of Ceylon.* Vol. 3. Colombo: Apothecaries Co.

————— 1981. *A History of Sri Lanka.* Delhi: Oxford University Press.

————— 1986. *Managing Ethnic Tensions in Multiethnic Societies: Sri Lanka 1880–1985.* Lanham: University Press of America.

Dumont, L. 1972. *Homo Hierarchicus.* London: Paladin.

Geertz, C. 1971. *Islam Observed.* New Haven: Yale University Press.

————— 1973. *The Interpretation of Cultures.* New York: Basic Books.

————— 1980. *Negara.* Princeton: Princeton University Press.

Gell, A. 1986. 'Newcomers to the World of Goods: Consumption among the Muria Gonds.' In *The Social Life of Things* edited by A. Appadurai. Cambridge: Cambridge University Press.

Gellner, E. 1983. *Nations and Nationalism.* Oxford: Basil Blackwell.

Gilsenan, M. 1976. 'Lying, Honor and Contradiction.' In *Transaction and Meaning* edited by B. Kapferer. Philadelphia: Institute for the Study of Human Issues.

————— 1982. *Recognizing Islam.* London: Croom Helm.

Gombrich, R. F. 1971. *Precept and Practice.* Oxford: Oxford University Press.

Goonatilaka, S. 1984. 'The Formation of Sri Lankan Culture: Reinterpretation of Chronicle and Archaeological Material.' In *Ethnicity and Social Change in Sri Lanka.* Colombo: Social Scientists' Association.

Goonetileke, H. A. I. 1975. *The April 1971 Insurrection in Ceylon. A Bibliographical Commentary.* Louvain: Centre de Récherches Socio-Religeuses, Université de Louvain.

————— 1984. 'July 1983 and the National Question in Sri Lanka: a Bibliographical Guide.' *Race and Class* 26, no. 1: 159–93.

Gunawardana, R. A. L. H. 1984. 'The People of the Lion: Sinhala Consciousness in History and Historiography.' In *Ethnicity and Social Change in Sri Lanka.* Colombo: Social Scientists' Association.

Halliday, F. 1971. 'The Ceylonese Insurrection.' *New Left Review* 69: 55–91.

Harriss, J. 1977. 'Social Implications of Changes in Agriculture in Hambantota District.' In *Green Revolution?* edited by B. H. Farmer. London: Macmillan.

Hellmann-Rajanayagam, D. 1986. 'The Tamil "Tigers" in Northern Sri Lanka: Origins, Factions, Programmes.' *Internationales Asienforum* 17, no. 1/2: 63–85.

Herring, R. J. 1983. *Land to the Tiller.* New Haven: Yale University Press.

Herzfeld, M. 1980. 'Honour and Shame: Problems in the Comparative Analysis of Moral Systems.' *Man* n.s. 15: 339–51.

Hobsbawm, E. 1972. 'Some Reflections on Nationalism.' In *Imagination and Precision in the Social Sciences* edited by T. J. Nossiter, A. H. Hanson and S. Rokkan. London: Faber.

Hocart, A. M. 1950. *Caste*. London: Methuen.

———— 1970. *Kings and Councillors* edited by R. Needham. Chicago: University of Chicago Press.

Horowitz, D. L. 1980. *Coup Theories and Officers' Motives*. Princeton: Princeton University Press.

Jiggins, J. 1979. *Caste and Family in the Politics of the Sinhalese 1947–1976*. Cambridge: Cambridge University Press.

Jones, G. S. 1983. *Languages of Class*. Cambridge: Cambridge University Press.

Joyce, J. 1971. *Ulysses*. Harmondsworth: Penguin.

Jupp, J. 1978. *Sri Lanka: Third World Democracy*. London: Cass.

Kannangara, A. P. 1984. 'The Riots of 1915 in Sri Lanka: a Study of the Roots of Communal Violence.' *Past and Present* 102: 130–65.

Kapferer, B. 1988. *Legends of People Myths of State*. Washington and London: Smithsonian Institution Press.

Kearney, R. N. 1967. *Communalism and Language in the Politics of Ceylon*. Durham, N. C.: Duke University Press.

———— ed. 1970. 'The 1915 Riots in Ceylon: a Symposium.' *Journal of Asian Studies* 29: 219–66.

———— and B. D. Miller. 1983 'Sex-Differential Patterns of Internal Migration in Sri Lanka.' *Peasant Studies* 10: 223–50.

———— 1985. 'The Spiral of Suicide and Social Change in Sri Lanka.' *Journal of Asian Studies*. 44, no. 1: 81–101.

Kedourie, E. 1966. *Nationalism* 3rd edn. London: Hutchinson

Kendrick, A. J. 1984. 'Caste and Temple Service in a Sinhalese Highland Village.' Ph.D. thesis, University of London.

Knox, R. 1681 [1911]. *An Historical Relation of the Island Ceylon*. Glasgow: MacLehose.

Leach, E. R. 1961a. *Pul Eliya*. Cambridge: Cambridge University Press.

———— 1961b. *Rethinking Anthropology*. London: Athlone.

McGilvray, D. B. 1982. '*Mukkuvar Vannimai*: Tamil Caste and Matriclan Ideology in Batticaloa, Sri Lanka.' In *Caste Ideology and Interaction* edited by D. McGilvray. Cambridge: Cambridge University Press.

MacIntyre, A. 1971. 'Is a Science of Comparative Politics Possible?' In *Against the Self-Images of the Age*. London: Duckworth.

Mahavamsa, The. 1960. *The Mahavamsa or the Great Chronicle of Ceylon*. Trans. by W. Geiger. Colombo: Ceylon Government Information Department.

Malalgoda, K. 1970. 'Millennialism in Relation to Buddhism.' *Comparative Studies in Society and History* 12, no. 4: 424–41.

Malalgoda, K. 1972. 'Sinhalese Buddhism: Orthodox and Syncretistic, Traditional and Modern.' *Ceylon Journal of Historical and Social Studies* n.s. 2: 156–69.

———— 1976. *Buddhism in Sinhalese Society 1750–1900.* Berkeley and Los Angeles: University of California Press.

Manor, J. ed. 1984. *Sri Lanka in Change and Crisis.* London: Croom Helm.

Marriott, M. and R. B. Inden. 1974. 'Caste Systems.' In *Encyclopaedia Britannica,* 15th ed.

Mathew, C. 1984. 'The Mathew Doctrine.' *Race and Class* 26, no. 1: 129–38.

Meyer, E. 1980. 'Dépression et Malaria à Sri Lanka 1925–1939'. Unpublished thesis, Paris, École des Hautes Études.

———— 1982. 'Bourgeoisie et Société Rurale à Sri Lanka (1880–1940).' *Purusartha* 6: 223–50.

———— 1983. 'The Plantation System and Village Structure in British Ceylon: Involution or Evolution?' In *Rural South Asia: Linkages, Change and Development* edited by P. Robb. London: Curzon.

———— 1984. 'Seeking the Roots of the Tragedy.' In *Sri Lanka in Change and Crisis* edited by J. Manor. London: Croom Helm.

Moore, B. 1978. *Injustice.* London: Macmillan.

Moore, M. P. 1981a. 'Politics in Sri Lanka: A Review Article.' *Modern Asian Studies* 15, no. 1: 163–9.

———— 1981b. 'The Ideological Function of Kinship: the Sinhalese and the Merina.' *Man* n.s. 16: 579–92.

———— 1985. *The State and Peasant Politics in Sri Lanka.* Cambridge: Cambridge University Press.

Morrison, B. M., M. P. Moore, and M. U. Ishak Lebbe eds. 1979. *The Disintegrating Village.* Colombo: Lake House.

Nairn, T. 1981. 'The Modern Janus.' In *The Break-up of Britain.* 2nd edn. London: New Left Books.

Neale, W. C. 1969. 'Land is to Rule.' In *Land Control and Social Structure in Indian History* edited by R. E. Frykenberg. Madison: University of Wisconsin Press.

Nissan, E. 1984. 'Some Thoughts on Sinhalese Justifications for the Violence.' In *Sri Lanka in Change and Crisis* edited by J. Manor. London: Croom Helm.

———— 1988. 'Polity and Pilgrimage Centres in Sri Lanka.' *Man* n.s. 23: 253–74.

———— and R. L. Stirrat. 1987. 'State, Nation and the Representation of Evil.' *Sussex Research Papers in Social Anthropology* 1.

Nyanawimala, K. 1967. *Saparagamu Darsana* Colombo: Gunasena.

Obeyesekere, G. 1963. 'The Buddhist Pantheon in Ceylon and its Extensions.' In *Anthropological Studies of Theravada Buddhism* edited by M. Nash. New Haven: Yale University Press.

Obeyesekere, G. 1967. *Land Tenure in Village Ceylon*. Cambridge: Cambridge University Press.

————— 1970. 'Religious Symbolism and Political Change in Sri Lanka.' *Modern Ceylon Studies* 1, no. 1: 43–63.

————— 1975. 'Sorcery, Premeditated Murder and the Canalization of Aggression in Sri Lanka.' *Ethnology* 14, no. 1: 1–23.

————— 1977. 'Social Change and the Deities: the Rise of the Kataragama Cult in Modern Sri Lanka.' *Man* n.s. 12: 377–96.

————— 1978. 'The Fire-walkers of Kataragama: the Rise of Bhakti Religiosity in Buddhist Sri Lanka.' *Journal of Asian Studies* 37: 457–76.

————— 1979. 'The Vicissitudes of the Sinhala-Buddhist Identity through Time and Change.' In *Collective Identities, Nationalisms and Protest in Modern Sri Lanka* edited by M. Roberts. Colombo: Marga.

————— 1981. *Medusa's Hair*. Chicago: University of Chicago Press.

————— 1983. 'The Goddess Pattini and the Parable on Justice.' Punitham Tiruchelvam Memorial Lecture Colombo: New Leela Press.

————— 1984a. *The Cult of the Goddess Pattini*. Chicago: University of Chicago Press.

————— 1984b. 'The Origins and Institutionalisation of Political Violence.' In *Sri Lanka in Change and Crisis* edited by J Manor. London: Croom Helm.

Peebles, P. 1973. 'The Transformation of a Colonial Elite. The Mudaliyars of Nineteenth Century Ceylon'. Ph.D. thesis, University of Chicago.

————— 1982. *Sri Lanka: a Handbook of Historical Statistics*. Boston: G. K. Hall.

Peiris, D. 1958. *1956 and After*. Colombo: Associated Newspapers.

Perera, S. G. 1938. *The Tombo of the Two Korales*. Ceylon Historical Manuscripts Commission Bulletin No. 4. Colombo: Ceylon Government Press.

Pieris, P. E. 1950. *Sinhale and the Patriots, 1815–1818*. Colombo: Apothecaries Co.

Pitt-Rivers, J. 1977. *The Fate of Shechem*. Cambridge: Cambridge University Press.

Radcliffe-Brown, A. R. 1940. 'Preface.' In *African Political Systems* edited by M. Fortes and E. E. Evans-Pritchard. Oxford: Oxford University Press.

Rahula, W. 1978. *What the Buddha Taught*. London: Gordon Fraser.

Roberts, M. 1973. 'Aspects of Ceylon's Agrarian Economy in the Nineteenth Century.' In *University of Ceylon History of Ceylon* III. edited by K. M. De Silva. Colombo: Apothecaries' Co.

————— 1979. 'Meanderings in the Pathways of Collective Identity and Nationalism.' In *Collective Identities, Nationalisms and Protest in Modern Sri Lanka* edited by M. Roberts. Colombo: Marga.

Roberts, M. ed. 1979b. *Collective Identities, Nationalisms and Protest in Modern Sri Lanka*. Colombo: Marga.

———— 1982. *Caste Conflict and Elite Formation*. Cambridge: Cambridge University Press.

———— 1984. ' "Caste Feudalism" in Sri Lanka? A Critique through the Asokan Persona and European Contrasts.' *Contributions to Indian Sociology* n.s. 18: 189–218.

Robinson, M. S. 1968. 'Some Observations on the Kandyan Sinhalese Kinship System.' *Man* n.s. 3: 402–23.

———— 1975. *Political Structure in a Changing Sinhalese Village*. Cambridge: Cambridge University Press.

Rogers, J. D. 1987a. *Crime, Justice and Society in Colonial Sri Lanka*. London: Curzon.

———— 1987b. 'Social Mobility, Popular Ideology, and Collective Violence in Modern Sri Lanka.' *Journal of Asian Studies* 46, no. 3: 583–602.

Russell, J. 1982. *Communal Politics under the Donoughmore Constitution: 1931–1947*. Dehiwala: T. Prakasakayo.

Ryan, B. 1953. *Caste in Modern Ceylon*. New Brunswick: Rutgers University Press.

Sahlins, M. D. 1972. *Stone Age Economics*. London: Tavistock.

———— 1985. *Islands of History*. London: Tavistock.

'Samarakone, P.' 1984. 'The Conduct of the Referendum' In *Sri Lanka in Change and Crisis* edited by J. Manor. London: Croom Helm.

Samaraweera, V. 1973. 'Land Policy and Peasant Colonization, 1914–1948.' In *University of Ceylon History of Ceylon* III edited by K. M. De Silva. Colombo: Apothecaries Co.

———— 1978a. 'The "Village Community" and Reform in Colonial Sri Lanka.' *Ceylon Journal of Historical and Social Studies* n.s. 8, no. 1: 68–75.

———— 1978b. 'Litigation, Sir Henry Maine's Writings and the Ceylon Village Communities Ordinance of 1871.' In *S. Paranavitana Commemoration Volume* edited by L. Prematilleke, K. Indrapala and J. E. Van Lohuizen-De Leeuw. Leiden: E. J. Brill.

———— 1981. 'Land, Labor, Capital and Sectional Interests in the National Politics of Sri Lanka.' *Modern Asian Studies* 15, no. 1: 127–62.

Sarkar, N. K. and S. J. Tambiah. 1957. *The Disintegrating Village*. Colombo: Ceylon University Press.

Sarkisyanz, E. 1965. *Buddhist Backgrounds of the Burmese Revolution*. The Hague: Nijhoff.

Scott, J. C. 1976. *The Moral Economy of the Peasant*. New Haven: Yale University Press.

———— 1985. *Weapons of the Weak*. New Haven: Yale University Press.

Selvadurai, A. J. 1976. 'Land, Personhood, and Sorcery in a Sinhalese Village.' *Journal of Asian and African Studies* 11, no. 1/2: 82–96.

Seneviratne, H. L. 1978. *Rituals of the Kandyan State*. Cambridge: Cambridge University Press.

————— and Wickremaratne, S. 1981. 'Bodhipuja: Collective Representations of Sri Lanka Youth.' *American Ethnologist* 7, no. 4: 734–43.

Siriwardena, R. 1984. 'National Identity in Sri Lanka: Problems in Communication and Education.' In *Sri Lanka the Ethnic Conflict* edited by Committee for Rational Development. New Delhi: Navrang.

Smith, B. L. ed. 1978. *Religion and the Legitimation of Power in Sri Lanka*. Chambersburg: Anima Books.

Solidarity. 1972. *Ceylon: the JVP Uprising of April 1971*. Pamphlet 42. London: Solidarity.

Southwold, M. 1983, *Buddhism in Life*. Manchester: Manchester University Press.

Spencer, J. R. 1984a. 'Representations of the Rural.' Paper presented at Conference on Material and Symbolic Aspects of Agrarian Change in Sri Lanka, July 1984, Anuradhapura.

————— 1984b. 'Popular Perceptions of the Violence: a Provincial View.' In *Sri Lanka in Change and Crisis* edited by J. Manor. London: Croom Helm.

————— 1986. *Tenna: Peasant, State, and Nation in the Making of a Sinhalese Rural Community*. D.Phil. thesis, Oxford University.

————— n.d.a. 'Telling Histories: Nationalism and Nationalists in a Sinhalese Village.' Typescript.

————— n.d.b. 'Collective Violence and Everyday Practice in Sri Lanka.' *Modern Asian Studies*. In press.

Stein, B. 1980. *Peasant, State and Society in Medieval South India*. Delhi: Oxford University Press.

Stirrat, R. L. 1977. 'Dravidian and non-Dravidian Kinship Terminologies in Sri Lanka.' *Contributions to Indian Sociology* n.s. 11, no. 2: 271–94.

————— 1982. 'Caste Conundrums: Views of Caste in a Sinhalese Catholic Fishing Village.' In *Caste Ideology and Interaction* edited by D. McGilvray. Cambridge: Cambridge University Press.

————— 1984. 'The Riots and the Roman Catholic Church in Historical Perspective.' In *Sri Lanka in Change and Crisis* edited by J. Manor. London: Croom Helm.

————— 1989. 'Money, Men and Women.' In *Money and the Morality of Exchange* edited by J. Parry and M. Bloch. Cambridge: Cambridge University Press.

Tambiah, S. J. 1958. 'The Structure of Kinship and its Relationship to Land Possession and Residence in Pata Dumbara.' *Journal of the Royal Anthropological Institute* 78: 21–44.

————— 1965. 'Kinship Fact and Fiction in Relation to the Kandyan Sinhalese.' *Journal of the Royal Anthropological Institute* 85:131–73.

Tambiah, S. J. 1976. *World Conqueror and World Renouncer*. Cambridge: Cambridge University Press.

———— 1986. *Sri Lanka: Ethnic Fratricide and the Dismantling of Democracy*. London: I. B. Tauris.

Tennekoon, N. S. 1988. 'Rituals of Development: the Accelerated Mahavāli Development Program of Sri Lanka.' *American Ethnologist* 15, no. 2: 294–310.

Thompson, E. P. 1968. *The Making of the English Working Class*. 2nd edn. Harmondsworth: Penguin.

———— 1971. 'The Moral Economy of the English Crowd in the Eighteenth Century.' *Past and Present* 50: 76–136.

Vimalananda, T. 1970. *The Great Rebellion of 1818*. Colombo: Gunasena.

Vitebsky, P. 1984. *Policy Dilemmas for Unirrigated Agriculture in Southeastern Sri Lanka: a Social Anthropologist's Report on Shifting and Semi-Permanent Cultivation in an Area of Moneragala District*. Cambridge: Centre of South Asian Studies. Mimeo.

Vittachie, T. 1958. *Emergency '58: the Story of the Ceylon Race Riots*. London: Andre Deutsch.

Weber, M. 1948. *From Max Weber* edited by H. H. Gerth and C. Wright Mills. London: Routledge and Kegan Paul.

Wickremaratne, L. A. 1970. 'The Rulers and the Ruled: a Study of the Function of Petitions in Colonial Government.' *Modern Ceylon Studies* 1: 213–32.

Williams, R. 1965. *The Long Revolution*. Harmondsworth: Penguin.

———— 1973. *The Country and the City*. New York: Oxford University Press.

———— 1977. *Marxism and Literature*. Oxford: Oxford University Press.

———— 1983. *Keywords*. 2nd edn. London: Fontana.

Wilson, A. J. 1979. *Politics in Sri Lanka, 1947–1979*. London: Macmillan.

Wolf, E. 1982. *Europe and the People Without History*. Berkeley and Los Angeles: University of California Press.

Wood, A. L. 1961. *Crime and Aggression in Changing Ceylon*. Transactions of the American Philosophical Society n.s. 51: 8.

Wriggins, W. H. 1960. *Ceylon: Dilemmas of a New Nation*. Princeton: Princeton University Press.

Yalman, N. 1960. 'The Flexibility of Caste Principles in a Kandyan Community.' In *Aspects of Caste in South India, Ceylon and North-West Pakistan* edited by E. R. Leach. Cambridge: Cambridge University Press.

———— 1962. 'The Structure of the Sinhalese Kindred: a Re-examination of the Dravidian Terminology.' *American Anthropologist* 64: 548–75.

———— 1967. *Under the Bo Tree*. Berkeley and Los Angeles: University of California Press.

———— 1969. 'The Semantics of Kinship in South India and Ceylon.' In *Linguistics in South Asia* edited by T. A. Sebeok. Current Trends in Linguistics 5. Paris: Mouton.

Index

282 / *Index*